LITURGICAL POWER

FORDHAM UNIVERSITY PRESS   NEW YORK 2018

COMMONALITIES
Timothy C. Campbell, series editor

LITURGICAL POWER

Between Economic and Political Theology

NICHOLAS HERON

THIS BOOK IS MADE POSSIBLE BY A COLLABORATIVE GRANT
FROM THE ANDREW W. MELLON FOUNDATION.

Visit us online at www.fordhampress.com.

Library of Congress Cataloging-in-Publication Data available online
at http://catalog.loc.gov.

Printed in the United States of America

20 19 18   5 4 3 2 1

First edition

CONTENTS

In societate angelorum omnia possidentur communiter; sed tamen quaedam excellentius habentur a quibasdam quam ab aliis.

[In the society of angels all things are shared in common, but some share in them in a more excellent way than others.]

—ST. THOMAS AQUINAS

Every heightening of direct power also thickens and condenses the vaporous circle of indirect influences.

—CARL SCHMITT

INTRODUCTION

Today, the question of political theology unexpectedly stands near the center of theoretical discussion in the humanities and social sciences.[1] And yet, ever since Carl Schmitt first pronounced his celebrated thesis according to which "all significant concepts of the modern theory of the state are secularized theological concepts"[2] it has almost exclusively been assumed that the vector charted by the theological-political travels in one direction and in one direction only. Whether the relation between the two terms has been understood according to the stronger model of genetic derivation or whether according to the weaker model of structural homology,[3] the orientation has remained always the same: from the heavens to the earth, from the religious to the secular, from the theological to the political. The present study, by contrast, offers a different account and a different trajectory. It examines a sequence of ostensibly theological concepts and figures, which assume their surprising political significance only if situated in a perspective articulated according to the inverse orientation. And not only on account of the fact, in itself insignificant, that these concepts and figures can be shown to have their provenance in the civic sphere (or at least in a context where the positing of a clear distinction between the "civic" and the "religious" would be meaningless); but also, and indeed above all, because they acquire their specific force—and hence, their particular hermeneutic value—only in the course of their Christianization as the more or less worldly instruments of a polis that has been definitively shifted out of this world.

A guiding premise of the following investigation is that the prevailing discourse around political theology has for the most part all too casually and uncritically accepted the pertinence and even self-evidence of the two structuring hypotheses that marked its twentieth-century point of inception:[4] on the one hand, the paradigmatic status of the theory of sovereignty; on the other, the hermeneutic necessity of the secularization thesis. Indeed, a close reading of Schmitt's *Political Theology* (and related texts from the same period) reveals to what extent the two apparently separate hypotheses were bound together by an imperative—at once genealogical and hermeneutical in character—strictly internal to Schmitt's own argumentative strategy. The revelation of the sovereign exception as the origin of modern politics in fact has its condition of possibility in the apprehension of modernity as the epoch of secularization: The assertion of a formal continuity between theological and political concepts in effect requires the supposition of their substantive discontinuity.[5] Secularization, in this sense, would function as the positive counterpart to the process of neutralization and depoliticization, which refers the besieged political, precisely at the moment of extreme crisis (represented, for Schmitt, by the progressive triumph of "economic-technical thinking"), back to its theological origin.[6] But what if it were the process of neutralization and depoliticization itself, which also, and indeed preeminently, had its origin in Christian theology? Such is the hypothesis that will be explored in the following pages.

The point of departure for this overhaul is a return to the protracted debate between Schmitt and Erik Peterson regarding the very possibility of a Christian political theology, whose stakes the contemporary Italian philosopher Giorgio Agamben has recently submitted to a major revaluation.[7] Opened in 1935 by Peterson's coded yet bracing critique of Schmitt,[8] and closed only in 1970 by the latter's belated response, some ten years after the theologian's death,[9] the debate has elicited an extensive scholarly coverage.[10] Yet outside theological circles it has been treated almost exclusively as an episode in the intellectual biography of Schmitt.[11] Following Agamben's intervention, the present book proposes to reverse this trend by concentrating instead on the position advanced by Peterson. For while the terms of Peterson's critique of political theology have been well rehearsed in the historiography, only rarely has it been noted[12] that his approach was in fact underpinned by a competing understanding of the relation between politics and theology, which was articulated in a sequence of brilliant articles dating from the very same period. Indeed, as we shall see, in this alternative rendering, Christian antipolitics is itself translated into a limit-form of politics. And while this in one sense explains the critique of political theology, in another sense it can be seen to open a new perspective on its current and future study, which simultaneously broadens its historical scope while refining its discrete point of application.

The critique itself—it is important not to forget—was carried out on two distinct, yet strictly interrelated, fronts. On the one hand, there was the well-known argument that with the proclamation of the orthodox dogma of the Trinity, early Christianity's brief flirtation with a political theology founded on the model of Hellenistic Judaism was brought to an abrupt and definitive end (for the reason that the triune God, unlike the "monarchical" God of the Jews, had no analogue in the created world). On the other hand, however, there was the lesser known, but no less significant, argument (and potentially even more devastating for its implicit target in Schmitt) concerning the triumph of St. Augustine's theology of peace over the prevailing interpretation of the Pax Romana as the fulfillment of the messianic prophecies of the Old Testament. According to this second perspective—which is treated only very briefly in the text, yet whose significance is underscored by the dedication to Augustine that graces the treatise's opening page—any peace, whether Roman or otherwise, that would be realized politically (and hence appear immanent to history) must necessarily be an illusion because true, authentic peace is to be attained only at the end of time, only in eternity.[13] But there could be no greater misunderstanding of the sense of his intervention than to suggest that with this rejection of concrete political eschatology (and the consequent elimination of monotheism "as a political problem"), Peterson had sought to exclude politics from the theological sphere altogether. To the contrary, it is the very suspension of the concrete eschatological that, by deferring the end of time and the advent of the kingdom of God, in effect makes secular politics possible. But this politics remains the unique prerogative of that public assembly whose very historical existence, in his account, is predicated on just this suspension: the Church.[14] Far from being aimed at preserving the purity of theological speculation against political contamination (as Schmitt perhaps willfully misrepresented it), Peterson's theological dismissal of all political theology was thus intended to counter the political instrumentalization of theology with a view to articulating the form of political action specific to Christianity itself.

For Peterson, then, contra Schmitt, politics cannot be theological, even in an occult manner, because theology itself is in a sense already political. Such a reorientation entails a number of important consequences for the study of the relations between the theological and the political. Most immediately, it decouples it from the attendant theory of secularization. The assertion of a politics specific to Christian theology means that its concepts are always already (albeit in attenuated sense that we will have to understand) political, and do not merely become so on account of having passed through the process of secularization. But this has the additional effect, evident from the erudite historical reconstruction through which Peterson's critique is conveyed, of expanding its field of application well beyond the limits of modernity.[15] Further to this double displacement that follows from Peterson's intervention, Agamben's recasting of its terms will nonetheless enable a final modification. The secular political activity mandated by Christian theology, he argues, in fact corresponds—terminologically, if not conceptually—to what in the ancient world, at least according to the Aristotelian definition, was thought to underlie politics in the strict sense, yet which was nonetheless sharply differentiated from it: economics, in the specialized understanding the Greeks had of this term.[16]

As we shall see in what follows, what stimulates Agamben's major contribution to the discussion of political theology is his discovery—substantiated by a point-for-point counter-reading of the same patristic texts that Peterson had analyzed—that the political activity whose undertaking the German theologian had reserved for the Church alone receives its theological justification by means of the very device through which the Fathers responsible for the first elaboration of the doctrine of the Trinity had sought to reconcile the unity of divine substance with a plurality of divine figures: the concept of *oikonomia*. The plurality of divine figures, they had argued, is a plurality without division: In terms of his "being" and his "substance," God is most certainly one; only in terms of his "economy"—which is to say, his salvific activity in time and in the world (in a word, his government)—would he instead be considered triple. That which "harmonizes" the trinity in unity is thus also, and at the same time, that which "disposes" the unity in trinity: The same term simultaneously encompasses both operations.[17] Monotheism—such would be the sense of Agamben's intervention (and here he emphatically parts ways with Peterson)—thus ceases to be a political problem only by virtue of its economic articulation. But this immediately feeds back onto the other aspect of Peterson's critique. The politics of the Church, in this sense—which coincides with the interim time inaugurated by the suspension of the concrete eschatological—would thus consist in nothing more, or nothing less, than mediating the theological economy.

For Agamben, in fact, nothing better describes the "economic theology" whose paradigm he seeks to reconstruct starting from Peterson's critique than the very formula that the theologian himself had employed in order to characterize the pagan variant of political theology he maintained had been definitively overcome with the proclamation of the Trinitarian dogma: "Le roi règne, mais il ne gouverne pas [The king reigns, but he does not govern]."[18] For him, it is the functioning of the Trinitarian *oikonomia* itself that is illustrated by this well-known expression of constitutional monarchy according to which the king abstractly reigns but does not concretely govern.[19] But this appropriation also in turn enables Agamben to stage another decisive rapprochement. With the same formula with which he displaces the prevailing model of political theology, Agamben thus seeks to integrate his analysis with Michel Foucault's contributions toward the genealogy of "governmentality." It is in the horizon opened up by this encounter that the following investigation will be situated. On the one hand, it seeks to unfold the profound overhaul of the conceptuality of political theology latent in the very formulation of an "economic theology." On the other hand, it attempts to delineate the defining features of a technology of power whose forms and whose modalities become discernible only in the light of this overhaul.

It is well known how, beginning above all with his 1977–78 lecture course at the Collège de France, Foucault had sought to shift the accent in the approach to the study of power away from the traditional orientation channeled through the framework of juridical and institutional models and toward an analysis of the more supple and variegated techniques and practices he would subsume (in accordance with the anti-Machiavellian literature of the sixteenth, seventeenth, and eighteenth centuries to which he refers) under the rubric of an "art of government."[20] Rather than focusing on the transcendent singularity that received its exemplary expression in Machiavelli's prince—who is characterized by a relationship of absolute exteriority with respect to his principality—the literature in question had sought instead to emphasize the multiplicity and plurality of practices of government immanent to society and the state itself.[21] In this sense, the research he would undertake in this direction sought to take up the challenge issued some years earlier, in the first volume of his *History of Sexuality*, to break free of the image of power grounded in the theoretical privilege of law and sovereignty.[22] It is significant that Foucault should speak, in this context, with respect to the specific exigency to which this new modality of power was intended to respond, of the need to introduce the "economy" into political practice—that is, of the necessity of integrating the management of the household with that of the state.[23] Between the too general and abstract framework of state sovereignty, on the one hand, and the too narrow and particular model of the domestic household, on the other, the art of government thus interposed itself as a third dimension (albeit one based on the latter), which took the economy in a first moment as its modality and its form and in a second moment as its privileged field of application. It was in order to register the stakes of this shift, as Agamben has observed, that he would adopt the same formula employed by Peterson. This privilege that government comes to assume with respect to rule, he writes, is such that "one day, in order to limit the king's power, it will be possible to say 'the king reigns, but he does not govern.'"[24]

In mobilizing the distinction between sovereignty and government, Foucault invokes a conceptual pair with an established tradition in the history of political thought.[25] Yet he brings a different emphasis to it, which inverts the usual hierarchy of relations between the two terms. Where, previously, it had been a question of deducing an art of government from the theory of sovereignty, he writes, with the increasing primacy that the former progressively comes to assume, it now becomes a question of providing the corresponding juridical foundation for an art of government already in existence.[26] For him, the formula thus serves to indicate the limit that had to be placed on the exercise of sovereignty in order to facilitate what he calls, in a striking phrase, "the unblocking of the art of government" (*le déblocage de l'art de gouverner*).[27] It is no coincidence, then, that the ensuing genealogy of governmentality he begins to trace should be concentrated on models whose domain has usually been conceived as subjacent to the political arena in the strict sense: the antique household, with its economy of persons and things,[28] and the Christian pastorate, with its economy of souls.[29] It is Agamben's contention, as we have seen, that these two models must nonetheless be complemented by the addition of a third—which, moreover, would be responsible for articulating the passage from the one to the other: the Trinitarian economy. If a redefinition of political theology will be carried out from the perspective of government, Foucault's own intuitions will thus in turn be furnished with a firm theological basis. In this way, as Roberto Esposito has summarized it, Agamben is able to open the theoretical construct of political theology "like a fan": "Just as the Schmittian paradigm needs to be expanded, horizontally, toward the economic lexicon, similarly, Foucault's investigation into governmentality needs to be taken backward, on the vertical plane, much further than the French philosopher did in reference to the pastorate, going back to the early Christian treatises of the first centuries on the double mysteries of the Trinity and Providence."[30]

As other commentators have rightly observed,[31] however, the shift in emphasis that Agamben introduces here with respect to Foucault's genealogy is in fact far more pronounced than that of a simple recalibration on the basis of amended temporal and metaphysical coordinates. Where for Foucault, as we have seen, the formula served to express the limitation that comes to be placed on sovereign power, for Agamben instead it is this very limitation that in effect precipitates an ulterior activity of government—one that is undertaken independently of the sovereign, as it were in his stead, yet that still formally pertains to him. Such that, in Agamben's rendering, it is still he who abstractly reigns, even though he does not—and indeed, according to a well-established tradition amply documented in his book, ought not to—concretely govern. Far from expressing a limitation of sovereign power, what Agamben's own deployment of the formula thus seeks to bring to light is what we could define as the paradox of sovereign or divine impotentiality, according to which—in a striking inversion of the sign—it is precisely what the King, or what God, *can* not do that in truth presents the index of his sovereignty.[32] Power is full only to the extent that it is divided, only to the extent, that is to say, that it is formally separated from its own exercise: This is the striking thesis that issues from Agamben's repurposing of the formula by way of the Trinitarian *oikonomia*, and that enables him to recast the distinction between sovereignty and government in terms of a bipolar relationship. Just as the Trinitarian *oikonomia* names both the disposition of the unity in trinity and the harmonization of the trinity in unity, so for Agamben, both with and against Foucault, the definition of power as administration and management (government) is thus revealed to be perfectly contiguous with its definition as ritual and ceremony (glory). The movement that runs from sovereignty to government must therefore be integrated with the strictly complementary line that runs from government to sovereignty.[33]

For this reason, despite being equally concerned with reorienting the thematic of power away from the paradigm of sovereignty and toward that of governmentality, Agamben's treatment nonetheless remains largely focused on the surprising implications that this shift entails for the figure of sovereign transcendence itself—which, far from being diminished, emerges as decisively amplified in this displacement, albeit in a very particular manner. Directly building on Agamben's highly sophisticated analysis, the present book is concentrated instead squarely on the governmental axis and its avatars. What I have sought to examine is how, starting from this double movement of the theological economy such as Agamben has theorized it, monarchical power is effectively diffused and apportioned, while at the same time raising those responsible for its concrete administration to a participation in it that is nonetheless strictly conditioned by this exercise. The principle of this diffusion and this apportioning, whose conceptual history I have sought to reconstruct in order to make its paradigm available for political theory, is *liturgy*.[34] Liturgy—understood in the broad, indeed etymological sense, as a "public service," which is performed only on behalf of another, yet solely for the sake of another again—I argue, is the device that enables the "economization" of power implicit in the elaboration of an economic theology. But it is also the operation that raises those charged with executing it to a participation in the divinity that in turn elevates them to a quasi-divine status. Crucially, however, this divinity is completely indexed to its performance. For, as we shall see, with the exception of Christ himself, whom the Letter to the Hebrews defines as the medium of a "more excellent liturgy,"[35] the minister (*leitourgos*) is divine, not according to its nature, but only according to its activity. In this sense, its figure presents the curious image of a wholly contingent divinity. If what defines sovereign power, according to Agamben, is the paradox of divine impotentiality, what defines liturgical power is thus a paradox of an entirely different order. Because it pertains to the subjects who administer it only accidentally, insofar as they are its executors, liturgical power, according to a refrain that will appear often in the course of the following pages, is a form of power that cannot be possessed but only enacted. Unlike God himself, in other words, the minister who acts in his stead cannot not act without thereby ceasing to be as such.

Placing the emphasis on liturgy in this way thus enables us to intervene directly at the level of the other structuring hypothesis of political theology in its Schmittian articulation: the theoretical privilege accorded to the concept of sovereignty. On the one hand, as we have already seen, it shifts the focus of the analysis away from the bearers of power in the strict sense, and toward its executors. Rather than attending exclusively to the question of sovereignty, in short, it concentrates instead upon that of governmentality. But it also supplies an important corrective with respect to Foucault's approach, which did not pay sufficient attention to the constitutively vicarious character of governmental power. The theme of vicariousness, to be sure, is not unfamiliar to the broader discourse of political theology. In an important 1952 study, Ernst Kantorowicz, for example, had already sought to examine the sense of the titles *vicarius Dei* and *vicarius Christi* in a theological-political context.[36] With respect to this established theological-political tradition, the theological-economical approach to the theme of vicariousness nonetheless maintains a distinct conceptual anteriority. It describes a vicariousness that takes place not only between the divinity and an element that is strictly external to it, but one that pulses, so to speak, internal to the godhead in its Trinitarian elaboration. Vicariousness here names not the position of the earthly representative—whether emperor or pope, king or bishop—with respect to the divine sovereign, but rather (in Agamben's striking phrase) "the intimate vicissitudinous articulation of the *archē* itself."[37] In this sense, it is the intra-Trinitarian relationship of the Father to the Son, and of the Son to the Father, that furnishes the theological paradigm for all vicarious power.[38] But this implies something like an "originary" economy, something like an "originary" vicariousness, which means that the *archē* of this power is always already split and does not simply become so in the course of its historical development. There is no original substance of power from which its various emanations and manifestations could ultimately be sourced, but only economy, only vicariousness. In the beginning was already the economy.

To speak of an originary economy, of an originary vicariousness of power, is thus not simply to shift the focus of the analysis from sovereignty to government, as was intimated above; it is rather, much more radically, to substitute the analysis of the relation between the two levels for that of the one usually understood to be primary. When viewed from the perspective of economic theology, it is now, however paradoxically, the relation itself that is primary (or at least that yields the paradigm through which the analysis is to be pursued). It is at the level of this relation that the question of liturgy is to be posed. The fundamental ambiguity that seems to define all liturgical practice—its being always on behalf of another, yet only to the extent that it is for the sake of another again (and vice-versa)—becomes fully explicable only by means of this model, even as it simultaneously attests to its ultimate irreducibility. There is no point beyond which the vicariousness of this power could ever finally be eradicated. Yet precisely this, as we shall see, is what enshrines its incessant circulation. But also its ethical indeterminacy. Liturgical power—as Hannah Arendt repeatedly observed of modern bureaucracy, perhaps its most ubiquitous contemporary manifestation[39]—is essentially unlocalizable and hence constitutively irresponsible.

The reconstruction of liturgical power encompasses five interlinked chapters. Building on these introductory remarks, the first chapter locates the intervention staged by Agamben's recuperation of the paradigm of economic theology in relation to both its ancient and modern intellectual-historical contexts. In the first instance, it situates Agamben's recuperation of this paradigm in the context of the late Hellenistic debates concerning the nature of the gods. Against the Epicureans, on the one hand, who maintained that the gods are improvident and hence inactive, and the Stoics, on the other, who argued instead that they are provident and thus active, the Trinitarian *oikonomia*, in Agamben's formulation, entails a god who is at once improvident and provident, at once inactive and active. It is this simultaneously inactive and active god—encompassing a Father who reigns but does not govern and a Son who governs but does not reign— which, in the second place, will be employed in order to intervene in the debate between Schmitt and Peterson regarding the possibility of a Christian political theology. As we have already seen, Peterson's theological dismissal of all political theology was not aimed at preserving the purity of theological speculation against political contamination, as Schmitt misrepresented it. Rather, it seeks to counter the political instrumentalization of theology with a view to articulating the form of political action specific to Christianity itself.

Further building on these premises, the second chapter seeks to deepen and extend Agamben's analysis by describing the terms of a specifically

Christian technology of power, which I call "liturgical power." The point of departure for this description is Peterson's suggestion that the form of political action specific to Christianity coincides with the Church's appropriation of the practice that in the ancient Greek polis was termed *leitourgia*, a suggestion that in turn stimulates a reappraisal of Foucault's influential notion of pastoral power. Pastoral power, I argue, on the basis of a detailed reconstruction of the semantic history of the term (*laos*) that in the Greek biblical tradition designates the "people" as the distinct referent of pastoral intervention, is more precisely conceived as "liturgical power." Only by emphasizing its liturgical dimension, I suggest, can we fully grasp the stakes of the process that Foucault himself suggestively described as the "institutionalization of the pastorate"; a process that is shown, finally, to coincide with its articulation—the first articulation, in the strictly lexical sense—in a hierarchy.

By disclosing the liturgical principle that articulates it, the next chapter is able to advance a novel interpretation of what is, arguably, the Christian tradition's most important, if surprisingly understudied, contribution to the theorization of power. As the angelological tradition from Pseudo-Dionysius through to St. Thomas Aquinas clearly demonstrates, hierarchy is neither simply the expression of ordered relations of natural superiority, nor merely a form of objective social organization, but a practice. A practice, moreover, which serves a distinctly soteriological function and whose elaboration thus constitutes a chapter of critical importance in the larger genealogy of governmentality. But because hierarchy is not only the practice of (internal) order, but also its (external) manifestation, its concept confirms the intimate yet unexpected link between "government" and "glory" that Agamben has sought to highlight.

The fourth chapter explores Foucault's passing remark that the problem of the relation between politics and religion in modernity is uniquely concentrated in the ambiguous figure of the "minister."[40] Its point of departure is Aquinas's definition of the minister as the "instrumental cause" of sacramental efficacy (the administration of the sacraments being the liturgical operation par excellence). Following a detailed examination of the philosophical history of the instrumental cause, this chapter is able to demonstrate how, far from constituting a mere adaptation of Aristotle's fourfold aetiology to the ends of Christian theology, the articulation of a notion of instrumental causality is in fact the vehicle through which theology seeks to assert its superiority with respect to philosophy. But to the extent that it defines the figure of the minister, it also in turn supplies the theoretical justification for the constitutively vicarious character of liturgical power.

But this constitutive vicariousness, which obtains its most extreme formulation in the doctrine of the *ex opere operato* efficacy of the minister's action, as the concluding chapter demonstrates, also entails a determinate shift in the ontology of power. If power is essentially liturgy and hierarchy, which is what the theory of the instrumental cause confirms, then it is strictly irreducible to the nature of the one who exercises it. As such, it has no separate existence outside each concrete enactment. Since what defines the liturgical office is the fulfillment of a function and not the expression of a substance, its bearer emerges as a thoroughly paradoxical being who must act in order to be able to be. Liturgical power is thus not only constitutively vicarious; it is also necessarily industrious. A reappraisal of the genealogy of the office, which encompasses both classical and Christian sources, thus provides the historical and theoretical framework for the intimation of a paradoxical anthropology that accompanies this profound displacement in the history of the ontology of power.

This study was initially undertaken with the understanding that (as has recently been observed apropos of Foucault's larger approach to the study of power) *postestas dicitur multipliciter* (power is said in many ways).[41] Liturgical power, from this perspective, would be but one further modality to be inscribed alongside the others that Foucault sought to delineate in the course of his research: psychiatric power, disciplinary power, biopower, and so on. Its concluding pages, and especially those dedicated to the reconstruction of the theory of the instrumental cause, encourage us to provisionally advance a hypothesis less circumspect. What would be at stake in the "liturgicization" of power, with its vicarious structure and the attendant ontological and even anthropological implications that follow from this, would be a transformation in its nature, which brings about a determinate collapse in the distinction between its active and its passive dimensions. Henceforth, it will no longer be possible to speak, according to a tradition that extends all the way from Plato and Aristotle up to Foucault himself, of a clear distinction between those who govern and those who are governed (even if only to affirm the latter over and against the former). The persistent misunderstanding of hierarchy as a structure, rather than as a practice, as a form of domination, rather than as a technique of governance—which is reflected everywhere (including even at the level of everyday speech)—has prevented proper analysis of the emergence of an important third category, which neutralizes the opposition between the two terms of the traditional distinction: those who govern only insofar as they too are governed. It is only with the appearance of this third category, only with the arrival of this integrally participatory model of power, that we can truly say, with Foucault, "power is everywhere," and precisely because it cannot be located anywhere.

1

THE ECONOMIC GOD

1.

Perhaps more than any other early Christian thinker, Augustine of Hippo found himself drawn time and again in his writings to the opening verses of the Book of Genesis. From the composition, in 388, of his short polemical treatise *De Genesis contra Manichaeos*, through to the completion, in 426, of his monumental *De civitate Dei contra Paganos* in twenty-two books, he turned to their exposition on no less than five separate occasions. Like Philo of Alexandria before him, he understood these verses, detailing the creation of the heavens and the earth, to be the most important of all divine scripture, the key to all wisdom; the right approach to them, moreover, would serve as the model of "proper" exegesis, in both its literal and allegorical modes. But not only for this. As the account of his first tentative approach to them, while still under the influence of Manichaeism, would appear to attest ("To feed my hunger," he wistfully records, "instead of you they brought me a diet of the sun and moon, your beautiful works"[1]), incorrect interpretation of these verses could equally serve as the model of "improper" exegesis as well.[2] This would be directly borne out in Augustine's own mature writings, where the two models would often be counterposed to one another, almost as if the correct interpretation could only proceed, on its own terms, by means of the exclusion of its "dark twin." St. Paul's dictum that there must be factions (*haireseis*) among those who purport to be the faithful so that those who are genuine may stand out among them, it would appear, was the *conditio sine qua non* for his inquiry into scripture.[3] As has often been observed, in the early Church as elsewhere (contemporaneously, for example, in Rabbinic Judaism), the discourse of orthodoxy proceeds hand in hand with the discourse of heresiology.[4]

Thus, the first of the three great exegetical books that conclude his *Confessions* is explicitly framed by what has been described as the "synecdoche"[5] of all improper questioning: Namely, what was God doing before he made heaven and earth? "See how full of old errors," he writes,

> are those who say to us: "What was God doing before he made heaven and earth? If he was unoccupied," they say, "and doing nothing, why does he not always remain the same forever, just as before creation he abstained from work?" For if in God any new development took place and any new intention, so as to make a creation which he had never made before, how then can there be a true eternity in which a will, not there previously, comes into existence? For God's will is not a creature, but is prior to the created order, since nothing would be created unless the Creator's will preceded it. Therefore God's will belongs to his very substance. If in the substance of God anything has come into being which was not present before, that substance cannot truthfully be called eternal. But if it was God's everlasting will that the created order exist, why is not the creation everlasting?[6]

The reproach that Augustine would bring to this question is justifiably famous. So famous, in fact, that it served to completely eclipse the very probity of the question that first gave rise to it. For it was here, in response to this improper question par excellence, that he would most forcefully expound his celebrated distinction between *tempus* and *aeternitas*, between time and eternity. The reasoning of those who, whether in good or in bad faith, seek to pose this question, he argues, rests upon a fundamental error: They act as if there were time before time. There cannot have been any time before God created heaven and earth, Augustine explains, for the simple reason that time itself had not yet been created. Like the heavens and the earth; like the sun and the moon; like the plants and the beasts; like the human being itself, the greatest of all his "works"—time is also, according to Augustine, but a creation of God. God (or rather, his Logos) created time, not before, but together with the world: "There can be no doubt," he writes, "that the world was not created in time but with time [*non est mundus factus in tempore, sed cum tempore*]."[7] There was thus a beginning of time, just as there will be—such is its necessary correlate—an end of time. For were there no beginning, were there no end to time, there could be no time; it would be indistinguishable from eternity. But time passes.

The very cause of its being, he memorably records, is that it will cease to be: It exists only in the sense that it tends toward nonexistence.[8] Like the created world itself, time is thus, for Augustine, essentially finite. The duration proper to changeable, corruptible beings, it is but the short interval between the two great, measureless expanses of eternity.

The sign of transience, of caducity, of death, time is thus, for Augustine, as Ernst Kantorowicz once remarked, a morally degraded concept.[9] At the same time, however, it is also that against which the incomparable majesty of God is made to appear as if in sharp relief. For change and motion are not predicable of God. The creator of all things, he is himself uncreated; and, unlike his creatures, has neither beginning nor end. Between time and eternity, there can be no common measure. Yet it is this very incommensurability that enables Augustine to transform the possible taint of heresy into the actual fount of glory. As he would write in a memorable passage of his *De civitate Dei* (a passage that, to be sure, nonetheless still indirectly betrays the incumbent difficulty that the so-called idleness question presented with respect to his thought):

> For God's pause before the creation of man was eternal and without beginning, so that compared with it an inexpressibly great number of centuries, which must still have an end and a defined extent, is not so much as the smallest drop of water compared with all the oceans of the world: for in this comparison, though one is tiny and the other is incomparably huge, still both terms are finite. But any space of time which starts from a beginning and is brought to an end, however vast its extent, must be compared with that which has no beginning, as minimal, or rather as nothing at all.[10]

2.

Augustine was, of course, neither the first Christian thinker to approach this question nor would he be the last. And, as brilliant and far-reaching as his riposte would be—it would remain virtually unchallenged, as the prevailing conception of time in Western culture, for close to a millennium (being then only partially displaced when the recovery of the Aristotelian notion of the "eternity of the world," principally through Averroes and his followers, necessitated certain modifications in its theory)[11]—it served more effectively to obscure, rather than to illuminate, the precise reasons why this question represented such a scandal for early Christian thought. Even worse, on this account, was the argument of Irenaeus of Lyons, advanced some two hundred years before Augustine. The answer to such a question, he maintained in the second book of his *Adversus haereses*, lies with God himself alone.[12] The scriptures inform us that the world, which was formed perfect by God, received a beginning in time; beyond that event, we know nothing. Even to inquire into how God was employed before he made the world, he argued, is to solicit "foolish, senseless and blasphemous emissions."[13] On one particular point, Irenaeus's account nonetheless remains indisputably valuable. For it makes palpably clear, as Edward Peters has demonstrated, at least one probable source of the question: the "Gnostic" heretics against whom his treatise was largely directed, and for whom it evidently presented no inherent difficulties. "If, however, we cannot find solutions to all the questions raised by Scripture," Irenaeus tellingly writes but a few lines before, "let us not on that account seek another God beyond He who is the true God. For that would be the greatest impiety."[14]

Much more illuminating is the discussion to be found in Origen's *De principiis*. Like Irenaeus before him, he cites the question as evidence of the gravest heresy; but unlike the former he also formulates a radical response to it. Even more important, however, is his singular characterization of the problem that it presents with respect to the Christian doctrine of creation. According to Origen, who here evokes the eschatological fervor of St. Paul as his witness, just as we must suppose an end to this present corruptible world, so we must also posit its beginning: The two extreme points in the continuum of creation reciprocally necessitate one another. The apostle, he observes, clearly asserts the end of the world, when he writes: "For the present form of this world is passing away" (1 Cor. 7:31). But in noting elsewhere that "the creation was subject to futility" (Rom. 8:20), he also in turn demonstrates its beginning. "If creation was subject to futility because of a certain hope, it was thereby submitted by a cause; and that which is on account of a cause must necessarily have had a beginning."[15] But then, he almost immediately adds, it is often objected: "If the world had a beginning in time, what was God doing before the world began?" Even while forthrightly rejecting, as at once impious and absurd, the very sense of the question, Origen nonetheless also indirectly points, in a manner that is far less oblique than the other Apologists, to certain incontestable difficulties that this question presents. "To say that it is God's nature to be idle and immobile," he writes, "is at once impious and absurd, just as it is to suppose that there was a time in which goodness did not do good and in which the omnipotent did not exercise its power [*vel putare quod bonitas aliquando bene non fecerit et omnipotentia aliquando non egerit potentatum*]."[16] There can be no time in which the divine goodness did not do good, no time in which the divine omnipotence did not exercise its power: With these twin assertions, Origen unambiguously signaled a pair of strictly interlaced imperatives that Christian piety must be committed to safeguarding at any cost, against all improper questioning.

This blessed and sovereign power, which exercises its dominion over all things, according to Origen, is what we call the Trinity, and it is impious to suppose that there was ever a time in which it was inactive: "It is at once impious and absurd to think that these powers of God were idle even for an instant. For it is impermissible to ask, even in passing, whether these powers, which principally enable us to grasp God in a worthy manner, have for one moment stopped producing works worthy of themselves and become inactive."[17] According to Origen's striking reading, God is—and must be—eternally active. He *is* his power: To suppose that there was a time in which he was inactive is thus to suppose that there was a time in which he was not; it is to contest his very existence. But in order to support this extreme vision, Origen was led to formulate a radical thesis later deemed unacceptable by the nascent Christian orthodoxy. In order to secure the perpetuity of God's power, in order to ensure that there was never a time in which he was inactive, it would be necessary, he argued, not only to postulate the existence of prior worlds anterior to the creation of the present world; even more drastically again, it would also be necessary to hypothesize the existence of future worlds that would assume their place after each successive passing of the one that preceded it. To support this vision, he appealed to the scriptural authority of Isaiah 66:22 and Ecclesiastes 1:9:

> It is not the case that God began to work when he made this visible world; rather, just as there will be another world after the corruption of this one, so we believe there were others before this one came to be. The authority of Divine Scripture will confirm these two points. Isaiah teaches that there will be another world after this one: "There will be a new heaven and a new earth, which I shall hold before me, the Lord

says." And Ecclesiastes shows that before this world there were many others: "What has been is what will be, and what has been done is what will be done; there is nothing new under the sun. Is there a thing of which it is said, 'See, this is new?' It has already been in the ages that preceded us."[18]

Such a solution was, of course, completely rejected by Augustine. Among other things, it implied that Christ's Passion must be repeated with each periodic succession of the ages, ad infinitum.[19] It is nonetheless surely an index of the difficulty that the problem of divine inactivity presented with respect to early Christian thought that, when in the twelfth book of his *De civitate Dei*, Augustine once again confronted it—but here, very distinctly, in the modified terms of Origen—he should find himself reduced to unwittingly repeating the gesture of Irenaeus. Just as I dare not submit that God were ever not sovereign, he observes, so I am equally bound to believe that man never existed previously and that he was created at a certain point of time. The two propositions must be made to be commensurate with one another. "But when I ponder the question," he writes,

> of what was the eternal subject of God's sovereignty, if creation did not always exist, I am afraid to give any positive answer, because I examine myself, and remember what the Scripture says, "What human being can know the counsel of God? Who will be able to think what God intends? For the thoughts of mortals are timorous, and our speculations uncertain. For the corruptible body weighs down the soul, and the earthly habitation depresses the mind as it ponders its many thoughts."[20]

In spite of his hesitation, the great Father of medieval Christendom will nonetheless proceed to advance a highly significant, if largely tentative, response. In order to ensure that there was always in existence some creature over whom God could exercise his sovereignty, while still observing the creation of man in time, it will be necessary, he suggests, to suppose the existence of a being that, while not coeternal with the creator, was nonetheless not created in time. In other words, it will be necessary to postulate the existence of a paradoxical entity that is at once created and eternal—an order of creation that would transcend the experience of time as such. The necessity that God be eternally sovereign coincides with the necessity of the angel.[21]

3.

That the divine being should appear as a figure of action is, in truth, anything but obvious. In Aristotle's *De caelo*, for example, we find the important argument, which would exert an enduring influence over certain currents of later thought (most notably, those associated with Epicureanism), that the complexity of action increases in inverse proportion with respect to its participation in the good—such that, at the limit, the being that finds itself in the best possible state has no need of action whatsoever. "Here on earth," he writes,

> it is the actions of man that are the most varied, and the reason is that man has a variety of goods within his reach, wherefore his actions are many, and directed to ends outside themselves. That which is in the best possible state, on the other hand, has no need of action [*outhen dei praxeōs*]. It is its own end, whereas action is always concerned with two factors, occurring on the one hand when there is an end proposed, and on the other hand the means toward that end.[22]

In this precise respect, however, his position differed starkly from that of his master. According to Plato, it would be absurd to reckon the gods as "indolent" (*tryphōn*) and "idle" (*argos*) and hence without "care" (*epimileia*) for human beings. Rather, like "pilots" (*kuberentais*) or "generals" (*stratēgois*) or "household mangers" (*oikonomeis*), they must be supposed as always provident, and with respect to great and small things alike: "Let us never suppose that God is inferior to mortal craftsmen who, the better they are, the more accurately and perfectly do they execute their proper tasks, small and great, by one single art—or that God, who is most wise, and both willing and able to care, cares not at all for the small things which are the easier to care for—like one who shirks the labour because he is idle and cowardly—but only for the great."[23] For the one, God is absolutely impassive, enduring no movement whatsoever; for the other, he is absolutely provident, superintending all beings, great and small alike.

By the time of the emergence of the later Hellenistic philosophies, however, the question as to whether the gods are active or inactive—and hence, whether or not they concern themselves with human affairs—had become not one question among many, but the question par excellence regarding their nature. As we learn from the opening pages of Cicero's *De natura deorum*—the volume that, in the absence of so many primary texts, provides the best summary account of these debates—the question concerning the actual existence of the gods presented comparatively little interest. This was something upon which almost all participants agreed. Regarding the question as to whether the gods are active or inactive, by contrast, the greatest disagreement reigned:

> Many views are put forward about the outward form of the gods, their dwelling-places and modes of life, and hence topics are debated with the widest variety of opinion among philosophers; but as to the question upon which the whole issue of the dispute principally turns, whether the gods are entirely idle and inactive, taking no part at all in the direction and government of the world, or whether on the contrary all things both were created and ordered by them in the beginning and are controlled and ordered by them throughout all eternity, here there is the greatest disagreement of all.[24]

Inactivity and activity, idleness and providence, considered here as divine attributes, are thus presented in the terms of a stark opposition. According to the Epicureans, on the one hand, the life of the gods is the "happiest conceivable, and the one most bountifully furnished with good things." As such, it is "entirely inactive and free from all ties of occupation."[25] They neither toil nor labor, but take pure pleasure in contemplating their own wisdom and virtue. The Stoic god appears to them, by contrast, to be strenuously overworked (*laboriosisimum*). If "repose" (*quietus*) is the essential condition of happiness, then to have to reside within the world as its "governor" and its "pilot," the Epicureans contend, can only be a business that is at once "irksome" (*molestis*) and "laborious" (*operosis*).[26]

According to the Stoics themselves, on the other hand, the gods must not only be conceived as active but as eminently so. For them, unequivocally, "the world and all its parts were set in order at the beginning and have been governed for all time by divine providence."[27] The argument runs as follows: Anyone who admits that the gods exist must grant them some activity; but if they are to be granted activity, it must be of the most distinguished kind, for otherwise this would be to suggest that there is an activity that is more distinguished than theirs. The most distinguished activity is the government of the world (*mundi administratione*); therefore, the world is governed by the gods.[28] The Stoic gods, however, are neither idle, like their Epicurean counterparts, nor do they "perform their activities with irksome and laborious toil," as the Epicurean argument would have it.[29] For unlike the Epicurean deities, with their "quasi-bodies" and their "quasi-blood," they are not weighed down with veins and sinews and bones; nor do they consume food and drink; nor can their bodies experience falls or blows or contract diseases on account of physical exhaustion. They have not human bodies, but are endowed with supreme beauty of form (which in the Stoic imaginary coincided with that of the sphere) and inhabit only the purest region of the heavens.

4.

In a recent study, which forms the point of departure for the present investigation, Giorgio Agamben has shown how the early Church Fathers were able to neutralize these debates regarding the nature of the gods by seeking to articulate together in a single, undivided paradigm the *deus otiosus* of Aristotle and the Epicureans with the *deus actuosus* of Plato and the Stoics. And he has done so, as we have seen, through the recuperation of an important chapter in the history of early Christianity, which saw the first attempt to coordinate the unity of divine substance with the threefold procession of divine figures, assume the curious form of an *oikonomia*. Michel Foucault—whose genealogy of governmentality Agamben expressly seeks to resume in these pages—had already drawn attention to the use of this term in the patristic context. In giving to the set of techniques and procedures characteristic of what he termed the pastorate, the "quite remarkable" name of *oikonomia psychōn* (economy of souls), the fourth-century Cappadocian Fathers, he observed, had invested the typically Greek notion of *oikonomia*—such as it had appeared above all in Xenophon and in Aristotle, where it referred to the effective management of the household—with a "completely different dimension" and a "completely different field of references."[30] A completely different dimension because, far from being confined to the delimited sphere of the household, the Christian *oikonomia* would now encompass, if not the whole of humanity, then at least the whole of Christendom; a completely different field of references because, instead of being restricted to securing the wealth and prosperity of the individual estate, it would be entrusted with a distinctly soteriological function.[31] In Agamben's extensive development and elaboration of

Foucault's suggestion, however, it is not just that the term itself comes to be invested with a different dimension and a different field of references. The converse is also true: It is that different dimension and that different set of references—which comprise nothing less than the entire providential schema of human history, from the beginning right up until the end of the world—that, starting from a certain point, begins to be administered and regulated in accordance with the principles that had governed the ancient Greek household.

With respect to its classical model, the Christian *oikonomia* nonetheless maintained a specific difference. As we have seen, it is Agamben's contention that the earliest patristic appropriation of this vocable particular to the domestic sphere in fact responded to an exigency far more fundamental than that to which Foucault himself had referred.[32] As he carefully demonstrates, the term *oikonomia* began to assume an unexpected and decisive importance in theology when the second- and third-century Fathers responsible for initiating the discussion regarding a trinity of divine persons were forced to confront a strong resistance internal to the Church itself that their doctrine entailed a lapse into polytheism. The argument, which received its most forceful and lucid expression in the heresiological writings of Hippolytus and Tertullian, went more or less as follows: that the plurality of divine figures is a plurality without division; and that God is most certainly one in terms of his "being," and triple only in terms of his "economy." This term, which in the classical Greek of Xenophon and Aristotle referred to the administration and management of the antique household, now serves to suture together, even while maintaining in their very separateness, the three distinct persons of the Trinity.

The unexpected significance that suddenly comes to be impressed upon this apparently modest word has nonetheless led scholars of the patristic period to distinguish between two distinct and even incompatible referents for the term, and even, in a modern variation, between the two distinct "Trinities" corresponding to this double reference. Either it would refer solely to the internal organization of the divine substance (the Trinity as it is "in and for itself") or else it would refer uniquely to its historical manifestation in time (the Trinity as it is "for us").[33] According to the advocates of the latter position, moreover, the latter usage would correspond to a specifically theological significance of the term, whose first practitioner had been the Apostle Paul. In a well-known sequence of his Letter to the

Ephesians, which quickly became a genuine topos in the discourse of the early Church Fathers, the apostle (or whoever its author might have been) had evoked the curious figure of an *oikonomia tou mystēriou* (economy of the mystery), hidden for the ages in God, which he had been entrusted as God's emissary to reveal.[34] Notwithstanding numerous instances both within the Pauline corpus itself and the New Testament more broadly where its application is perfectly consistent with the everyday secular use,[35] scholars have usually understood this striking construction to mark a new point of departure in the semantic history of the term. Henceforth—so the standard account runs—*oikonomia* would acquire the highly specialized significance of "divine plan of salvation," particular to its use within the theological sphere. As Agamben has argued, however, the supposition of such a dramatic shift cannot be justified—either from a conceptual or from a linguistic perspective. Indeed, the insistence upon the emergence of a new and specifically theological meaning for the term, he suggests, is but the result of the projection of a later theoretical elaboration onto the semantics of a term that retained the pragmatic sense it had in the profane sphere. Only the latter has now been displaced onto a new, hitherto undemonstrated, field of application.[36] For Agamben, both in Paul and in the Church Fathers (who, importantly, were responsible for inverting the juxtaposed terms of the Pauline syntagm), the economy of the mystery names not the extratemporal and extramundane plan of salvation, but the concrete activity of its realization in time and in the world.[37]

In the strict sense, then, the use of the term *oikonomia* in the early patristic corpus thus refers neither simply to the Trinity as it is "in and for itself" nor simply to the Trinity as it is "for us," neither simply to its "essence" nor simply to its "existence." Rather—and this would be Agamben's contention—it is what enables the two polarities to cohere in a unitary paradigm, even at the cost of making God's action in the world equally as inscrutable as his being. It is what allows for God, that is to say, to remain forever as he was, is and always will be, impassive and unchanging, while at the same time assume upon himself that most distinguished of all activities that is the providential government of the world. If God can appear simultaneously as three in one and as one in three, it is only by virtue of his *oikonomia*.

5.

In this sense, the use of *oikonomia* in this context is perfectly consistent with what we find in classical Greece (and above all in Aristotle). As in Aristotle, so in the patristic texts, *oikonomia* would denote an "art" (*technē*) and not a "science" (*epistēmē*); it would refer to an administrative practice at once eminently variable and unconditioned by any necessity.[38] In the strictest sense of the term: a pragmatics.[39] In Hippolytus, for example, we see the term employed in exactly this manner, in the service of his refutation of the argument of a theological adversary, Noetus, who had carried the assertion of the identity of the Father and the Son as far as to suggest that the Father had also died on the cross. From the very beginning of his refutation, the strategic importance of the key term is already in evidence. No one, he argues, would deny that there is a single God; but not everyone would also in turn "scrap the economy [*oikonomian anairēsai*],"[40] as his adversary had proposed to do. It is only in the conclusion to this exercise, however, that he delivers the thesis that had evidently guided his demonstration from the start. On the weight of the evidence presented, he writes, even an unwilling person is obliged to confess—contra Noetus—that the Father, the Son, and the Holy Spirit are not one but three. "But if," he continues, "he wants to learn how God is shown to be one, he must know that there is a single power [*dynamis*]. As far as the power is concerned, God is one; but in terms of the economy the manifestation is triple [*kata tēn oikonomian trichēs ē epideixis*]."[41] Although there is no doubt, as Agamben observes, that the strategic function performed by the term in this passage attests to its technical character, there is still no need to argue for a specifically theological significance even in this instance. Its meaning remains perfectly perspicuous. Even here the term retains the strictly practical sense that it has in Aristotle.[42]

In a later passage, however, Hippolytus will institute an even closer correspondence between his usage and that of the philosopher, by articulating the intra-Trinitarian relations according to a "despotic" chain of commandment and execution. The simultaneous unity and distinction of God, he argues, has a scriptural basis and is best illustrated in the famous incipit to the Gospel of John. When the Evangelist claims that the Word, which was there in the beginning, was with God (*pros tōn theon*), Hippolytus writes, he certainly does not intend to suggest that there were two gods. Rather, he means that there is one Father (*patēr*); but two persons (*prosōpa*), including the Son (*yios*); to which one may add a third, the Holy Spirit (*hagion pneuma*).[43] And the relative functions of the three persons may thereby be revealed:

> The Father gives orders, the Word performs the work, and is revealed through the Son, through whom belief is accorded to the Father. By a harmonious economy the result is a single God. This is because there is one God. For the one who commands is the Father, the one who obeys is the Son, and the one who promotes mutual understanding is the Holy Spirit. He who is the Father is over all things, and the Son is through all things, and the Holy Spirit is in all things.[44]

In this extraordinary sequence, which finds an almost exact parallel in Tertullian,[45] the stakes of the recourse to the vocabulary of economy appears as if completely laid bare. The Father alone commands the work that will be executed through the Son and the Holy Spirit. But all three are unified in accordance with a "harmonious economy" (*oikonomiai symphōnias*). In the space of a single paragraph, *oikonomia* is thus simultaneously employed for the purpose of two distinct ends. It is, at one and the same time, what "disposes" the unity in trinity and what "harmonizes" the trinity in unity: The same term encompasses both operations.[46] Yet it is only its originally administrative significance—this is the sense of Agamben's intervention, over and against the prevailing scholarship—which enables it to concurrently fulfill these two separate, and seemingly incompatible, demands.

If it is true, then, that there is no specifically theological meaning of the term *oikonomia* that would be distinct from what we find in the classical Greek texts, it is nonetheless the case that the specific technology of power that it incarnates—this is the thesis that we will seek to substantiate in the ensuing pages—emerges as completely transformed on account of passing through its Trinitarian elaboration. The "despotic" character of the economic theology that may be recuperated from the textual examples of Hippolytus and Tertullian is ultimately only apparent; in truth, an altogether quite different paradigm to that which had defined the ancient household is at issue here. It is starting from the revelation of this paradigm, whose theoretical reconstruction will form the subject matter of the present book, then, that we will argue for the necessity of a profound overhaul of the prevailing conceptuality of political theology. Our intention, however, is not simply to substitute a theological-economical vocabulary for a theological-political one. For, from a certain point of view, even Schmitt's own understanding of political theology, with its emphasis on the figure of sovereign transcendence, may ironically be characterized—pace Schmitt himself—as economic. According to this perspective, which has been attributed to Hannah Arendt, political theology would be "the outcome of a process of scission that gives rise to transcendence-effects within the political world."[47] But this "process of scission," which manifests itself through the appearance of the distinction between ruler and ruled—and the consequent division, in the field of action, between those who know but do not act and those act but do not know—is itself only the result of the installation of a prepolitical relationship in the midst of the political sphere.[48] Where there is a distinction between ruler and ruled, according to Arendt, there is an attempt to transpose the paradigm of the *oikos* into the *polis*.[49] And thus it is the prepolitical relationship between master and slave that becomes the model for all political relationships. In this sense, as Erik Peterson has rightly observed (albeit according to an different register), the emergence of "political theology" in the Schmittian sense—a political theology whose origin, as we shall see, he will trace back to the formation of a conception of "divine monarchy," above all in the milieu of Hellenistic Judaism—would not only significantly predate the advent of Christianity; it would have nothing uniquely Christian about it. It would represent a perennial scourge from which no polity from ancient Greece through to the present would be fully insulated, and with which all would remain at least virtually threatened.

As we shall see, something like a specifically Christian political theology can appear only with the elaboration of the Trinitarian *oikonomia*. Which is to say that, with Christianity, political theology can only assume the form of an economic theology. In order to substantiate these claims, however, it will be necessary to examine Agamben's reading of the very critique of political theology that, as we have seen, served as the point of departure for his recuperation of the tradition of economic theology: that undertaken by Erik Peterson in his important 1935 study on "Monotheism as a Political Problem." More specifically, it will be necessary to consider the sense of his repurposing of the very formula ("Le roi règne, mais il ne gouverne pas") that Peterson had employed to describe the political theology he intended to discredit in order to characterize the economic theology whose evidence he sought to suppress. With respect to the master who knows but does not act, the Trinitarian institution of a monarch "who reigns but does not govern" represents a subtle, yet decisive shift whose significance we shall have to bring out.

Excursus: On Divine Improvidence

In the context of their fierce polemic with the Gnostics, to which the ante-Nicene uptake of *oikonomia* in large part pertains, the heresiologists of the early Church would not unsurprisingly seek to identify the Gnostic conception of the deity with that of Epicurus. As Agamben has shown, however, what they sought to emphasize through this identification was less the opposition between a good god and an evil god, as that between a god who is extraneous to the world and one who governs it according to an immanent economy.[50] According to Irenaeus, the Gnostics envisage a god who is beyond god, a god whom no one can know because he communicates nothing of himself to human beings and plays no part in the administration of earthly affairs; yet whose purported greatness is premised upon exactly this unknowability. But it is not the god of Scripture whom they have discovered, he argues, but the god of Epicurus: "a God who provides nothing either for himself or for others; in short, a God who is improvident [*oudenos pronoian echonta*]."[51] According to Tertullian, who is even more explicit again, Marcion had deigned to call by the name of Christ "some god out of the school of Epicurus." But the notion of a god who "gives no trouble either to himself or to others," he continues, paraphrasing one of the sayings of Epicurus himself, is completely incompatible with the life of the Jesus that is recounted in the Gospels, who gave trouble both to the Jews "on account of his doctrine [*per doctrinam*]" and to himself "on account of his passion [*per crucem*]."[52] But if the Gnostics thereby sought an absolute rupture between the planes of creation and salvation—for them, the God who creates is not the God who saves—the Epicurean account is even more radical again.

As we have seen, the characteristic feature of Epicurean "theology" is its insistence upon the necessity of divine inactivity. Not without exaggeration can it be described as a doctrine of divine improvidence. Because the Epicureans value happiness above all else, and because happiness is thought to reside in a complete tranquility of mind, their gods are presented as absolutely exempt from all duties (*in omnium vacatione muneram ponimus*).[53] Not only did the gods not create the world ("To say that they conceived the wish to create the world . . . for the sake of men," Lucretius observes, "is folly"); but they take no interest in human beings whatsoever ("For what profit could imperishable and blessed beings gain from our gratitude to take on any task for our sake?").[54] To be a god, according to the teachings of Epicurus, is thus to be relieved of any duty with respect to human beings. But since it is inconceivable that the gods should ever act malevolently, it follows that they must be excused from all acts of beneficence as well. With respect to human beings, the Epicurean deities can only be utterly indifferent. But if the gods are thereby relieved of every obligation regarding human beings, the converse is also true: Human beings, too, are relieved of every obligation regarding the gods. And this, as Lactantius was to observe, is effectively to dissolve all religion. "But if God never does anything good to anyone," he writes, "if he returns no thanks for the devotion of a worshipper, what is so empty, so foolish, as to build temples, make sacrifices, bestow gifts, deplete one's private fortune, for no gain?"[55] Epicurean theology is thus resolutely and unapologetically a-liturgical.

Perhaps nowhere do the profound consequences that follow from this doctrine of divine improvidence appear more starkly, however, than in the remarkable critique of natural teleology that appears in the fourth book of Lucretius's *De rerum natura*. Carrying to an extreme Aristotle's inquiry into whether there is a "function" (*ergon*) particular to man as such ("as eye, hand, foot and in general each of the parts has an function," the philosopher had written, "may one lay it down that man has an function apart from these?"[56]), Lucretius here seeks to call into question even the "functions" particular to each of the specific parts of the body as well. It should not be supposed, he writes, that the clear light of the eyes was expressly created in order that we might be able to see; nor that the thighs, calves and feet were purposefully joined together in order that we might be able to walk; nor, finally, that the arms were deliberately fixed, together with the hands, on either side of the body in order that we might be able to do all that is useful for living.[57] All such explanations, he observes, are ultimately back to front:

> For nothing has been engendered in our body in order that we might be able to use it. It is the fact of its being engendered which creates its use

[*nil ideo quoniam natumst in corpore ut uti possemus, sed quod natumst id procreat usum*]. Seeing did not exist before the light of the eyes was engendered, nor was there pleading with words before the tongue was created. Rather, the origin of the tongue came long before speech, ears were created long before sound was heard, and all our limbs, in my view, existed in advance of their use.[58]

In this respect, he continues, the different parts of the body should be distinguished from the various instruments (shields, beds, cups, for example) expressly created by human caprice. These, by contrast, according to Lucretius, were created solely for the sake of their use: shields for the avoiding of wounds; beds for the resting of weary bodies; cups for the quenching of thirst.[59] To conceive of an inherent functionality of the different parts of the body on the basis of its evidence in manmade objects, however, is to pursue a false analogy. If it is true that certain manmade objects are indeed designed to facilitate functions that have been acquired through the use of the different parts of the body, the same cannot be said of those different parts themselves. The gods neither design nor do they create. Nor, finally, do they take care of what they have not created. Nothing, then, Lucretius concludes, should induce us to believe that the different parts of the body were engendered solely "for the function of utility [*utilitatis ob officium*]."[60] At the limit, the Epicurean doctrine of divine improvidence contests even the ordered disposition—the *oikonomia*—of the various different parts of the human body itself.

6.

In 1935, the German theologian Erik Peterson advanced a withering critique of the conception of "political theology" promoted in the writings of his former colleague at the University of Bonn, Carl Schmitt (who, at the time of publication of Peterson's short monograph, remained a committed member of the National Socialist Party). As has been much remarked, Peterson would wait until the final footnote of his incomparably erudite treatise to make explicit the very critique toward which the entire course of the argument would appear in retrospect to have been consciously directed.[61] "To my knowledge," he wrote, "the concept of 'political theology' was introduced into the literature by Carl Schmitt, *Politische Theologie*

(Munich, 1922). His brief arguments at that time were not intended to be systematic. Here we have tried to show by a concrete example the theological impossibility of a 'political theology' [*die theologische Unmöglichkeit einer 'politischen Theologie'*]."[62] Although the text contained not a single reference to contemporary events, the implication was nonetheless clear enough: By placing themselves in the service of the Reich, he warned, German theologians risked repeating the gesture of Constantine's panegyrist, Eusebius of Caesarea—whom Franz Overbeck had memorably described as the hairstylist of the Emperor's theological wig—in illegitimately surrendering strictly theological considerations to purely political concerns. But it went further than that. As Jacob Taubes was to observe many years later in a personal letter to Schmitt, the reference to *De civitate Dei* 3, 30, through which the critique of Eusebius is carried out—a reference that yields nothing historically, yet that in 1935 was almost "shockingly contemporary"—in fact addresses itself directly to Schmitt in a coded warning, albeit one that failed to reach him.[63] The suggestion was that his fate might end up mirroring that other "eloquent expert on the art of government"—Marcus Tullius Cicero—who, as Augustine had written, showed himself to be quite "blind and unforeseeing [*caecus atque improvidus futorum*]," when betrayed in the name of the very master he thought himself to be serving.[64]

At the level of the text itself, Peterson's analysis was nonetheless located entirely in the late antique world. His argument, which is crystallized only in the final two pages of the treatise, can be easily summarized. With the proclamation of the orthodox dogma of the Trinity, early Christianity's brief flirtation with a political theology founded on the model of Hellenistic Judaism was brought to an abrupt and definitive end. And for two principal reasons. In the first instance, because the triune God, unlike the "monarchical" God of the Jews, had no immediate analogue in the created world, and hence could not so easily be appropriated for the purpose of political instrumentalization. In the second instance, owing to the triumph of Augustine's theology of peace, with its attendant eschatology of deferral, over the prevailing interpretation of the Pax Augusta as the concrete fulfillment of the messianic prophecies of the Old Testament. "The doctrine of the divine monarchy," he writes, in conclusion, "was bound to founder on the Trinitarian dogma and the interpretation of the Pax Augusta on Christian eschatology. In this way, not only was monotheism as a political problem resolved and the Christian faith liberated from bondage to the Roman Empire, but a fundamental break was made with every 'political theology' that misused the Christian proclamation for the justification of a political situation."[65] "In only two pages," as Agamben has observed, "the political theology to whose reconstruction the book had been dedicated is completely demolished."[66] Yet a close examination of this seemingly exhaustive reconstruction, which encompasses pagan, Jewish, and Christian sources alike, also reveals the significant lacunae upon which his account rests. And while these do not discredit the substance of his argument, as we shall see they do allow it to be oriented in a different direction.

According to Peterson, the initial uptake of political theology in the patristic tradition was facilitated by two distinct, yet related, factors. The first was the singular amalgamation of the Hebrew conception of God with the monarchical organization of Aristotle's "theology," and the resulting mobilization, largely for rhetorical purposes, of the figure of a "divine monarchy," which was accomplished in the milieu of Hellenistic Judaism (which is to say, in the writings of Philo of Alexandria). In this case, the Peripatetic material that Philo had employed for the purpose of making the abstract concept of Jewish monotheism comprehensible to the proselyte was easily and conveniently appropriated by the Christian Apologists for the same end.[67] The second factor can also be traced back to a Peripatetic origin. In the pseudo-Aristotelian treatise *De mundo*, whose composition is usually dated around one hundred years after the philosopher's death, we encounter a God who, in a subtle yet decisive divergence from the Aristotelian teaching, is presented as the "principal" (*archē*) according to which "power" (*dynamis*) is active in the cosmos, but who, for precisely this reason, nonetheless does not coincide with it. It is Peterson's contention that, starting from this example, the pagan world too would arrive at a political theology, according to which the invisible divine monarch—who is indeed described, in certain sources, with a striking political image, as a *basileus basileōn* (king of kings)[68]—abstractly "reigns" (*herrscht*), while the so-called national deities allocated to the different parts of the earth concretely "govern" (*regiert*) in his stead.[69] According to a formula that Peterson inexplicably borrows from a characterization of constitutional monarchy in nineteenth-century France to apply in this context: "Le roi règne, mais il ne gouverne pas."[70] In this case, however, the pagan political theology was not adopted in the apologetic literature, but was completely liquidated by the competing Christian political theology for which Eusebius was again the representative spokesperson. According to this vision, in which the destiny of the Christian faith was profoundly and decisively conjoined with that of the Roman Empire, the national deities could no longer govern because national identities had themselves been dissolved by the Pax Augusta over which Constantine presided.

In both cases, then, the concept of the divine monarchy evidently constituted an irresistible pole of attraction for the early Christian authors, whether in their attempt either to justify the monotheistic credentials of the Christian teaching, or else to appraise the concrete political realities in messianic terms. But with the consolidation of the orthodox Trinitarian creed, all of this came to an abrupt and definitive end. It is not the case, to be sure, that the Christian authors suddenly stopped speaking of the divine monarchy, but rather that in the wake of the Arian controversy (in which monotheism, in Peterson's striking expression, was transformed into "a piece of *Reichspolitik*"[71]) it ceases being expressed in a theological-political key. The final word is given to the Cappadocian Father, Gregory of Nazianzus:

> Gregory of Nazianzus gave [the divine monarchy] its ultimate theological depth when he declared, in his *Third Theological Oration*, that there were three opinions about God: anarchy, polyarchy, and monarchy. The first two assumptions unleashed disorder and revolt in God, and ultimately dissolution. Christians, on the other hand, confessed the Monarchy of God. To be sure, not the Monarchy of a single person in the godhead, for this bore the seed of schism within itself, but the Monarchy of the triune God. This conception of nature had no correspondence in the created world. With such arguments, monotheism is laid to rest as a political problem.[72]

7.

"This conception of nature had no correspondence in the created world": For Peterson, as we have seen, this is the critical point. Following the proclamation of the orthodox dogma of the Trinity, the divine monarchy, he contends, can no longer be realized politically—not least because such a realization would, by definition, be impossible. The specifically Christian monarchy is a wholly singular unity in trinity, constituted—to quote directly from Gregory himself—"by the equal dignity of nature, the agreement of will, the identity of movement and the return to unity of all that comes from it, which is impossible in the case of created nature."[73] And what Gregory had accomplished with respect to the concept of God, Peterson continues, Augustine would in turn achieve with respect to the concept of peace.[74] Not only is the Augustan peace a false peace (in the sense that even during his reign numerous civil wars were waged), but there can be no peace in this world, only in the world that is still to come. Only in the kingdom of heaven, as in the monarchy of the triune God, will the scourge of civil war finally be obviated.

In the discussion of Aristotle's "theology" that initiates his treatise, Peterson had duly noted the absence of the term *monarchia* from the philosopher's exposition. Yet while the term itself does not yet appear in this context, he insists, the notion is nonetheless already there in substance—and in a double sense: "In the divine monarchy," he writes, "the single rule (*mia archē*) of the ultimate single *principle* coincides with the actual hegemony of the single ultimate possessor of this rule (*archōn*)."[75] It is nonetheless surprising that he does not pause to consider the one place where it definitely does appear. And where, as we have already seen, it describes the organizational structure not of the political realm but of that against which the former is sharply differentiated: the antique household.[76] This is all the more striking when one considers that it is the example of the household, together with that of the army, that Aristotle himself employs in the general context of his theology, in order to illustrate how the paradigm of the transcendence of the good may be reconciled with that of its immanent order.[77] "We must also consider," he begins Book Lambda of the *Metaphysics*,

> in which of two ways the nature of the universe contains the good or the highest good, whether as something separate and by itself, or as the order of the parts. Probably in both ways, as an army does. For the good is found both in the order and in the leader, and more in the latter; for he does not depend on the order but it depends on him. And all things are ordered together somehow, but not all alike. . . . [N]ot such that one thing has nothing to do with another, but they are connected. For all are ordered together to one end, as in a household [*en oikia*].[78]

Yet as Agamben has argued, Peterson's elision of the "economic" articulation of the divine monarchy is even more flagrant again in the case of his analyses of the Apologists who first sought to appropriate this notion for the benefit of the Christian message.[79] For, as we have already seen, it was by means of this very articulation that the same authors would seek to defend the nascent doctrine of the Trinity. Given the importance that the Trinitarian dogma comes to assume in Peterson's argumentative strategy, Agamben contends, it is simply remarkable that he neglects to speak of it. Indeed, he not only neglects to speak of it, but he even appears to intentionally avoid any reference to it—leaving Agamben to suppose something like a "conscious repression."[80]

Consider the example of Tertullian. While drawing attention to Tertullian's attempt in his *Adversus Praxean* to reclaim the term "monarchy" from its appropriation on the part of his theological adversaries—the so-called Monarchians, who, like Hippolytus's opponent Noetus, had insisted on a complete identification of the Father and the Son—Peterson includes not a single reference to the other term through which, in apparent continuity with the Aristotelian tradition, such a reclamation will be accomplished. Indeed, as Agamben has shown, so intent is Peterson on avoiding any reference to the "economy" that he will even go to the extreme length of deliberately interrupting his citations.[81] Where he quotes, for example, "'We hold', they say, 'to the monarchy', and even Latins so expressly frame the sound, and in so masterly a fashion, that you would think that they understood monarchy as well as they pronounce it," the text continues: "but while Latins are intent to shout out 'monarchy', even Greeks refuse to understand the *oikonomia*."[82]

But the larger context is even more illuminating again. For, as we have seen, *oikonomia* is the very term through which Tertullian, developing indications already to be found in Irenaeus and Hippolytus, had sought to reconcile the unity of divine substance with a plurality of divine figures. "For all the simple people," he had written,

> that I say not the thoughtless and ignorant (who are always the majority of the faithful), since the Rule of Faith itself brings us over from the many gods of the world to the one true God, not understanding that while they must believe in one God only yet they must believe in him along with his economy, shy at the economy [*sed cum oeconomia esse*

credendum, expavescunt ad oeconomian]. They claim that plurality and ordinance of the trinity is a division of unity—although a unity which derives from itself a trinity is not destroyed but administered by it [*non destruatur ab illa sed administretur*].[83]

In almost identical terms to what we have seen in Hippolytus above,[84] here the divine monarchy is administered by an economy. And even if this economy should be dispensed by a plurality, Tertullian continues, the monarchy would not thereby be destroyed on this account. The monarchy would not cease if were to be ruled in partnership with a son; but neither would it cease if it were to be administered by other closely related persons who had been appointed as "officers." Even in the case that it were to be administered by so many legions and hosts of heavenly angels, as is suggested in the Bible (Dan. 7:10)—even then, according to Tertullian, it would not cease:

> Therefore if also the divine monarchy is administered by so many legions and hosts of angels (as it is written, "Ten thousand times ten thousand stood before him and thousands of thousands ministered to him"), yet has not therefore ceased to belong to one, so that it ceases to be a monarchy, because it is managed by so many thousands of authorities, how could God be thought to experience division and dispersion in the Son and in the Holy Spirit, who occupy the second and third rank and who are partners in the Father's substance, when he does not experience it through so great a number of angels who are alien to the Father's substance.[85]

The implication should be clear: The monarchy is not destroyed when it is administered by many, but only (according to an argument that should by now be familiar) when another ruler is introduced in opposition to the first, or when another God is revealed in opposition to the creator God—in which case, the monarchy would enter into civil war with itself.[86]

Much as Peterson would later find in Gregory of Nazianzus, so there appears already in Tertullian—one of the principal targets of his polemic—a monarchy that is articulated in Trinitarian terms. A monarchy of one God alone, yet subject to an economy, as the Aristotelian tradition would have it. It is nonetheless important to note the subtle difference that Tertullian introduces with respect to this received knowledge.[87] In Tertullian, there is no longer, as there was in the Aristotelian tradition he takes up and modifies in turn, an attempt to define the economy in monarchical terms; rather, according to a curious strategic reversal whose sense we shall have to clarify, it is the monarchy itself that now proceeds only by means of an economy. It is not that the economy is monarchical, but that the monarchy is economical.

8.

It is Peterson himself who suggests that the French formula "Le roi règne, mais il ne gouverne pas," which he had employed to characterize the pseudo-Aristotelian *De mundo*, might also be applied to Tertullian as well. According to him, when Tertullian argued that the divine monarchy may be administered by a son, or by other specially appointed intermediary persons (or, indeed, by innumerable legions and hosts of heavenly angels), without the unity of substance thereby being imperiled, he not only directly borrowed his argument from the Peripatetic-Platonic tradition of which the *De mundo* was the preeminent expression; much more disturbingly still, he sought to explain the intra-Trinitarian relations using a paradigm previously employed to justify polytheism.[88] Evidence of such a defense, Peterson suggests, was widespread throughout the late antique world, and is attested even in Tertullian himself. In his *Apologeticus*, for example, the North African author had observed that this is how most men, Plato included, had "apportioned the divinity" (*disponunt divinitatem*): "They hold that the control, the supreme sway," he writes, "rests with one, the various functions with many [*esse penes unum, officia eius penes multos*]."[89] But everywhere, according to Peterson, the idea is the same: "Le roi règne, mais il ne gouverne pas."[90] For him, it is astonishing that Tertullian would in turn employ the same image to describe the Trinity.[91] As the Tertullian of the *Apologeticus* would record, albeit in accordance with a tradition that stretches at least as far back as Philo, the incipient risk of such an account is that "the procurators and prefects and presiding officers" would be worshipped on equal standing with the one supreme being.[92]

For Peterson, Tertullian had illegitimately sought to transpose the monarchy-concept of the pagan political theology onto the Trinity, without realizing that the latter requires its own independent conceptual development. By restoring to Tertullian's text, precisely where Peterson had censored it, the discourse pertaining to the "economy," Agamben, by contrast, is able to repurpose the formula to describe the operation of the Trinitarian *oikonomia* instead. In so doing, however, he completely reorients the sense in which the formula is to be understood. On the one hand, it registers the displacement of a division that had been supposed at the level of the divine being itself: The king reigns, but he does not govern. On the other hand, however, it indicates the subsequent recomposition and rearticulation of the two divided elements at an ulterior level: that of divine praxis. In this sense, the formula is no longer to be understood in terms of a simple division (whether this is conceived as a dualism or even as an opposition), but rather, only in terms of the functional coordination of its constituent elements. As Agamben has argued, however,[93] such a coordination has its condition of possibility in the reappearance of the very division that had been avoided at the level of God's being, at the subsequent level of the relation between his being and his action. As opposed to the Aristotelian theology with which Peterson's own exposition had begun, in which divine being and acting had reposed together in perfect unity, the latter being but the "expression" of the former, with the elaboration of the Trinitarian *oikonomia* this is no longer the case. Henceforth, God's action—his "economy"—has no foundation in his being. Yet it is precisely the ungrounded and even anarchical character of this economy that enables it to function as a mechanism of governance.[94] By virtue of a striking paradox, the necessity for the divine government of the world is secured with the very gesture that makes it possible.[95]

The present book, which seeks to deepen and extend Agamben's analyses, is concerned less with tracing out the consequences that follow from this transformation of the paradigm of classical ontology, which coincides with the sundering of being and acting, than with theorizing the singular form of action that issues from the latter and the particular technology of power that it incarnates. A form of action, that is to say, that fully participates in the divinity, yet without coinciding with it completely. Against Peterson, who maintained that the Trinity encompasses a monarchy without parallel in the created world, Agamben has argued that the Trinity is a monarchy that is nonetheless administered by an economy. In this way, as we have seen, he is able to repurpose the formula that Peterson had employed to describe the pagan political theology he seeks to discredit in order to characterize the economic theology he wants to repress. The properly Christian political theology—this is what Agamben's intervention leads us to conclude—can only assume the form of an economic theology. And not least because—as we shall see in what follows—once the one true polis has been definitively shifted out of this world, as happens with Augustine, the *saeculum* itself must be conceived only in economic terms. From this perspective, the transformation of the public realm into an integrally economic space, which reaches its apex with the emergence and triumph of the sphere of civil society in modernity, can be shown to form part of the Christian heritage of the West.

2

LITURGICAL POWER

1.

There could be no greater misunderstanding of the sense of Peterson's theological-political injunction than to suggest that what the theologian sought was to expunge politics from the theological sphere altogether.[1] A quick glance at the first lines of the preface to his treatise is sufficient to confirm this. "The European Enlightenment," we read, "retained nothing of the Christian belief in God except 'monotheism,' a retention as dubious in its theological substance as it is in its political consequences. For the Christian, there can be political action [*politisches Handeln*] only under the condition of the belief in the triune God."[2] As has been observed, what is striking in this passage is not so much its foregrounding of the critique of Schmitt—a critique that, as we have seen, will have to wait until the book's infamous final footnote to become explicit—as the positive assertion that unexpectedly penetrates through it: the surprising suggestion that there is a distinctly Christian "political action," but that it may be grounded on the Trinitarian dogma alone.[3] For Peterson, there is, unequivocally, a uniquely Christian politics; to critique political theology, then, means to critique the particular form that it has been typically understood to assume: that of political monotheism.[4] Above all, it means to critique the transpositive model, whereby theological concepts would be illegitimately transferred from the religious sphere and installed at the heart of the political. In short: the thesis regarding secularization. For the Christian, there can be no correspondence, whether by analogy or otherwise, between religious and political monotheism, no continuum between the theological concept of divine monarchy and the political concept of secular absolutism. In no instance may the Christian proclamation be placed in the service of secular politics. The specific locus of an expressly Christian politics must instead be sought elsewhere.

For Peterson—such is the striking thesis he will advance in a sequence of influential publications more or less contemporaneous with the treatise on monotheism—the distinctly Christian form of political action coincides instead with the practice that the ancient Greeks called *leitourgia*. Its specific locus, accordingly, will be that institution that Peterson was also accustomed to denominating by its Greek name: the *ekklēsia*. Already in his 1926 doctoral dissertation, dedicated to the meticulous examination of the appearance of the "one God" formula in late antique epigraphical, liturgical, and literary sources, Peterson had sought to underscore the juridical character of the Christian liturgy through an analysis of its acclamatory aspect.[5] But it was only with his important 1929 essay on "The Church"—the text that arguably precipitated his own imminent conversion to Catholicism—that this discovery would come to assume an expressly theological significance. Significantly, his argumentation adopts an orientation inverse with respect to that of the secularization thesis. Here it is the Christian *ekklēsia* itself that is presented as a reflection of its profane counterpart, the great assemblies of the ancient Greek city-states. And, as with the latter, so what is decisive in the former is the "public" and "political" character of the deeds carried out there: "The secular *ekklēsia* of antiquity is familiar to us as an institution of the polis. It is the assembly of the fully enfranchised citizens of a polis, gathered together to perform legal acts [*Rechtsakten*]. In an analogous fashion, one could call the Christian *ekklēsia* the assembly of fully enfranchised citizens of the heavenly city, gathered together to perform particular acts of worship [*Kulthandlungen*]."[6] Far from being opposed, in this striking sequence law and worship are presented as perfectly continuous with one another, owing to their shared acclamatory form. For Peterson, it is the liturgy that thus attests to the political and juridical character of the Christian assembly.

That this thesis presents one of theoretical nuclei of his entire theology is further attested by the fact that it serves at once as the point of departure and as the interpretative matrix for what is, arguably, the most important of all his theological tractates: the "Book on the Angels."[7] Right from the outset of this remarkable essay, the determining theme is already announced. In accordance with the schema first articulated in the Letter to the Hebrews—but most readily associated with its subsequent elaboration in the writings of Augustine—Peterson would again seek to define the "essence" (*Wesen*) of the Christian *ekklēsia*, only starting from its "existence" (*Existenz*), its liminal position between the earthly and the heavenly cities: "The Church's way leads from the earthly to the heavenly Jerusalem, from the city of the Jews to the city of the angels and saints. The Church's existence between the earthly and the heavenly city determines its essence. Its character is conditioned by the fact that Christians have left the earthly Jerusalem, and, because they have no lasting city on earth (Heb. 13:14), like Abraham they seek the city to come, whose builder is God (Heb. 11:8–10)."[8] Having departed the earthly Jerusalem (a reading that Peterson grounds dogmatically on the Twelve Apostle's actual departure from Jerusalem, as recorded in the Pentecostal narrative of Acts), the Church has nonetheless not yet been absorbed into the heavenly Jerusalem—an event that will only take place at the end of time. And yet, having left the earthly city behind as a "political entity," it is nonetheless already figured as an "institution" of the heavenly city: the city that is still to come, but into which the heavenly high priest has already entered. It is primarily toward the latter, according to Peterson, that Christians' eyes are turned:

> Perhaps we could also say that, just as the profane *ekklēsia* of antiquity is an institution of the polis, so the Christian *ekklēsia* is an institution of the heavenly city, the heavenly Jerusalem. Just as the profane *ekklēsia* is the assembly of the citizens of the earthly polis to perform legal acts, the Christian *ekklēsia* could analogously be defined as the assembly of the citizens of the heavenly city to perform acts of worship—the legal acts of the Christian *ekklēsia* also being acts of worship.[9]

The Church is not yet the Kingdom. But there is nonetheless something of the Kingdom that, in Peterson's words, "clings to the Church."[10] On the one hand, a sharp distinction is made; at the same time, however, a connection is formed. Through its sacraments and through its worship—in short, through its liturgy—the Church, according to Peterson, in effect participates temporally, together with the holy angels, in the eternal cult celebrated by the "citizens" of the heavenly polis.[11] In a remarkable gloss on the use of the verb *apographesthai* in Heb. 12:23, he even goes as far as to suggest that, through the baptismal rite, Christian children are, as it were, "enrolled" in the civil registry of the celestial city.[12] Hence the surprising thesis—whose significance Agamben has again sought to underscore[13]—which the theologian repeats multiple times in the course of his exposition and whose import he seeks to verify through detailed scriptural and patristic analysis: Namely, that through its worship and its liturgy, the earthly assembly as it were participates in the heavenly assembly and that it thereby maintains, in his words, "an original relation with the political world [*eine ursprüngliche Beziehung zu der politischen Welt*]."[14]

2.

To illustrate this thesis, Peterson advances a striking "political" reading of Chapters 4 and 5 of Revelation, beginning with a consideration of the liturgical-hymnic "inserts" which intermittently punctuate its text to interrupt the eschatological visions. The point of departure is already instructive: Just as "from the standpoint of narrative economy," the inserts serve "a retarding function [*eine retardierende Funktion*]," so too, in this way, according to Peterson, they reflect early Christianity's relation to the eschatological events.[15] Intoned first by the four "living creatures" (*zōa*) of Jewish prophecy and then by the twenty-four "elders" (*presbyteroi*) who represent the "spiritual" Israel (that is, the Church)—the sequence is important—they make manifest, in the form of the heavenly praise in which the earthly Church's worship participates, the glory of God's eternal world, which has not yet broken through but against whose backdrop the eschatological events must be seen to unfold.[16] In one sense, the twenty-four responsible for the chanting of these hymns must be viewed as priests. But they are also kings, Peterson contends; as such, they are presented as laying down their crowns.[17] In the same sense, the setting for their worship is not so much a temple as a throne room; a throne room, however, of a very particular kind, in which there appears, in addition to the one throne, a further twenty-four on which the elders themselves are seated. Not only, then, do the twenty-four deliberately cast aside their crowns; while intoning their hymn ("You are worthy, our Lord and God, / To receive glory and honor and power"), they also fall in unison before the venerated throne.[18] Their hymn, according to Peterson, is thus "fundamentally an acclamation [*im Grunde eine Akklamation*]."[19] What they acclaim is the sovereignty of the king of the heavenly city, the king who is to possess his throne for all eternity.

It is this eschatological detail that furnishes the hermeneutic key for Peterson's entire interpretation. As the next of the inserts further consolidates,[20] the triumph of the Lion of Judah is a triumph over all of "the kings of the earth" (Rev. 6:6): Precisely this is what the elders—casting aside their crowns and prostrating themselves before the throne—acclaim through their song. "The 'victory' of the Lamb," Peterson writes, "founds a new polis."[21] But it also calls forth a new people, a new people of God. "By [the Lamb's] blood," he writes, "we are purchased from the 'tribes, tongues, peoples and nations,' that is, we have been freed from the natural captivity [*natürlichen Verhaftetsein*] to 'tribes, tongues, peoples and nations.' The blood of the Lamb has created a new people, the people of the Christians, as the Church Fathers are forever saying. Over against all national hymns, the hymn of the Church is thus a 'final,' eschatological hymn, just as the people that intones this hymn is a final 'holy people.'"[22] Just as the Church's language is the transcendence of all natural languages, and just as the Church's anthem is the transcendence of all national anthems, so too this "new people," according to Peterson, must be seen as the transcendence of all other peoples. In exactly the same sense, so too the heavenly doxology—that for which the people "assemble," that which indeed first constitutes them as a "people"—must be viewed as the transcendence of every merely political acclamation.[23] Or rather, as the transcendence of the acclamation of bounded, terrestrial, national polities in favor of that of the one true polity, which is in heaven and not on earth.

Perhaps nowhere so much as in this sequence does the contrast that Peterson's vision presents with respect to the paradigm of secularization (and the theological-political tradition that is consubstantial with it) appear with such starkness. With his insistence on interpreting the function of the Christian liturgy from the perspective of political acclamations, he rejects the thesis of the genetic anteriority of the theological relative to the political, which constitutes the tacit axiom of modern political theology. At the same time, however, drawing on a tendency already present in the longer development of Christian thought—yet nonetheless carried to an extreme point in the singular prominence he attributes to the figure of the "celestial Jerusalem"—he asserts the metaphysical superiority of the theological over the political, even to the point of wholly absorbing the latter within the remit of the former. It is only in this perspective that the expressly political significance that Peterson ascribes to the heavenly congregation of intoning and acclaiming angels—the angels into whose "fellowship" the faithful yearn to be taken—becomes fully explicable.

According to Peterson, even their presence alongside Christ, at the celebration of the Eucharist, to which the testimony of certain Church Fathers bears witness, serves simply to emphasize the public character of Christian worship.[24] The singing of psalms, the celebration of marriage, the election of bishops, the rites of baptism and consummation: These are all, for Peterson, irreducibly public, and never merely private, devotions.[25] There is, then, even for the Church itself, a "heavenly publicity" (*himmlische Öffentlichkeit*). Yet it certainly does not owe the latter to the endowment of the secular authorities.[26] Rather, it pertains intrinsically to the Church as such, and stems once again from the fact that, through its worship and its liturgy, the former manifests an *ursprüngliche Beziehung* with the political world. It acts, that is to say, and it acts publicly, in its singular capacity as the one worldly "institution" of the polis that is in heaven.

3.

As the theologian was doubtless well aware, *leitourgia* was also an important convention of the ancient polis. Although the original sense of the term has been largely forgotten today, it is important to observe that, with it, the Church Fathers (and presumably also the unknown author of the Letter to the Hebrews) had inherited, via the Septuagint, an expressly political term pertaining to the sphere of public administration, which referred to the compulsory "public services" that the wealthiest citizens of the Greek polis were obliged to undertake for the benefit of the larger public. As has often been observed, such a definition was preserved *in nuce* in the popular etymology of the term, which was widespread already in antiquity: A compound of *laos* (people) and *ergon* (work), the *leitourgia* was a service—democratic in the first instance, although susceptible to an antidemocratic drift—performed by the people and for the people itself. As opposed to the system of fixed taxation, it designated the financial burden assumed by the most prominent residents of the city, usually at fixed intervals and often at considerable personal cost, for the provision of a delimited set of highly specialized services. Thus, although compulsory, liturgies were not seen as economic obligations, but rather as civic duties, which carried with them a strong honorific dimension.[27] In classical Athens, the major liturgies were the *triērarchia*, which entailed building, equipping, and manning the trireme of a naval vessel during wartime; the *chorēgia*, which involved assembling and preparing of a group of performers for the annual dramatic festivals; and the *gymnasarchia*, which comprised recruiting and training a team of competitors for the athletic contests. Others again—considerably less expensive, and as a direct corollary, significantly less important—were related to public works and religious observance.

The sheer scale of the expenditure associated with even the least costly of liturgies has led some scholars to suppose a complete identification of the *leitourgantēs* (the liturgy performers) with the *euporous* (the rich), and even to speak of a "liturgical class" as such.[28] Yet the very passages that most sharply attest to the existence of such a distinction at the same time also anticipate its future inversion. Thus, a highly sardonic sequence of the pseudo-Xenophonian *Constitution of the Athenians* speaks of the "wealthy" (*plourioi*) who preside over the liturgies in which the "people" (*dēmos*) participate, becoming increasingly poorer as a result of them, while the people themselves grow progressively richer.[29] Indeed, so great was the cost of certain liturgies, and so willing were the citizens to undertake even the most lavish and extravagant of them, that the ancient Greeks were compelled to coin a distinct verb, *kataleitourgeō*, to describe someone who had been, as it were, "ruined in liturgies."[30] Conversely, Aristotle will include among his enumeration of the moral virtues a category that refers precisely to the appropriate performance of a liturgical office: He who displays a magnitude in his liberality that is in accordance with the means of his wealth thus demonstrates his "munificence" (*megaloprepeia*).[31]

The liturgical system remained an integral part of the administration of Greek cities throughout the Hellenistic and Roman periods, reaching its broadest extension in Roman Egypt, where it obliged, at one time or another, almost the entire populace.[32] From the compulsory yet laudable acts of pure gratuity performed by the city's elite in service of the people, it was thus gradually transformed into a vast bureaucratic apparatus that obliged almost everybody, regardless of personal status or fortune. In his reconstruction of the early semantic history of the word, Naphtali Lewis has shown how, together with this expansion in its remit, the scope of the term itself was also gradually extended and generalized so as to encompass service "of any kind, for any beneficiary, not necessarily for the benefit of the community."[33] It was out of this general atmosphere that we find the emergence of the highly specialized sense of "cultic service to the divinity," the sole meaning that the term preserves to this day (yet that was already attested as early as the fourth century BCE).[34] It is significant that under Constantine's rule bishops, priests and deacons—in short, all the members of the nascent ecclesiastical hierarchy—were accorded highly coveted exemptions from these cumbersome and time-consuming services, which so tightly constrained the broader population.[35] The suggestion being that once Christianity had become the religion of the empire, the clergy immediately became the bearers of a liturgy (in the political sense) of almost unparalleled importance, and hence ought to be free to pursue their worship of God unencumbered for the benefit of the larger community. Like the imperial liturgy, the ecclesiastical liturgy was thus also viewed as a "public" service, a labor performed by the people and for the people. It is nonetheless important to observe that in this instance the execution of one particular liturgy went hand in hand with "immunity" from every other public obligation.[36] The ecclesiastical liturgy is thus not one liturgy among others, but already, even here, in a sense the transcendence of every other liturgy.

When Peterson asserts that the specifically Christian form of political action coincides with the liturgy of the Church, it is this historical backdrop that he in one sense evokes and in another sense modifies. For the liturgy of the Church, in his reading, certainly does not owe the attribution of its political character to its contribution to the this-worldly polis below, but rather to its participation in the otherworldly polis above, which englobes and transcends it. Far from representing the simple negation of Schmitt's political theology, Peterson's political ecclesiology in fact constitutes the most definitive twentieth-century expression of a specific branch of political theology (although perhaps, in his case, it would be more accurate to speak of a "theological politics"[37]); one with its own distinct history and its own particular tropes, which locates the one true polis of the Christians in the celestial city of Jerusalem, yet that maintains, for the faithful, a unique point of contact in the liturgy of the sole worldly institution of the celestial city that is the Church. If liturgy remains a "public service" for Peterson, however (and he would appear to be insistent on this), it is important to observe that, for him, such a service would be performed not for the benefit of a public that is already in existence, but would instead be constitutive of the "people" as such. Liturgy, in this sense, would thus not merely describe the particular form of Christian political action; more specifically again, it would name the very operation by which an originally unpolitical element (and hence, a "non-people") is, as it were, "politicized": the operation by which it becomes political, the operation by which it is constituted in a political community.

This is the sense in which we must understand the reference to Cicero's classic definition of the *res publica* in an important sequence of Peterson's 1926 doctoral dissertation that sets the tone for all that follows. "The *laos* that takes part in the *eucharistia*," he writes, evoking the specific Greek term for people that we have seen forms one of the constituent parts of the compound *leitourgia*,[38]

> is *laos* only to the extent that it has a juridical capacity. I recall Cicero, *De re publica*, 1, 25, where it says: *populus autem non omnis hominum coetus quoquo modo congregatus, sed coetus multitudinis iuris consensus sociatus.* That the legal acts of the *laos* in later times were limited solely to the rights of acclamation changes nothing in the fundamental determination, namely, that one may speak in an originary sense of a *populus* (*laos*) or an *ekklēsia* only where there exists, for a people, the possibility of carrying out legal acts.[39]

"But a people is not any assembly of human beings brought together in any way, but an assembly of the multitude associated through agreement of law"[40]: When Peterson quotes Scipio's definition it is important to observe that he does not merely cite Cicero's text; more specifically again, although his name remains unmentioned in this context, he cites Augustine's citation of it. In an important chapter from the nineteenth book of his *De civitate Dei*, the bishop of Hippo had sought to fulfill a promise made earlier in his treatise by demonstrating that there was never any Roman republic answering to Scipio's definition.[41] His reasoning went as follows: Since there is no law without justice, and no justice without God, there could have been no people in the sense that Scipio described and hence no republic in Rome. Instead, he argues, there must have prevailed "some kind of mob, not deserving the name people [*qualiscumque multitudinis quae populi nomine digna non est*]."[42] For Augustine (and also for Peterson as well), the Roman state was thus composed of a nondescript *multitudo*, which only the *iuris consensu* that God alone could have provided would have succeeded in transforming into a *populus*.[43] What is genuinely new in Peterson's account, however, is the unprecedented role assigned to the liturgy in articulating this shift. As he continues:

If one day someone were to write the history of the word "lay" (*laos*), they would have to pay attention to all the contexts evoked here, and at the same time also understand that the *laos* is precisely the *ochlos*, insofar as it must cry out liturgical acclamations. They will at the same time further understand that when the *laos* cries out liturgical acclamations, it establishes its ecclesiastical-legal status in same manner in which, in public law, the *laos* signals its status through its right to express its *ekboēseis* to the *despotēs* in the profane *ekklēsia*.[44]

For Peterson, the *laos* constitutes itself as such—which is to say, as a public and political entity—solely through the chanting and intoning of liturgical acclamations. In his singular conception, the "people" literally shouts itself into existence.[45] But a history of the word *laos*, such as Peterson proposes here, would in fact show that the Church concept of Christianity ends up separating the *ekklēsia* from the people who would compose it, with the result that the acclamations ultimately lose their constitutive force (retaining, at best, a merely accessory value).[46] If these acclamations nonetheless remain political in the sense that Peterson describes, it is only to the extent that they now supplement, precisely by giving their assent to it, a liturgy that is performed by priests alone and that articulates a technique of government hitherto unrecognized as such. Liturgy ceases once and for all to be a service performed by the people and for the people itself; rather, it becomes a service for the people—but only to the extent that it is also a service to God, the two finally having become undecidable—that is performed by those who, in a very determinate sense, are not the people. It is in precisely this sense, however, as we shall see, that Peterson's affirmation of the political character of the liturgy may be shown to coincide with the mediation of the theological economy.

4.

Among the signature achievements of Michel Foucault's important 1977–78 lecture course at the Collège de France—the very course, that is to say, in which he first announced the theme of *gouvernementalité*, which would remain at the center of all his subsequent research—was the reconstruction of a distinct technology of power, whose operation he would seek to present as irreducible to that of state.[47] If the latter constitutes a centripetal force, inexorably drawing everything into its radiant core, what the French philosopher termed "pastoral power" (*le pouvoir pastoral*) would instead present the paradigm of something like a centrifugal force: In diffusing itself throughout the entire social body, it would describe a modality of power oriented outwards toward individuals, individuals whose conduct it would seek to administer in a continuous and permanent manner. As distinct from sovereignty, what Foucault called government is never exercised over a state, over a territory, or indeed over any political structure; it is exercised only over men, at both the individual and the collective levels.[48] And the pastorate is the form in which it would receive its originary elaboration.

In the strict sense, then, government is not a political concept. Nor, furthermore, are its origins to be sought at the beginnings of Western culture, whether in ancient Greece or Rome. For it, one must project a different genealogy. The image of the shepherd king who watches over his "people" as a herdsman watches over his "flock" emerges in the first instance, according to Foucault, in the ancient Near East (specifically, in Egypt, Assyria, and Mesopotamia).[49] But it was the Hebrew Bible that would advance the "most developed ideology" of the shepherd king, reserving this title for Yahweh alone (with the important exception of the prophetic books, where it frequently served, significantly enough, as a designation for the Messiah).[50] There, as Foucault has sought to underscore, it was employed in a strictly religious, and never in a political, sense. Indeed, at no point across its twenty-four books does the royal title "shepherd" ever appear in a positive form.[51] It is God, and God alone, who is the "shepherd of Israel"[52]; it is exclusively he who appears before his people, who leads and who guides them; who "restores Israel to its pasture."[53] "The pastoral relationship," Foucault writes, "in its full and positive form is therefore essentially the relationship of God to men. It is a religious type of power which finds its principle, its foundation and its perfection in the power that God exercises over his people [*son peuple*]."[54]

As the exclusive relationship that obtains between God and his chosen people, the pastoral paradigm, in its Hebrew form, encompasses four distinctive features.[55] To begin with, it is neither territorial nor static: The shepherd wields his power over the flock itself, and not over the land upon which they graze. And he wields it over the flock insofar as it is perpetually in movement. In contradistinction to the pantheon of Greek Gods, who are always attached to a specific place, the Hebrew God is not a territorial God: He is "the God who walks, the God who moves, the God who wanders."[56] Secondly, it is the action of the shepherd, who gathers together and directs his flock, that in effect causes it to exist: The flock has no consistency outside of him; it would immediately scatter were it not for his constant vigilance. Its continuity is thus dependent on the permanence of his presence and the regularity of his action. Thirdly, the shepherd's action articulates a mode of power that is defined entirely by its beneficence. It serves an exclusively soteriological function: Its essential aim and objective is nothing less than the eternal salvation of the flock. The shepherd thus appears as the intermediary between the flock and its salvation. For this reason, fourthly, and finally, his action assumes the form of a duty or an obligation that must be fulfilled with respect to each and every one of the members of his flock. The shepherd must be devoted to his sheep. He must ensure the salvation of all of them indifferently; to achieve this end, however, he must attend to each of them in their individuality. His, then, is a strictly "individualizing" power. Not a single sheep may be lost from view. He must be willing to sacrifice himself in order to save the whole; at the same time, he must also be willing to sacrifice the whole in order to save a single sheep. One for all and all for one: Such, according to Foucault, defines the ethical and religious paradox of the shepherd.

The importance of this last aspect for nascent Christianity hardly needs to be emphasized. Jesus is, par excellence, the "great shepherd" who, "by the blood of the eternal covenant,"[57] sacrifices himself for the sake of the entire flock.[58] But he is also the author of the parable of the lost sheep, who, in taking up the Mosaic theme, declares his willingness to sacrifice the entire flock for the sake of a single sheep: "Which one of you," he boldly inquires of the Pharisees, "having a hundred sheep and losing one of them, does not leave the ninety-nine in the wilderness and go after the one that is lost until he finds it?"[59] In adopting, and thereby adapting to its own purposes, this Hebrew model,[60] the Christian pastorate, as Foucault acutely observes, nonetheless accomplished with respect to it something hitherto unprecedented in its history: It transformed it into a Church. It is together with this process, which Foucault adroitly describes as the "institutionalization of the pastorate [institutionnalisation du pastorat],"[61] that the history of governmentality in the strict sense may be said to begin:

We should no doubt say . . . that the pastorate begins with a process that is absolutely unique in history and no other example of which is found in the history of any other civilization: the process by which a religion, a religious community, constitutes itself as a Church, that is to say, as an institution that claims to govern men in their daily life on the grounds of leading them to eternal life in the other world, and to do this not on the scale of a definitive group, of a city or a state, but of the whole of humanity. . . . With this institutionalization of a religion as a Church, fairly rapidly, at least in its broad outline, an apparatus was formed of a kind of power not found anywhere else and which was constantly developed and refined over fifteen centuries, from the second and third centuries after Jesus Christ up to the eighteenth century.[62]

For the Hebrews, there was no shepherd outside of God. To that extent, there could be no pastoral "institution" in the strict sense: It was the relationship of God to his people alone that could assume this form. With the development and spread of Christianity, on the other hand, according to Foucault, a concurrent "autonomization" of the shepherd theme takes place. The relationship of the shepherd to his flock, he suggests, thus becomes the fundamental, encompassing relationship, employed not just to describe God's relationship to his people, but a whole sequence of further relationships, extending from top to bottom of the Church, modeled on that of the first. It is not only Christ but the apostles, not only the apostles but the bishops, not only the bishops but the abbots, not only the abbots but the priests, who act as shepherds with respect to their flocks.[63] The Church thus assumes a pastoral organization. Finally, and decisively, this pastoral power, according to Foucault, will come to assume a sacramental form. What is baptism, he asks, if not the power of calling sheep to the flock? What is penance, if not the power of reintegrating those who have momentarily strayed? Although this aspect in the genealogy of governmentality has elicited almost no commentary, it is important to observe that for Foucault the institutionalization of the pastorate coincides with the "sacramentalization" of the specific technology of power that it incarnates. From a certain point on, pastoral power becomes sacramental power.[64]

5.

For Foucault, the pastorate is of strictly Eastern provenance. It was uniquely through Christianity, according to his account, that it would come to enter the West and thereby exert its determining influence over the formation and deployment of the specific technology of power whose paradigm he seeks to designate. "The real history of the pastorate," he writes, "as the source of a specific type of power over men, as a model and matrix of procedures for the government of men, really only begins only with Christianity."[65] Not only is the conspicuous absence of the pastoral theme in Greek political reflection underscored, but Foucault goes further to show that even in the rare instances in which it does appear—for example, in Plato's *Statesman*, which devotes many lines to considering the appropriateness of this metaphor for representing political activity—it resolves to exclude any positive identification of the lowly figure of the shepherd with the majesty of the king.[66] "The demands of pastorship," Foucault concludes, "are too trifling to be suitable for a king."[67] There is, to be sure, the well-known epic formula *poimen laōn* (shepherd of the people), which appears frequently in Homer (often with specific reference to Agamemnon) and which will be regularly cited by later Greek authors.[68] But Foucault dismisses even this designation as merely a "ritual title" and, in any case, as itself a distinct borrowing from the East.[69]

Yet even if it does reflect an Eastern influence, the Homeric epithet nonetheless does contain a specific element that would come to assume a decisive importance in the language of Hellenistic Judaism; an element that, moreover, would in turn be transmitted, by way of the New Testament, to the patristic tradition, where it would assume an even greater significance. The connection is not at first glance obvious, since it concerns the figuration not so much of the "shepherd" as that of its referent, the "flock." When the Alexandrian rabbis responsible for translating the Hebrew Bible into Koine Greek came to the passages that related the story of the "people" of Israel's divine election, over and against the other "nations," they opted almost uniformly to render the Hebrew *'am* with the Greek *laos*.[70] By virtue of an obscure process whose history remains largely to be written, the "people" of Homer becomes the "people" of God.[71]

It is not our intention to reconstruct this history here. Rather, we intend simply to register, starting from this confluence, the importance of the differing inflections of the flock for the elaboration of the paradigm of pastoral power.[72] The genealogy of the figurations of the shepherd must be integrated with a genealogy of the figurations of the flock, the genealogy of those who exercise pastoral power with a genealogy of those who over whom it is exercised. Only in this way, we shall suggest, will it become possible to concretely grasp the stakes in what Foucault so suggestively termed the "institutionalization of the pastorate"—but which, for reasons we will have to consider, he left largely unexamined—and to assess its significance for the broader history of governmentality. To the extent that it names the "people" (*'am*) insofar as they have forged a covenant with God, Israel becomes *laos*; all the other "peoples" (*goyim*), by contrast—the plural, once again, is significant—become *ethnē* (nations). Agamben has suggested that a "fundamental chapter" in the semantic history of the term "people" begins with this translation, or rather, this pair of translations, which could be traced right up to the contemporary use of the adjective "ethnic" (as, for example, in the syntagm "ethnic conflict"). But it would be equally worthwhile, he continues, to investigate the circumstances that led the translators to avoid taking recourse, in either instance, to that other more familiar Greek term for people that has retained such prestige throughout the Western political-philosophical tradition: *dēmos*.[73] In seeking to attend to the differing figurations of the flock, we shall attempt to advance a specific response to this question. And in so doing we shall hint at the profound, if largely unremarked, consequences that issue from this startling terminological choice.[74] As we shall see in what follows, what is at issue here is nothing less than the institution of a division—which today has become almost impossible to discern, owing to the fact that one and the same problematic term refers indiscriminately to both realities—between the "people" (*dēmos*) insofar as it is political entity and the "people" (*laos*) insofar as it is an economic entity in the sense that we have been describing. That is: between the people insofar as it is the subject of sovereignty and the people insofar as it is the object of government.

At first glance, the reasons for this terminological choice are anything but obvious. Aside from direct citations from Homer, the term *laos* appears only rarely in Herodotus and in the later Greek dramatists, and is almost completely absent from Attic prose. It is attested only twice in Plato (in the Attic form, *leōs*) and appears nowhere in Aristotle, Thucydides, Xenophon, or Demosthenes. In later authors, both contemporary with and subsequent to the production of the Septuagint (Polybius, Plutarch, Epictetus, among others), its usage is only marginally more frequent.[75] By the time of the third and second centuries BCE, it has thus been suggested that the term clearly already pertained to "an archaic and poetic mode of speech" and that it played "almost no role at all outside the sphere and influence of this mode."[76] In the Septuagint, by remarkable contrast, it appears more than two thousand times and almost exclusively in the singular (the plural *laoi*, which is the more common term in Homer, is attested only a comparatively infrequent 140 times). It is this increased prevalence that is adduced as evidence of a profound semantic shift: In the Septuagint—so the conventional theological interpretation runs—the "archaic" and "poetic" *laos* was thus revivified and repurposed so as to become (in Hermann Strathmann's words) "a specific term for a specific people," serving exclusively to designate the unique and privileged position of the people of Israel within God's providential plan.[77] And yet, even granting that this was the case (and, as we shall see, from a strictly linguistic perspective, there is sufficient reason to contest such a reading), the question nonetheless remains: What sense can we give to this startling terminological choice? What led the translators to assume this, and no other term, as the exclusive name for the people of God?

The two principal Greek terms for designating the "people" as a political entity—*dēmos* and *laos*—were in fact equally well represented in Homer. Yet, as Émile Benveniste has observed in an important chapter of his *Vocabulaire des institutions indo-européennes* (dedicated, precisely, to "Le roi et son peuple"), the *poimen* is never represented as ruling over a *dēmos*, but only over a *laos*. The same holds for the many other ritual designations for the king: *orchamos, koiranos, kosmētor*, and so on.[78] The two terms are thus not only morphologically, but conceptually, distinct. *Dēmos* is a strictly territorial concept. It refers primarily to the portion of land and only secondarily to the people who inhabit it. And only through this last aspect does it acquire its political significance: Generically, it names the "people" insofar as they inhabit a certain territory, a certain country. In contrast to *ethnos*—which, significantly enough, could be employed indifferently to refer to any more or less permanent grouping of living beings, whether human or otherwise (even, in one sequence of *The Iliad*, to a "tribe"[79] of swarming bees)—*dēmos* thus designates the grouping of men united by common social status, rather than by bonds of kinship or by membership of a distinct political collectivity.[80] *Laos*, on the other hand, is an expressly military concept. In this sense, unlike *dēmos* it preserves an originally political meaning: More than anything else, it is to the close link between the grouping of men as a political community and their capacity for military service that the use of the term bears witness.[81] In contrast once again to *ethnos*, however, which was frequently employed to refer generically to any band of combatants, *laos* has the distinct specificity, Benveniste writes, "of expressing the personal relationship [*la relation personnelle*] of a group of men with a leader [*chef*]."[82] A leader who—to adopt Max Weber's terminology—must be said to possess a distinctly "charismatic" authority.[83] *Laos*, in this sense, names the people insofar as they stand assembled and unified behind a leader; conversely, the leader only appears as such to the extent that he receives the backing and support of the *laoi*. The two are thus bound together in a relationship of mutual dependence. In this sense, Benveniste suggests, the use of the term *laos* marks the resurgence, at the heart of the antique Hellenic world, of the structure and organization particular to the ancient warrior societies made famous by the analyses of Georges Dumézil. It is never employed to refer to the elderly or children, but solely to men of a virile age; very distinctly, *laos* is thus the name of the people insofar as it is capable of bearing arms.[84]

At stake, then, in the epic distinction between *dēmos* and *laos* is the separation between two distinct conceptions of regal authority: the one that refers to the territory over which the king's power extends (*dēmos*); the other that refers to the group of warriors upon whose fidelity his power depends (*laos*).[85] Hence the exclusive use of royal titles such as *poimen* (but also *orchamos, koiranos, kosmētor*) with unique reference to the *laos*.[86] If the king is to be designated as shepherd, it can only be with respect to the flock (and never simply with respect to the portion of land on which they graze): Such, as we have seen, was the most basic insight of Foucault's description of pastoral power specifically and of governmentality more generally. As he writes: "One never governs a state, a territory, or a political structure. Those whom one governs are people [*gens*], individuals, or groups."[87] But it is also this sense of the term that makes discernible and explicable its otherwise unlikely transposition into the text of the Bible of Alexandria. It was not owing simply to a predilection for arcane and solemn words that the translators were led to adopt this particular term as an equivalent for the Hebrew *'am*, as has so often been insisted; there were precise reasons for their doing so, even if they have rarely been investigated or even acknowledged as such.

6.

Indeed, it is not even strictly the case that, at the time of the Septuagint's production, the term was no longer a word of everyday use. Nor is it true that its use therein was reserved exclusively for the people of Israel alone. If it is undeniable that, with the Septuagint, the term acquires "a new lease of life and a specific sense that became normative in the usage of the early Church," it is nonetheless not correct to speak of a determinate "shift in meaning."[88] As we shall see, the basic meaning of the word remains more or less invariant. What does change, however, is its specific point of application and, as a direct corollary of this, the precise nature of the relationship that it designates. It is the latter, we suggest, which merely gives the appearance of a shift in meaning—all the more palpable, in this instance, on account of the apparent revivification of an archaic term. Indeed, as Orsolina Montevecchi has shown in a carefully documented study,[89] while it is certainly true that by the time of the Septuagint's redaction the Attic form *leōs* had become obsolete, use of the Doric-Aeolic form *laos*—the same as had appeared in Homer—remained widespread throughout the Hellenistic kingdoms, including especially in Ptolemaic Egypt. There, as in Asia Minor and Syria, it was employed predominantly to refer to the indigenous, non-Hellenized population in opposition to the immigrants of Greek or Macedonian descent who also inhabited the territory but who remained *katoikoi* (citizens) of the city-states of their respective homelands. Evidence of this usage is to be found in a distinction traced in the decree of Memphis (196 BCE), which is preserved in a sequence from the Greek text of the Rosetta Stone, between the *laos*, on the one hand, and *hoi alloi pantes*, on the other—a distinction that Montevecchi interprets in the following manner: *Laos* names the people in the strict sense, which is to say the Egyptian population, whereas *hoi alloi pantes* refers instead to all the other remaining residents of the country who remain unspecified and unnamed precisely because the decree's content does not concern them.[90] Employed principally by the conquering Macedonian sovereigns themselves, the term thus entered the common language of the Eastern Hellenistic kingdoms, Montevecchi suggests, because it responded "better than other terms to a reality very different from that of the *dēmos* and the Greek *poleis*."[91]

It is on this basis that she is also able to explain, as never before, the newfound vigor with which the term *laos* would come to be employed in the Septuagint. The choice of this apparently archaic term cannot have been motivated by mere literary considerations—not least because, as we have seen, it remained a term of use in the very milieu in which the translators, purportedly at the instigation of the cultured Ptolemy II himself, completed their labors. Moreover, its choice responded to a particular exigency: Neither *ethnos* nor *dēmos* were entirely appropriate terms to reflect the specificity of the nature of the relationship that the Bible (and the Book of Exodus, in particular) described. To the extent that it had been employed ever since Aristotle to refer to "foreign" peoples (that is, to those who are not Greek), *ethnos*—whose usage in the Septuagint, predominantly in the plural form *ethnē*, is almost as prevalent as that of *laos*—thus furnished the apt oppositive term: It served principally, if not exclusively, to designate that against which the unique situation of the people of Israel would be asserted. *Dēmos*, on the other hand, to the extent that it described the territorial and political reality of the Greeks themselves, carried a connotation that was itself completely foreign to Jewish experience and was thus deemed completely out of the question. In any case, as Montevecchi observes, it would itself be put to a very specific use in the Septuagint. In continuity with the popular etymology of the word, it would be employed (above all, in Numbers) to indicate the various "clans" into which the twelve "tribes" (*phylai*) of Israel had themselves been divided.[92] Among available options, *laos* alone remained.

But even here, as Montevecchi continues, we should be careful not to see its application to be reserved exclusively for Israel alone. Indeed, it is those instances in which it is applied to people who are not Israel that clarifies the prevailing sense with which it was employed—both for Israel and for others. It is the exception that proves the rule. Just as the Bible speaks of the "people of Sodom," of the "people of Abimelech," of the "people of Schechem" and, above all, of the "people of Pharaoh"[93]—expressions for which the Septuagint each time reserves the term *laos*—so does it speak of Israel as the "people of Yahweh" and, indeed, by extension, as the "people of God."[94] What counts, in each instance, is the character of possession or, alternatively, that of belonging. As Montevecchi writes:

Laos is thus always accompanied by a specification: the name of a city, or that of its god . . . or, more frequently, that of its king. In this way, the notion either of an organization under a leader [*capo*], or, more often, of a belonging (the people is the king's people) is emphasized. At another level, but perfectly analogously, we find the position of Israel, *laos tou theou*, the people for whom Yahweh is king, the people who belong to Yahweh.[95]

Israel is thus the *laos tou theou* because it is God's possession, because it belongs to God, and not (as the practitioners of "sacred lexicography" would maintain) because it is, in and of itself, holy.[96] It is worth emphasizing this point: If Israel is indeed represented as holy it is exclusively on the basis of the divine distinction itself. "You are a holy people [*laos hagios*] for the Lord your God, and the Lord your God has chosen you to be for him a special people [*laos periousias*], as compared with all the nations [*para panta ta ethnē*] to be found on the face of the earth."[97] Moreover, should it wish to maintain this distinction, the people must conduct itself in such a manner as is deemed worthy of the divine attribute. "You shall be holy," runs one of the most constant refrains throughout the Pentateuch, "for I the Lord your God am holy."[98] The people becomes holy insofar as it is possessed, it is not possessed insofar as it is holy.

Exemplary, from this perspective, is the Septuagint version of Exodus 33:12–13, the very text, that is to say, in which the distinction between *laos* and *ethnos* appears in its paradigmatic form:

> And Moses said to the Lord: "Here, you have said to me, 'Raise this people,' but you have never indicated who you will send with me. Now, you have said to me, 'I know you above all and you have favor with me'. If I have found favor before you, show yourself to me; that I may see you as you know me; that I may be in the state of having favor before you and in order that I may know that this great nation is your people."[99]

"In order that I may know that this great nation is your people" (*oti laos sou to ethnos to mega touto*): Perhaps nowhere, as in this passage, does the distinction between *ethnos* and *laos* appear with such clarity. This great *ethnos* (Israel) *becomes* a *laos* when, and only when, Yahweh takes possession of it. Or, alternatively, when it forms a covenant with him and pledges obedience to his laws. There is nothing, in and of itself, negative in the Septuagint's usage of the term *ethnos*, just as there is nothing, in and of itself, positive in its use of the term *laos*. It is, rather, but a reflection of the people's "belonging" to God. In this sense, as Montevecchi has suggested, it was simply the most suitable word in the language of the time to express the particular nature of this relationship.[100] Yahweh is with respect to the people of Israel, and the people of Israel are with respect to Yahweh, as Ptolemy is with respect to the people of Egypt, and the people of Egypt are with respect to Ptolemy. In an attenuated sense, by liberating Israel from its Egyptian servitude, he even appears as their conqueror. But he is their conqueror only to the extent that he is also, and at the same time, their shepherd, their pastor; in the final analysis, their savior: "Through your righteousness you have led your people [*laon sou*], those whom you have delivered; through your strength you have invited them to your holy habitation [*kataluma hagion sou*]."[101]

7.

It is, to be sure, precisely through the Septuagint that *laos* (together with its oppositive term, *ethnos*) enters the vocabulary of the Christian tradition. Scholars generally distinguish between three distinct uses of the term in the New Testament writings. In the first place, there is the generic use of the term as a synonym for *ochlos*, which appears frequently in the writings traditionally ascribed to Luke.[102] In the second place, there is the use of the term with specific reference to the "people" of Israel, as carried over directly from the Septuagint, whether as set over and against the other "nations" or otherwise.[103] Finally, and most importantly, there is a third use of the term, specific to the New Testament but modeled on that of the Septuagint, with specific reference to the nascent Christian community. It is with this third usage, according to the prevailing scholarship, that we enter a new phase in the term's semantic history. Here *laos* is no longer opposed to the *ethnē*, but is in fact composed from them. And yet, even here, in this most theologically significant of the three prevailing New Testament usages, it is easy to see (contra Strathmann, among others) the basic pattern of the Alexandrian model, as exemplified in the Septuagint's version of Exodus 33:13, penetrating through. The key text is Acts 15:14. Its speaker is James, the brother of Jesus and the principal representative of so-called Jewish Christianity. The context is the Council of Jerusalem, the opening remarks of his apostolic decree: "My brothers, listen to me," he begins:

Simeon has related how God first looked favorably on the Gentiles [*ethnon*], to take from among them a people [*laon*] for his name. This agrees with the words of the prophets, as it is written, "After this I will return, and I will rebuild the dwelling of David, which has fallen; from its ruins I will rebuild it, and I will set it up, so that all the remaining men may seek the Lord—even all the Gentiles over whom my name has been called."[104]

Exactly as in the Septuagint's Exodus pericope, God takes a *laos* for himself from among the *ethnē*. And again, it is the character of possession that is decisive. 1 Peter will even speak of the followers of Jesus, in terms almost identical to the Septuagint, as a *laos eis peripoiēsin* (a people for his possession).[105] Above all, however, it is the Letter to the Romans that is called upon to lend theological weight to this interpretation. Just as it is not the "children of the flesh" but the "children of the promise" who are presented as the true descendants of Israel, so, following the apostle's citation of the prophet Hosea, it is those who were "not my people" (*ou laon mou*)—the Gentiles, according to the prevailing interpretation—whom the Lord will now call "my people" (*laon mou*).[106] In the Letter to the Hebrews, as 1 Peter, the transfer is apparently complete: The epithet *laos tou theou* can now be applied without reservation to the Christian community, which at points even appears to take the place of Israel (a conclusion at which the genuine Pauline epistles would never have arrived).[107]

There can be little doubt that the assumption of this title reflected the genuine self-understanding of the earliest Christian communities. As we have seen, in the nineteenth book of his *De civitate Dei*, Augustine will even audaciously attempt to wed the biblical notion with Cicero's celebrated definition of the people in the first book of his *De re publica*. According to Augustine, only the Christian assembly—the *populus Dei*—properly realizes the *coetus multitudinis iuris consensus et utilitatus communione sociatus* that alone, for Cicero, constitutes a *populus*.[108] It is to the Church, in its totality, that the designation *laos tou theou* now exclusively applies. Such an interpretation, however, leaves almost inexplicable a concurrent development in the history of the Church that not only takes place by virtue of the same terminology, but that also gives rise to the sole form in which the term *laos* will survive in modern languages.[109] It is only by emphasizing the character of possession that defines the people insofar as it is designated as *laos* that we will succeed in grasping the stakes in what, according to Foucault, characterizes Christianity's institutionalization of the pastorate in a very specific manner: its formation of a strategic and functional "dimorphism," within the pastoral field itself, between the "clergy," on the one hand, and the "laity," on the other.[110]

To the sequence of shifting figurations of the pastoral function (leader, God, clergy) there thus corresponds an equally decisive sequence of shifting figurations of its object (followers, people, laity). In a sense, then, obviously without intending it as such, Foucault's analysis of pastoral power constitutes a significant contribution toward the project first advanced by Peterson in his 1926 doctoral dissertation for a history of the *laos*. At the same time, however, when viewed in this light, Foucault's own project receives an impetus otherwise lacking from his investigation.[111] Together with the "autonomization" of the shepherd theme that, according to Foucault, constitutes the specificity of the Christian pastorate, we see the emergence of two distinct categories of persons within the one people of God: on the one hand, an entire "class" of shepherds, endowed with a whole swath of specific privileges—civic, economic, and above all, spiritual—owing to the particular function that they perform within the economy of salvation (the clergy); on the other, a subordinate "class" of persons who are expressly excluded from exercising this function—being, instead, its very object—to whom, on this account, these manifold privileges clearly do not extend (the laity).[112] The history of the laity coincides with the history of the governed; pastoral power is liturgical power. If it is true, as Foucault has suggested, that the problem of the relation between religion and politics in modernity is to be sought not so much in the relation between the pope and the emperor, but rather in that between "these two figures who in our language, and also in others, share one and the same name of minister,"[113] then this problem may be adequately confronted only by situating it against its liturgical backdrop. The minister is precisely the *leitourgos*. The problem of the relation between religion and politics in modernity must be construed liturgically.

Excursus: The Angels of the Nations

Together with this pair of translations (of 'am into *laos* and of *goyim* into *ethnē*), there also begins that fascinating chapter in the history of the

Church, which is the doctrine of the angels of the nations. According to this doctrine, which receives its clearest expression in that *Summa* of early Christian apologetic literature that is Origen's *Contra Celsum*, while Yahweh reserved Israel exclusively for himself, the remaining nations were entrusted, as a result of sin, to presiding "national" angels under whose guardianship they would remain until the end of time. The point of departure for this obscure doctrine was once again the Septuagint, specifically its version of Deuteronomy 32:8–9. But here it was a question less of a translation than of a genuine textual corruption (or, at the very least, of an imported interpretation). Where the Hebrew text had read: "When the Most High apportioned the nations [*goyim*], when he divided the sons of Adam, he fixed the boundaries of the peoples [*ammim*] according to the number of sons of Israel," the Septuagint instead had: "When the Most High apportioned the nations [*ethnē*], when he dispersed the sons of Adam, he fixed the boundaries of the nations [*ethnon*] according to the number of angels of God [*aggelōn theou*]." And the latter had continued: "And the Lord's share was his people [*laos*], Jacob, the portion of his inheritance, Israel."[114] For Origen, who had been trained in rabbinic hermeneutics, this text clearly appeared as a *midrash* on the story of the Tower of Babel, as related in the eleventh chapter of Genesis. The rupture of the original national unity and the consequent "scattering" of the nations coincided, for him, with the rupture of the original linguistic unity and the consequent "scattering" of tongues: Significantly enough, a single Greek verb— *diespieren*—was employed in the Septuagint in reference to both. Not only, then, were the presiding angels (whose degree of sternness, Origen noted, increased in direct proportion to the scale of the corresponding people's degree of sin) responsible for administering and managing their respective nations; they were also responsible for imparting to each their particular languages.[115]

While undoubtedly of Jewish origin, the doctrine of the angels of the nations thus assumed a very distinct physiognomy in the perspective of Christian eschatology. Indeed, as none other than Erik Peterson has observed in an important essay dedicated to this theme, in their respective readings, the two messianisms—Jewish and Christian—decisively confront one another.[116] While, in the Jewish interpretation, at the end of time all the nations will be restored to their original language before the fall (namely, Hebrew), in the Christian perspective of an Origen such an interpretation is, so to speak, "spiritualized": The blessed who will enter the messianic kingdom, who will compose a *laos tou theou* that encompasses Gentiles as well as Jews, shall speak a language, Peterson observes, that is not conditioned by the union of body and soul—"perhaps the language of the angels."[117] In other words: the language of divine praise.[118]

8.

The place in which the transformation that would lead to the institutionalization of the pastorate may be said to begin is the First Letter of Clement to the Corinthians, one of the earliest documents of the Christian tradition (if we accept the traditional dating of its composition toward the end of Domitian's reign in 96 CE, then it predates many of the so-called canonical books of the New Testament). It is a transformation that is marked in two distinct, yet nonetheless interrelated ways. First of all, through its characteristic reference to the nascent Christian community as the "flock of Christ" (*poimniō tou Christou*), a designation that appears at three separate points in its text and that serves principally to distinguish the mere followers from those who would act as their leaders.[119] And secondly, through the introduction of a new term as a synonym for the former, which is unattested either in the Septuagint or in the New Testament (but which is present, significantly enough, in certain papyri and in the later, second-century translations of the Hebrew Bible); a term that is employed but twice in a single sentence of the letter, yet that will nonetheless enjoy a protracted afterlife both in the history of Christianity and beyond: the term *laikos*.[120] In both cases, as we shall see, the role of *leitourgia* in articulating this transformation will be critical.

The circumstances that led the author of the letter, an official representative of the church in Rome, to intercede on behalf of his counterparts at the church in Corinth, are well documented in the opening paragraphs of the letter itself. Where previously the Corinthians had enjoyed (on account of their "virtuous and stable faith," their "temperate and gentle piety," their "magnificent hospitality" and their "perfect and unwavering knowledge") a venerable and revered reputation, deemed worthy of widespread love and admiration, they have now been assailed by a desperate and deleterious internecine conflict, a *stasis* that threatens to irrevocably split their church from top to bottom.[121] It is as if, according to Clement, this esteemed church—the addressee of not one but two of the most significant of the genuine epistles of the Apostle Paul—had fulfilled, on account of its particular eminence, what had been prophesied of Israel in the Bible: It had grown fat off its own glory and kicked out with its heels in defiance of its maker.[122] As a result, all righteousness and peace had been removed, and jealousy and discord had instead appeared in their place. "And so," Clement recounts, "the dishonorable rose up against the honorable, the disreputable against the reputable, the senseless against the sensible, the young against the old."[123] The honorable, the reputable, and the sensible, of whom Clement speaks and to whose defense he promptly comes, are the vanquished church elders, the *presbyteroi*, whom a "vile and profane faction" has unlawfully removed from their posts. It is against this unlawful deposition that he rallies, preaching an immediate return to the proper order, which had been instituted by the Lord himself.

In the course of Clement's impassioned plea for an end to division and discord and the return to peace and order at the church in Corinth, a special emphasis is placed on the notion that it is the Christian people who now constitute God's "chosen portion." It is they whom he has taken for himself from among all the other nations. In perfect continuity with the Jewish backdrop that informs his intervention, Clement thus argues that since the followers of Christ now constitute a "holy" people, they must act and conduct themselves accordingly. This he grounds on the authority of Deuteronomy 32:8–9 in the Septuagint version. "And so," he writes, "we should approach him with devout souls, raising pure and undefiled hands to him and loving our gentle and kind-hearted Father who made us his own chosen portion. For so it is written: 'When the Most High divided the nations and scattered the descendants of Adam, he established the boundaries of the nations according to the number of the angels of God. His people, Jacob, became the portion of the Lord; Israel became the allotment of his inheritance.'"[124] Not without a certain inconsistency, Clement maintains that it is even through "righteous deeds"—and not through "mere words"—that the holy people should acquire and preserve their holiness.[125] Just as the creator and maker of all things rejoices in his "works," so, he argues, those whom he has stamped with his own image "should hasten with fervor and zeal to complete every good work."[126] In this respect, and in contrast to the "idle" and the "slovenly," they should model themselves on the example of the host of heavenly angels, who, according to Clement, stand forever alongside of God, endlessly "administering his will [*thelēmati autou leitourgousin*]."[127] "For the Scripture says," he writes, "'Myriads upon myriads stood before him, and thousands upon thousands were ministering to him; and they cried out, "Holy, holy, holy, Lord of the Hosts, all of creation is full of his glory."' So too we should gather together in harmony, conscientiously, as we fervently cry out to him with one voice, that we may have a share in his great and glorious promises."[128]

Like angels: If they are to preserve their holiness, the chosen people, too, according to Clement, must administer God's will, continuously and without delay; and they must do so by engaging in righteous works, whether through song or otherwise. In this sense, the letter reflects a theology that is consistent with the Jewish (or Jewish Christian) circles out of which it undoubtedly emerged. Not incidentally does the passage cited immediately above constitute the first appearance of the Jewish *Qedushsha* in an unequivocally Christian text. What is genuinely new here, however, is the distinctive introduction of the hierarchical theme—a theme that receives its specific impetus, above and beyond the ambiguous analogy with the Levitical priesthood, from the glorious ascension of Christ.[129] It is through him who is superior, even to the holy angels themselves, according to Clement, that the faithful are guided toward the "heights of the heavens." Yet it is nonetheless not the case, on account of this, that all must aspire to commensurate degrees of holiness. One need only consider, for example, the relationship between a group of soldiers and their leader. Not all men, Clement observes, employing a military metaphor much favored by Aristotle (but that would also enjoy great fortune in the subsequent history of the Church), need act as commanders-in-chief with respect to a thousand, a hundred, or even fifty troops. Not all men order, but rather, "each one, according to his own rank [*en tō idiō tagmati*]," accomplishes, for his part, what is ordered, whether by their king or by their leaders.[130] The two—those who order and those who are ordered—thus wholly depend on one another: "Those who are great cannot survive without the lowly nor the lowly without the great."[131] In this sense, the order itself, he observes, in a decisive shift of metaphorical register (which, if possible, would assume an even greater significance in the subsequent history of the Church), is comparable to our own body. Just as the head is nothing without feet, so the feet, according to Clement, are nothing without the head. All parts, including even the most insignificant, must work together—in unison and in accordance with a single overarching order—to ensure that the body, in its totality, remains healthy.[132]

By this point, the pertinence of Clement's remarks with respect to the concrete situation in which he is intervening should be evident. Just as it has one God and one Christ and one spirit and one calling, so too, according to Clement, the Christian community forms a single body, which is united in Christ. And when it creates strife and division among its own members, it follows that it is its own body that it mutilates.[133] And so, he concludes, all Christians must unfailingly act in accordance with the prescribed order—an order that, furthermore, has been secured for them in advance:

> Since these matters have been clarified for us in advance and we have gazed into the depths of divine knowledge, we should do everything the Master has commanded us to perform in an orderly way and at appointed times. He commanded that the sacrificial offerings [*prosphoros*] and liturgical rites [*leitourgias*] be performed not in a random or haphazard way, but according to set times and hours. In his superior plan he set forth both where and through whom he wished them to be performed.... For special liturgical rites [*leitourgias*] have been assigned to the high priest, and special places have been designated for the regular priests, and special ministries [*diaikoniai*] for the Levites. The lay person is assigned matters enjoined on the laity [*Ho laikos anthrōpos tois laikois prostagmasin dedetai*].[134]

"Each one, according to his own rank" (*en tō idiō tagmati*): When this characteristic phrase appears again for a second time in the very next sentence, it is the "established rule" of one's own *leitourgia* that his Christian "brothers" are exhorted not in any circumstance to violate.[135] For Clement, the hierarchy is ordered and administered according to liturgy. Hierarchy is always a hierarchy of function, and never a hierarchy of substance; as such, has it been instituted by God. To transgress this order is thus to transgress the divine will, even (to the extent that they are one and the same thing) the divine law itself. Which is exactly what "the dishonorable, the disreputable and the senseless" stand accused of at Corinth. According to Clement, the deposed *presbyteroi* are only the most recent in a sequence that stretches back to the "ministry" of Christ and that thus issues directly from God himself. In this way, in a manner that is wholly consistent with what has been described as the "discursive institution" of orthodoxy in the early Church,[136] the conflict at Corinth becomes the place in which the letter's author, himself later anachronistically inscribed in the long line of bishops of Rome extending right up to the present, grounds his famous teaching regarding apostolic succession. A single, unbroken line, according to Clement, runs from the Father to the Son, from the Son to the apostles, from the apostles to the bishops and deacons, and from the bishops and deacons right up to the presbyters themselves.[137] And what links these apparently disparate figures together is solely the liturgy that, in each instance, is entrusted to them from above and that they are expected to fulfill. The peculiar process whereby that which, in the great city-states of ancient Greece and Rome, was an occasional, if compulsory public service, at times (as in the limit case of Roman Egypt) obliging the entire populace, came progressively to be transformed into a more or less permanent "office," has one of its points of departure here.

But it was also in this context that the notion of the "laity" appeared for the first time in the history of Christian literature. This was no minor innovation. In the New Testament, the whole Christian people had been defined as *klēros* to the extent that all were equally considered "heirs" (*klēronomoi*) according to the promise.[138] It is in this sense that 1 Peter could adopt the Septuagint's inadvertent inversion of the messianic concept of the "priestly kingdom" (*mamleket kohanim*) into the "royal priesthood" (*basileion hierateuma*) and apply it to the Christian assembly without broaching any contradiction.[139] In the same epistle, moreover, the "elders" (*presbyteroi*)—a position with which the author of the letter himself (almost certainly not the Apostle Peter) clearly identified—would be implored not to "exercise lordship" (*katakyrieuontes*) over "those who are in their charge" (*klēron*), but to act instead as "examples" (*typoi*) with respect to their "flock" (*poimniou*).[140] Here, very distinctly, it is the *klēros* (the term from which the later "clergy" evidently derives) with which the "flock" is identified. Altogether different, however, is the situation that Clement describes. For him, the community of the faithful is instead articulated into a sequence of distinct classes, whose divisions he clearly models on the order of the Levitical priesthood (*archiereus, hiereus, leuites*)—willfully ignoring the fact that, according to the teaching of Hebrews, cited just a few paragraphs earlier, the high priesthood of Christ has in effect sublated the entire composite of the former.[141] But he also introduces a new, as it were unmarked category with respect to these. For while special liturgies and ministries have been reserved, as we have seen, for the high priest and for those who directly issue from him according to the model of apostolic succession, the "laity" are instead defined only negatively. In the absence of a specific function to fulfill, they are but generically assigned, according to a curious chiastic construction, the "precepts" incumbent upon them qua laity. From the very beginning, then, the laity will be defined as those who have no specific liturgy to perform—or rather, more precisely, as those whose only specific liturgy is to be the object of the liturgy of those who are not the laity.

That, in a very precise sense, the process that Foucault so astutely termed the institutionalization of the pastorate coincides with the invention of the laity, is confirmed, moreover, beyond any doubt, in the very passage in which Clement expressly returns his discussion to the concrete situation prevailing at Corinth. It is not right, he argues, to remove from their posts those whose appointments can be traced back directly to the apostles, and who, in any case, he adds, have "ministered blamelessly over the flock of Christ [*leitourgēsantas amemptōs to poimniō tou Christou*]."[142] Here, in this striking passage, it is the *laikoi*—in sharp opposition to the *klērikoi*—who are now clearly positioned as the flock.

9.

The adjective *laikos* has nonetheless presented particular difficulties for later interpreters. While scholars are in general agreement that it derives from the noun *laos*, the absence of the term itself from the New Testament canon has led theologians, in a kind of linguistic transference, to wholly identify it with its etymon and thereby bestow upon it the same lexicological overdetermination that we have already seen characterizes the semantic history of the latter. As Ignace de La Potterie has shown in an important study, this has resulted in a narrative of extreme semantic evolution—suggesting a veritable *Gegensinn*, in Carl Abel's and Sigmund Freud's sense[143]—whereby, in the course of its history, the term has come to figure at once as a synonym for the sacred (the people, according to its scriptural connotation, as consecrated to God), and at the same time, by virtue of a spectacular reversal, as a synonym for the profane (the laity in contrast to the clergy, and by extension the secular in contrast to the religious).[144] Such a narrative, according to La Potterie, nonetheless rests on a double misunderstanding. In the first place, it falsely assumes that the term *laikos* emerged only with the earliest Christian communities. In the second place, it seeks to explain the formation of the neologism solely on the basis of a general sense of *laos* supposedly attested in the Septuagint and the New Testament. In truth, as we shall see, its history is much older, and a quick survey of earlier attestations easily demonstrates the more restricted sense with which it was exclusively employed prior to the Christian epoch.[145]

As with other adjectives ending in–*ikos*, La Potterie observes, following the analyses of the linguist Pierre Chantraine, *laikos* always has a "classifying value" and a "categorizing sense."[146] Absent from the classical literary texts in which its "poetic" etymon often appears, but present in several third-century BCE papyri, in each instance it indicates that which pertains specifically to the people in the restricted sense that we have seen, understood as those who are not the leaders. One, for example, speaks of the beasts of burden of the people of a certain district, which a minor official is urged to make use of in order to speed up the delivery of wheat; another refers to the aid of the people, which the debtor is bound by contract not to have recourse to. Even more important again is the formula *laikē syntaxis*, which will assume a technical character in the later Roman epoch and which refers to the per capita tax that each member of the population is obliged to pay to the civil administration.[147] In each of these fragments, which predate 1 Clement by more than three centuries, *laikos* thus retains a very specialized sense, not without significance for its etymon. In the papyri, *laos* too always has a particular (and hence, restricted) meaning: It refers not to the people in its totality, but only to a particular part of it. *Laos* is never the whole people; it is always a people within the people: Very distinctly, it is those who are governed, as opposed to those who govern.

This reading would appear to be again confirmed in the later second-century revisions of the Septuagint preserved in Origen's so-called Hexapla, where *laikos* features three times. To that extent, however, it must have already been minimally present in the use of *laos* attested in the Septuagint itself. And indeed, as La Potterie observes, even in the very sequence in which Israel is first defined as a *laos periousias* "above all the other nations," it is already clearly applied to the people only as distinct from their leaders, and above all from those charged with exercising a *leitourgia*: namely, the "priests" (*hiereis*).[148] But it is to the Septuagint's use of *laos* in the context of the worship conducted in the Temple that the unknown later scribes' employment of the adjective *laikos*, where it had not been present before, may be traced. In all three cases, *laikos*—at times supplemented with a wholly unprecedented verb, *laikoō*, found nowhere else at any other time—translates the Hebrew *hol* (profane). In 1 Samuel 21:5–6, it is employed, where the Septuagint had used *bebēloi*, to distinguish the *artoi* (bread) specifically not reserved for religious purposes; in perfect continuity with this usage, in two separate passages of Ezekiel (22:26 and 48:15), it is again employed to mark that which is profane in opposition to that which is sacred. In the first case, the priests are reproached for having neglected their duties in not sufficiently maintaining this distinction; in the second, by contrast, the fulfillment of such duties in the future city is premised on their capacity to reassert it. In the broader context of the last example, in fact, *laikos* refers to the specific part of the city that will be reserved for the people (*laos*) in its more restricted sense, in opposition to that which will be reserved for the priests and the Levites (and even for Yahweh himself), thereby more or less reproducing the distinctions that we have already seen at work in Clement. The same distinction, which is predicated of Israel in its totality, in its relation to the other nations, is here clearly retraced, internal to the *laos hagios* itself, to distinguish that which pertains to those who are endowed with a cultic function from that which pertains to those who are not.[149]

The very paucity of attestations of *laikos* among the Apostolic Fathers and the Apologists, by contrast (in addition to Clement himself, it appears only a single time each in the Pseudo-Clementine writings, in Clement of Alexandria and in Origen), would appear to suggest that it is not an especially significant theological term. In 1 Clement, as we have already seen, the categories against which *laikos* is negatively defined repeat those already present in the second-century Greek versions of Ezekiel. With a single caveat: Where, in the latter, *laikos* referred exclusively to things reserved for "profane" usage—in this instance, to a portion of the holy city itself—it is now referred to a particular portion of the people itself: *ho laikos anthrōpou*.[150] An important paleographic discovery from the late nineteenth century has underscored the unprecedented significance of this gesture. In 1893, a Benedictine monk, Germain Morin, discovered in the Grande Séminaire of Namur in Belgium a Latin codex containing versions of all the Clementine writings, including, most importantly, an edition of the genuine Epistle. And although the codex itself was dated to the comparatively recent eleventh century, Morin, who subsequently edited and published his "découverte sensationnelle" under the title *Sancti Clementis Romani ad Corinthios epistulae versio antiquissima*, immediately sought to date the Latin Clement as early as the first half of the second century—a dating later corroborated by no less an authority than Adolf von Harnack himself—thus making it one of the earliest documents of Christian Latinity.[151] As La Potterie, among others, has observed,[152] such was the strangeness of the language of 1 Clement 40, 5 that the anonymous translator evidently felt compelled to employ two discrete strategies in an attempt to distinguish between what he evidently perceived to be two distinct uses of the adjective *laikos* in its single sentence. While, in the second instance, the reference was clearly to an inanimate "thing" and could therefore be handled by simple transliteration (*tois laikois prostagamasin* thus became *laicis praecepta*, thereby marking the first appearance of the adjective *laicis* in the Latin language), the first—referring, as it did, unmistakably, to human beings—would have presented the translator with a largely unprecedented usage, one to which he would seek to attend by rendering it with a very particular term already completely loaded with implications at the time of its redaction. *Ho laikos anthrōpou* duly became *plebeius homo*.

In spite of the claims of those theologians who attempt to secure, for the adjective *plebeius*, as for the substantive *plebs*, the same general sense that we have seen they advocate for *laikos* and *laos*, in the language of Imperial Rome the term clearly served to designate—negatively, as was the case with *laikos* in 1 Clement itself—those who did not belong to the patrician class.[153] Even granted that there is, then, both a "general" and a "restricted" sense of the term *laos* (and, from the linguistic point of view, as we have seen, this would appear to be highly doubtful), in none of the cases that La Potterie examines, whether pagan, Jewish, or Christian, can the derivation of *laikos* from *laos* in its supposed general sense be observed. "The meaning of *laos* from which *laikos* derives," he concludes, "is not its general meaning (*people*, in contrast to another people), but its restricted, 'categorizing' meaning: 'a certain part of the people.' . . . The contrast we find in the texts is always the same: that of two categories, within the people of God."[154] Yet theologians (including, astonishingly, La Potterie himself)[155] nonetheless still seek to retain both significations: a general *laos* and a restricted *laos*. According to Christian theology—such is its peculiar paradox—*laos* is, at one and the same time, the whole of the people and a part of the people.

On the one hand, all Christians: the people of God, precisely. On the other, only a particular portion of them: the laity as opposed to the clergy.[156] The semantic ambiguity that, as Agamben (and others) have shown, traverses many European languages, and that sees the "people" positioned at once as the constitutive political subject and as the class that must be excluded from politics, finds an unexpected anticipation here, which must be integrated with the analysis of its concept.[157] To the fundamental "biopolitical" fracture that Agamben has discerned in the concept of the people insofar as it appears as the subject of a political will, there thus corresponds an equally fundamental "theological-political" (or rather, "theological-economical") fracture that passes through the people insofar as it is the object of an *oikonomia*. The whole of the people, a part of the people: What links these two, apparently incommensurate, indeed mutually exclusive, significations together is, once again, the distinctly pastoral, which is to say governmental, function that they each distinctly serve within Christianity's soteriological machine. *Laos* would name the people insofar as it willingly submits, in view of future salvation, to the non-natural partition of the people into those who govern and those who are governed. In other words, and in a very precise sense, it names the people insofar as it is governable.

In this way, however, an unexpected theoretical reversal can nonetheless be demonstrated to have taken place; only it is the symmetrical inverse of that which the theologians had sought to document. If the restricted sense of *laos* cannot be inferred from the general sense, this is precisely because, with the advent of Christianity, it is the opposite inference that must be drawn: It is the general sense that must be inferred from the restricted sense. The people—if we may express it thus—becomes the "people of God" only insofar as it is governable. But this introduces a further distinction, which becomes fully explicable only in this light. It is only insofar as only a part of the people has come to coincide with the whole of the people, only insofar as "people" now names that which is governable, that the missing remainder—which encompasses those who have assumed a liturgical power with respect to the former—will in one sense come to transcend this categorization, even as in another sense they may be said to preeminently belong to it. The figure of the "priestly kingdom" will thus have truly yielded a "royal priesthood."

3

THE PRACTICE OF HIERARCHY

1.

We can now state with precision what in a certain sense was already obvious: The institutionalization of the pastorate coincides with its articulation in a hierarchy. But hierarchy is not only the form that the pastorate thereby assumes; it is also, and above all, its medium. In a sense that remains to be clarified, to govern—but also to be governed—means to be "uplifted" (*anagogikē*) into the hierarchy. Such, in any case, was the sense in which the scholastic tradition sought to approach this concept. Not only, for example, did Aquinas's most sustained reflections on hierarchy, occupying *quaestiones* 106 through 109 of the *Summa theologiae*, form a significant part of his treatise on the divine government, but even the term itself—a term that curiously enters the Latin tradition by way of transliteration, rather than translation—means nothing other than "sacred power," or even "sacred government" ("hierarchia est sacer principatus," as Aquinas writes).[1] For Aquinas, the term *principatus* encompasses both governor and governed: Owing, once again, to that decisive sequence of Aristotle's "theology" in which the philosopher sought to reconcile the immanent order of the good with the necessary transcendence of its source, it reflects their mutual, if asymmetrical co-implication.[2] "Two things," he writes, "are denoted by the term *principatus*: both the governor himself [*ipse princeps*] and the multitude ordered under him [*multitudo ordinata sub principe*]."[3] But in what sense should we understand the attribution of "sacredness" here? In what, exactly, does the "sacredness" of this power consist?

To begin to approach this question, we must turn to the *auctoritas* on whom Aquinas uniquely grounded his speculations. For even if, as a result of the rhetorical strategy of its author—who sought apostolic authority for his writings by presenting himself as the Athenian disciple of St. Paul who reportedly converted to Christianity following the Apostle's speech before the Areopagus[4]—the exact date of its first circulation cannot be located with precision, the first appearance of the term *hierarchia* can nonetheless be traced back to a single, and singularly influential, text: the *Peri tēs ouranias hierarchias* of the mysterious late fifth- or early sixth-century Christian Neoplatonist known to later tradition as Pseudo-Dionysius the Areopagite. This is far from being of mere historical-philological interest. As Ronald F. Hathaway has underscored, Pseudo-Dionysius is, in fact, "the virtual author of the term with the lexical meaning which it has possessed ever since."[5] The formation of this neologism, moreover, marks the sole terminological innovation of an author whose vocabulary is otherwise entirely dependent upon his Neoplatonic precursors (and Iamblichus and Proclus, in particular).[6] Not for nothing was he known by the epithet "doctor hierarchicus" throughout the Middle Ages. But such a conceptual novelty was evident even to the very first commentators and glossators of the *Corpus Areopagiticum*. Where previously the term *hierarchēs*, although extremely rare, had been employed to refer to the position of the *episkopos* (bishop), in both its Christian and pagan variants, in relation to his subordinates, its Pseudo-Dionysian derivation entailed a much broader extension in which the entire ecclesiastical order itself appears restricted to a merely subsidiary role. Thus, while attesting to this derivation, John of Scythopolis—the very first of the glossators, whose extensive scholia accompanied even the earliest circulation of the corpus—is nonetheless careful to distinguish the sense of the Areopagite's coinage with respect to it. *Hierarchia*, according to John, denotes the "power" (*archē*) over "sacred things" (*hierōn*), and almost the "care" (*phroneis*) that is taken of them. The *hierarchēs*, then, is not the *archiereus*: He is the "authority" (*archōn*), not over "priests" (*hiereōn*), but over "sacred things" (*hierōn*); the one who "cares" (*phrontizōn*) and "provides" (*pronoōn*) for them.[7] What is "sacred," according to John's precious suggestion, is thus not simply the subject of power, but also, and above all, its very object. In the terms of Pseudo-Dionysius himself: not simply those who "initiate," but those who are "initiated." Or again— what is the same thing—not simply those who "hierarchize," but those who are "hierarchized." As a form of power, hierarchy would thus be as impervious to the distinction between subject and object as it would to that between active and passive. To hierarchize would mean, at one and the same time, being hierarchized.

Such an interpretation would appear to be confirmed by the text of the treatise itself, which devotes an entire chapter not only to defining "what, in our opinion, the hierarchy itself is," but also—the caveat is important—to explaining "what benefit the beings who are members of the hierarchy derive from it."[8] "In my opinion," we read, "hierarchy is a sacred order [*taxis hiera*], a knowledge [*epistēmē*] and an activity [*energeia*], which is assimilated, as much as is possible, to the divine form, and which, in accordance with the illuminations divinely granted to it, is raised, to the extent of its capacities, toward the imitation of God."[9] The hierarchy is but an effect of God; it issues directly from him as from its cause. To the extent, however, to which (according to the late Neoplatonic schema that Pseudo-Dionysius somewhat crudely attempts to graft here onto the biblical narrative of creation and salvation) every effect must necessarily "remain" in its cause—for otherwise, were it to secede completely, it would retain no identity with it—not only must it directly "proceed" from him (*proodos*), but it must also seek to "revert" to him (*epistrophē*).[10] The hierarchy thus has a "purpose" and a "goal" (*skopos*); and, as in Proclus, this is to be attained only through degrees of "assimilation" (*aphomoiōsis*) to the divine cause.[11] Hierarchy therefore demands an unprecedented extension and exercise of the mimetic faculty. Its members must become, to the extent that is possible, "images of God," "perfectly transparent and spotless mirrors" capable of receiving his primordial light and of reflecting it in turn.[12] They must become, for themselves and for others, imitators of the divine. But imitating him who is inimitable can only mean conforming absolutely to the divine dispensation, participating in its power, making its operation manifest in themselves:

> Thus, when we speak of hierarchy, we generally mean a certain sacred disposition, an image of thearchical splendor, which sacredly carries out [*hierourgousan*] in hierarchical orders and knowledges the mysteries of its own illumination, and which is assimilated, as much as is permitted, to its own source [*archōn*]. Since, for each of the beings whose lot it is to belong to the hierarchy, perfection consists in being uplifted, according to what its own capacities allow, to the imitation of God and—what is surely more divine than anything—in becoming, in the words of

scripture, a "divine co-worker" [*theou synergon*], and in showing the divine operation manifesting itself in them as far as is possible [*deixai tēn theian energeian en heautō kata to dynaton anaphainomenēn*].[13]

Hierarchy serves a distinctly soteriological function. But the salvation of the governed, according to Pseudo-Dionysius, also coincides with their divinization: "The blessed Thearchy, which . . . is the source of all divinization . . . has granted the gift of hierarchy to every substance endowed with reason and intelligence to ensure its salvation [*sōtēria*] and divinization [*theōsei*]."[14] The ultimate goal of the hierarchy is thus "the divinization of the saved [*theoumenōn tēn sōzoumenōn*]."[15] And yet, for precisely this reason, although certainly divinely instituted, it cannot be said simply to coincide with the order of creation. It is, instead, but a divine "gift," which is granted only in addition to, or rather, beyond nature. As has been astutely observed, hierarchy is never the simple expression of the inherent superiority of one living being with respect to another, but nor is it the mere reflection of their objective social organization.[16] It is not an onto-logical fact; it is a form of *practice*. A form of practice, moreover, which is itself divided, in accordance with the triadic (or, indeed, Trinitarian) obsession of its author, into three discrete movements, themselves hier-archically coordinated with one another. Every hierarchy, according to Pseudo-Dionysius, is at once "purifying," "illuminating," and "perfect-ing." In order for the divine operation to manifest itself, it is nonetheless necessary, he writes, that some purify and that others are purified; that some illuminate and that others are illuminated; that some perfect and that others are perfected—that each, in other words, should imitate God in accordance with the function that has been assigned to them.[17] At the same time, however, it is also necessary that those who have been purified should purify in turn; that those who have been illuminated should illu-minate in turn; that those, finally, who have been perfected should perfect in turn. "In this way," he writes, "each order of the hierarchical disposition is uplifted, to the extent of its powers, toward cooperation with God."[18] Here we begin to glimpse the distinctive paradox that characterizes every hierarchy: It is a form of power whose executors must manifest the very order their ultimate aim can only be to transcend. The paradox of hierar-chy would thus double, in its uneasy finitude, that of the very theological economy whose expression it would be.[19]

2.

The articulation and elaboration of hierarchy coincides with the articulation and elaboration of the very particular beings that exhibit it. As scholars and theologians, both ancient and modern alike, have never ceased to repeat, the term "angel" (from the Greek *aggelos*, which translates the Hebrew *mal'ak*) means simply "messenger." Charged with filling the otherwise unbridgeable gap that separates the human from the divine, the angel, then, would be the being that is naturally endowed, above all else, with the power of communication. And yet, according to the extraordinary suggestion of Gregory the Great, "the word 'angel' is the name of a service, not a nature [*officii, non naturae*]."[20] Mere "angels," then, would be distinguished, by degree, from those who would communicate the most important messages, the "archangels." Even more important again would be those particular archangels (Michael, Gabriel, Raphael) blessed with the added distinction of personal names. But even here it is not really a question of proper names in the strict sense. "Archangels are distinguished by personal names to indicate by the word the service they are able to perform."[21] Whether Michael ("he who is like God"), Gabriel ("God's strength") or Raphael ("God's healing"), these archangels, Gregory writes, assume the particular names by which they are known to us solely according to the specific *ministerium* they are called upon to fulfill.[22] More than those beings naturally endowed with the power of communication, then, we should more accurately say that the angels are those beings defined by their participation in the communication of power. What the hierarchy communicates, that is to say, is principally and preeminently itself. Only in this way, as we shall see, will it be possible to resolve the seeming aporia of a form of power that appears directed toward its own dissolution.

Such a definition would seem to be confirmed by the distinct position that they occupy in the order of creation. The angel is, in a very precise sense, the medium between the human and the divine. But, for just this reason, their existence is circumscribed by a kind of double exclusion: Less than divine but more than human, they act solely in the name of the one and solely for the sake of the other. There is nothing that is truly their own. As we have already seen, not even their very "nature." Yet this extreme impersonality is the source of their incomparable efficiency. As Emanuele Coccia has argued, the necessity of the angel coincides with the necessity of a form of power—"sacred power," precisely—that is irreducible to the nature of the one who exercises it.[23] While in God nature and power must coincide absolutely (his power being but an expression of his nature and his nature but a reflection of his power[24]), the angel, by contrast, would mark the impossibility of such a coincidence. Indeed, if God's power finds its most immediate expression in the very nature of the things that he has created, the angels are, not incidentally, according to Coccia, the sole created beings that are themselves incapable of creating anything or even of reproducing their own kind. Sacred power—angelic power—is the power that is absolutely extraneous to nature (and hence to creation). It is power "only insofar as it concerns the execution and not the institution of things, power that begins only after the seventh day, only after the *opus naturae* has definitively concluded."[25] Because God has created the heavens and the earth, because he must now order and administer what he has created—this is why the angels exist. The angel, then, is the cipher for the exercise of power beyond nature, beyond the originary act par excellence that is creation.

For this reason, however, the exercise of angelic power is necessarily conditioned by a double exigency: It must come from above and it must be conveyed below. Incapable of possessing it naturally, the angel can "have" power only to the extent that it is capable of receiving it from above and only to the extent that it is capable of transmitting it below.[26] Angels, then, are not simply hierarchical beings; they are the very being of hierarchy. This means that, on the one hand, their power is necessarily vicarious. What God has ordered is what the angels must execute: Whether it be internal or external,[27] theirs is a "service" which is always undertaken in the strictest conformity to the will of God. Functionaries in an absolute sense, they can never act at their own behest but only at that of the one who has sent them. Their only possible comportment is thus an unconditioned obedience (or, as in the case of the fallen angels, an equally unqualified disobedience).[28] On the other hand, it means that their power is one that must be constantly exercised if it is to be maintained. Above everything else, it is the possibility of the fall—a possibility that is inscribed in their being as such—that attests to this. As Coccia once again has observed, the angel is the divine being that is capable of losing its own divinity. "Being able to fall," he writes, "means being able to lose one's own divinity."[29] But it also means being able to gain it. It is *taxis*, and not *physis*, that defines the angel in its being, whether good or bad. Sacredness, in other words, is never a natural attribute of the angel, but something that is entirely contingent upon its action: For the angel, being divine means acting divine. In the same sense, having power means participating in it.

Whether with respect to the human beings over whom they minister or, indeed, as is more often the case, with respect to those of their own kind who pertain to a lower hierarchy, angels can never stand in a relation of mere natural superiority; they must seek constantly to assert their sovereignty. Unlike the divine creator who, on the seventh day, according to the book of Genesis, can rest from his work (indeed, for whom this rest is "sacred"),[30] the angels must continuously exercise their power in order to preserve it. Theirs, then, is a perennial service, a service that knows no end (or rather, whose end would coincide with that of the angelic function itself). Hence their particular industriousness, for which the endless beating of wings provides the fitting symbol. It is certainly not in order that they may move about from place to place that the angels are represented with wings—these beings who, in the absence of bodies, are tethered neither by time nor by space.[31] They are there to signify the irreducible excess of activity with respect to the nature that could find expression in it. Extraneous to nature, sacred power can never be the "expression" of the one who exercises it. Conversely, it can only ever manifest the will of the one who is not its executor. Sacred is that power that cannot be possessed but only exercised, or that can be possessed only insofar as it exercised. Sacred power—that is, angelic power—is liturgical power.[32]

3.

The executors of a sacred, liturgical power, angels thus act as God's go-betweens, his emissaries, his intermediaries. But why does God need intermediaries? In a sense the question is poorly posed, for he who is without privation certainly does not *need* intermediaries. Well prior to vast elaboration of Christian angelology, the great Hellenistic Jewish thinker of the first century Philo of Alexandria had already sought to underscore this point. Since God seeks to fill all parts of the universe with living beings, he argued, and since he set land animals upon the earth and aquatic creatures in the rivers and in the seas, it is necessary to suppose the existence of those aerial beings that the philosophers called "demons" but that Scripture more aptly termed "angels" (and whom it presented as variously descending and ascending Jacob's Ladder, carrying messages from the "father" to his "children" and from the "children" to their "father" in turn). But this does not therefore mean that God, "who is already present in all directions," he added, has any need for such informants. So great, in fact, is the extent of our awe and dread before the universal monarch, he explains, that it is indeed a boon to us in our miserable state to have mediators to act on our behalf.[33] According to this interpretation, God does not need mediators; rather, he needs to be mediated.

Indeed, the larger Neoplatonic tradition to which Philo in a sense belonged considered the appearance of intermediaries to represent an augmentation, rather than a diminution, of the splendor of divine sovereignty. God is not an *autourgos*, he is not someone who works for himself; but there is nonetheless nothing that he does by way of intermediaries that he could not otherwise have done directly. It is he who chooses to act indirectly, in order to avoid involving himself in things unworthy of his majesty. Which includes, above all, engaging in any form of direct intercourse with human beings. According to Plato himself, the necessity of the intermediary can be ascribed to just this exigency: "God with man," he has Diotima inform Socrates in a well-known passage of the *Symposium*, "does not mingle; but the demon is the means of all society and converse of men with gods and of gods with men, whether waking or asleep."[34]

But the necessity of the intermediary could also be demonstrated by more elaborate means. As we read in Plutarch's *De defectu oraculorum*, Plato's companion Xenocrates had employed the curious example of the order of triangles to this end: "The equilateral he compared to the nature of the gods, the scalene to that of man, and the isosceles to that of the demons; for the first is equal in all its lines, the second unequal in all, and the third is partly equal and partly unequal, like the nature of the demons, which have mortal passions and godlike power."[35] Others again would infer its necessity from the existence of the moon, which was also understood to occupy an intermediary position, midway between the heavens and the earth. Just as to remove the air between the earth and the moon, Plutarch observes, would be to destroy the unity and consociation of the universe, since it would leave an empty and unconnected space in the middle, so to withdraw the ministering and interpreting nature of the demons would be either to make the relations between gods and humans too alien and remote or to introduce a disorderly confusion into things by entangling the gods too deeply in human affairs.[36] But we should neither consider that the gods disregard religious ceremonies nor that they are somehow present in these rituals and participate in them. Rather, we should commit these matters, he writes, to those "ministers of the gods" (*leitourgois theōn*) to whom it is appropriate to undertake them.[37] If the gods remain utterly transcendent in relation to the world of human affairs, yet are nonetheless somehow able to intervene with respect to it, it is thanks to the mediation of the *leitourgois theōn*.

It is this last aspect, in particular—the "liturgical" aspect, in the broad sense that we have been describing—that the Christian tradition will seek to develop and extend, by entrusting the intermediary with a genuinely governmental function. Here the intermediary will be figured as an "executive agent" of divine providence, thereby articulating a two-tiered model for the functioning of power in the sense that we have intimated above. As Aquinas has argued in an important chapter of his *Summa contra gentiles*—to choose but one illustrative text among many possible examples—two distinct elements are required for the dispensation of providence: the ordering (*ordinatio*) and the execution of that order (*ordinis executio*). The first, he writes, is accomplished by the "cognitive power" (*virtutem cognoscitivum*), which is to say, by God alone. Such is the perfection of the divine wisdom that it arranges the orders for all things, even down to the smallest, most insignificant details. But the execution of this order, particularly as pertains to the smallest, most insignificant details, will be accomplished by means of other inferior agents—what he calls the "operative power" (*virtutem operativum*)—"through whom he himself works, as does a universal and higher power through a lower and particular power."[38] The reasons for this apparent delegation of power are manifold. In the first place, as is clear from the discussion above, the inferior agents will be responsible, as in the Jewish and Neoplatonic traditions, for performing those operations that God, in his incomparable majesty, ought not to perform. But their participation also allows for an extension and increase of his power—and precisely on account of their medial position. The stronger the power of an agent is, Aquinas explains, the farther away will its operation extend (as, for example, the stronger a fire is the farther away will the things that it heats extend). "But this is not the case," he explains, "with an agent who does not act through a medium [*non agit per medium*]; for whatever it acts upon is adjacent to it."[39] As is evident still today the extension and increase of power thus requires the participation of the media.[40] But their participation will also be required to ensure the perfection of divine providence. For since order itself is its effect, such perfection, Aquinas writes, will be made manifest only where there is a higher order of causes that would be responsible for executing it. Without the interposition of what Aquinas here calls "intermediary causes" (*causae mediae*), that is to say, there would not be an order of causes, but only an order of effects. In which case, the order of divine providence would not be the best.[41]

The divine government of the world will thus be more perfect when the "operative power" of the intermediary causes—which Aquinas will seek to illustrate, in the very next chapter, through the important metaphor of an instrument, "which does not move unless, through being moved, it participates somewhat in the power of the principal agent"[42]—is responsible for concretely executing it. When he again returns to this theme in the *Summa theologiae*, in the context of the treatise on divine government, he is even more emphatic again. "Since the carrying out of government," he writes, "is for the sake of bringing the governed to their perfection, that form of government will be better which communicates a higher perfection to the governed [*tanto erit melior gubernatio quanto major perfectio a gubernante rebis gubernantis communicatur*]."[43] And the manner in which a higher perfection is communicated to the governed, as we have already seen, is through the elevation of a certain portion of them to the rank of causes in the government of others. Just as a teacher causes his students not only to learn, but also to be teachers of others in turn, so God, without his government thereby ceasing to be unified,[44] governs in such a way that a part of the governed comes to actively participate in the bringing of others to their perfection.[45] Indeed, if the effect of God's government is certainly one when viewed from the perspective of its end (which is the assimilation of all things to the highest good), there are nonetheless two distinct ways in which such an assimilation is effectively carried out. The creatures attain "likeness" to God, he writes, with a clear appropriation of the vocabulary of Pseudo-Dionysius, in the first instance to the extent that they imitate God insofar as he is good (*quod Deus bonum est, inquantum creatura est bona*), and in the second instance to the extent that they imitate God insofar as he is the cause of good in others (*quod Deus est aliis causa bonitatis, inquantum una creatura movet aliam ad bonitatem*).[46] There could be no clearer theoretical justification than this for the introduction of a "third" category to the traditional distinction between those who govern and those who are governed, which is arguably Christian theology's most important contribution to the genealogy of governmentality. For here it is the governed themselves who govern, in accordance with a particular modality of the *imitatio dei*, by imitating God insofar as he governs.

But this is also the place in which the intimate yet unexpected link between government and glory, upon which Agamben has insisted, begins to become apparent.[47] For, as Aquinas immediately proceeds to specify, by way of an analogy with the political sphere, that an earthly king should have many ministers need not only be an indication of imperfection, but also of majesty: "For the order of ministers," he writes, "makes the king's power even more illustrious [*quia ordine ministrorum potestas regia praeclarior redditur*]."[48] Or again, in the *Summa contra gentiles*, where—to borrow a concept from Walter Benjamin—its "exhibition value" is even more emphatically affirmed: "It belongs to the dignity of the ruler to have many minsters and a variety of executors for his rule, for, the more subjects he has, on different levels, the higher and greater is his dominion shown to be [*tanto altius et maius ostendetur suum dominium*]."[49] Far from being the expression of a deficiency or a lack, God's governing by way of intermediaries thus makes the plenitude of his power all the more manifest.

4.

With this last observation, we rejoin our point of departure for the present chapter: the interpretation of the concept of hierarchy, such as it has been elaborated in that privileged laboratory that is Christian angelology. But we do so with the capacity to add a further specification to it, one that has nonetheless been latent in our discussion from the beginning. Hierarchy, we have suggested, is neither an ontological fact nor an objective structure; it is a practice. More specifically, it is a practice of ordering—of purifying, of illuminating, of perfecting—that is applied not only to those who are its object, but also to those who are its subject. But it is not merely a practice of ordering; it is also its *manifestation*. It is a practice of ordering that shows itself as such. To put it in grammatical terms, "order" (*taxis*)—which is not only what the hierarchy does, but also what it shows—functions at one and the same time as a verb (in the imperative form) and as a noun. The former produces the latter, but only to the extent that the latter exhibits the former: The two lexical categories thus mutually reinforce one another. The "economic" practice of government thus generates a distinctly "non-economic" supplement, a kind of sublime double of itself.[50] And in this doubling the liturgical power of the intermediary causes—for which the figure of the angel furnishes the decisive emblem—occupies an essential place. In accordance with the double exigency to which it responds, their liturgy, as we have seen, is always simultaneously for the sake of the human and the divine. In other words, it is not only an external service with an internalizing effect (being the cause of perfection in the government of others); it is also, and to the same extent, an internal service with an externalizing effect (making God's power even more illustrious). And the latter is no mere epiphenomenon of the former: The supplement in fact forms an integral part of the hierarchical apparatus. Indeed, between the internalizing and externalizing effects of every hierarchy there is a tension that would appear irresolvable, if not for the ultimate absorption of the former by the latter, which is to say, of the "economic" whole by its "noneconomic" supplement.

It is no coincidence, then, that the apex of the angelic hierarchy should coincide with the orders of the cherubim and seraphim, executors of a purely doxological liturgy. As a distinctly soteriological technology of power, hierarchy must show itself, must exhibit itself, must communicate itself; otherwise, were it to succeed in absolving its task completely, it would also thereby dissolve its own concept. But this specification of a necessary supplementary dimension to all hierarchical practice (which for Erik Peterson, as we have seen, coincides with its "political" dimension) also reveals the occluded "katechontic" logic that it must observe.[51] This means, of course, that the salvation that hierarchy confers (and this holds equally for both its religious and secular variants) can ultimately only ever be apparent. Hierarchy is the organ, not of salvation itself, but only of its promise. It institutes a paradoxical form of salvation without end, of salvation without deliverance—something like an infinite *oikonomia*. What is truly saved is only the hierarchy itself. The dimension of power that Agamben has sought to inscribe under the rubric of "glory" (and whose unexpected continuity with the economic practice of government he has sought to underscore) is indeed what secures, over and against the apparent finitude of liturgical power's exercise, the paradoxical permanence of its institution. But it is not only the form in which the functioning of power survives its own exercise, as Agamben wants to suggest; it is also the form in which the function itself—the *officium*, to employ the term with which the Latins would translate the Greek *leitourgia*—survives the discrete time and place of the one who would exercise it.

Excursus: Marx and Bureaucracy

Karl Marx demonstrated a perfect awareness of the absolutely insubstantial character of every hierarchy in his brief analysis, in the *Critique of Hegel's 'Philosophy of Right,'* of the modern and profane hierarchy par excellence: bureaucracy. For him, the fact that Hegel develops no "content" of the bureaucracy in his remarks on the executive, but offers instead only some general indications regarding its "formal" organization, is in itself symptomatic. For the bureaucracy—so his striking definition reads—is merely "the 'formalism' of a content which lies outside of the bureaucracy [*der 'Formalismus' eine Inhalts, der außerhalb derselben liegt*]."[52] This content "which lies outside of the bureaucracy" coincides with that of the state, and so Marx can immediately further specify his definition of bureaucracy as "the state formalism," or rather, "the state as formalism."[53] And because this state formalism becomes itself a real power in the form of the bureaucrats themselves, the latter are accordingly defined as "the Jesuits and theologians of the state."[54] It is Marx's great insight, in fact, to have observed how the aims of the bureaucracy, to the extent that they coincide with the formal aims of the state, can enter into conflict with its real aims—a conflict that can only be resolved through the transformation of the aims of the state into those of the bureaucracy itself. In this way, however, the state comes to coincide with its own formalism, which is to say, with its own executive. It is important to observe, then, that when Marx, by way of a distinct appropriation of the terminology of Christian angelology, presents "the divinization of authority" (*der Vergötterung der Autorität*) as bureaucracy's specific ethos,[55] such a divinization can only mean: the divinization of itself. For even though authority is something "which lies outside of the bureaucracy"—being instead, as Marx observes, the hierarchical principle of its knowledge[56]—the only content of the bureaucracy is, as we have seen, precisely what lies outside of it. Bureaucracy, then, coincides with that which lies outside of it, whose formalization it is. According to the aporetic circular logic that its concept observes, the only content of the bureaucracy is the state, even as the only content of the state is the bureaucracy. Exactly as in the angelic hierarchies, bureaucratic power must be incessantly exercised in order to be possessed. For since it receives its content from without, it can only manifest its existence through the constant manipulation of this content[57]—which is to say, through an incessant activity of government. But bureaucracy's "crass spiritualism," according to Marx, may also in turn be accompanied by an equally "crass materialism." To the extent that the aims of the state come to coincide with those of the bureaucracy, so too, for individual bureaucrats, the universal interests come to coincide with their own private interests: with the pursuit of ever higher posts—in short, with the building of a *career*.[58]

It is here that Marx's critique of the Hegelian account of bureaucracy begins to become apparent. The bureaucracy is not the universal class, as Hegel wrongly supposed; it is a "pseudo-universal": the dispensation of the universal assuming the form of a particular class.[59] It is significant, in this sense, that Marx should directly employ the example of the clergy/laity "dimorphism" to illustrate this state of affairs. That every citizen has the theoretical possibility of joining the ranks of the civil service, according to Marx, is certainly no testament to its universality. For while it is true that every Catholic maintains the possibility of becoming a priest (and thereby of separating himself from the laity), the clergy does not confront the laity, on this account, as any less of an oppositive force: "That each and everyone has the potentiality [*Möglichkeit*] of acquiring the right of another sphere," he writes, "only proves that his own sphere is not the actuality [*Wirklichkeit*] of this right."[60] As is well known, it is nonetheless the case that Marx would take the notion of a class within society whose interests would truly be universal, and whose appearance would thus coincide with the dissolution of all classes, very seriously.[61] The affirmation of the classless society thus distinctly passes through the deactivation of liturgical power.

4

INSTRUMENTAL CAUSE

1.

The problem of the relationship between politics and religion in modernity, according to Foucault, is not the problem of the relationship between the emperor and the pope; it is the problem of that ambiguous figure who, significantly enough, retains the same name across both spheres: the figure of the minister. Within the context of Foucault's own oeuvre, this curious remark, which seems to present almost the key to his reflections on pastoral power (and hence, by extension, to the larger genealogy of governmentality, of which the former is but a part), remained entirely without continuation. Uniquely concerned with constructing the passage that led from the pastoral government of souls to the political government of men, and with tracing the emergence of the population-wealth dyad that would become the privileged object of the new governmental reason—what, starting from Antoine de Montchrestien, would come to be termed, however incongruously, "political economy"—the problem of the minister as such was left completely unelaborated and even unexamined. Its appearance in effect coincided with its disappearance.

But what is a minister? According to the important definition of Aquinas, a minister is an "instrument with intelligence" (*minister est sicut instrumentum intelligens*).[1] He is an instrument because (as we have already seen in the case of those intermediary beings par excellence that are the angels) he is moved by another (*ab alio movetur*), yet solely for the sake of another again (*ad aliud ordinatur*). But he is an instrument with intelligence because, unlike simple material instruments (an axe, for example), which must be employed by force, he nonetheless acts in his instrumental capacity incontrovertibly of his own free will. He is not only moved (*movetur*), but he also moves himself (*movet seipsum*). The caveat is important: If the minister can indeed be defined as a "servant of God," it is only on the condition of having freely chosen his own servitude. To be a minister—to be an *instrumentum intelligens*, whether human or divine—means to freely place oneself in the service of God: This, among other things, is what the doctrine of the fall of the angels teaches with eloquence.

The minister, then, never simply acts, but always necessarily doubly acts. Every ministerial action—every liturgical action, in the strict sense—is necessarily preceded by a prior action in which the minister formally conjoins his will to that of the one on whose behalf alone he acts. Nowhere is this more apparent than in that sphere of liturgical action that, more than any other, presents the paradigm of a specifically human ministry: the administration of the sacraments. Precisely because a sacrament is, in one respect, a material, physical thing (water, for example, in the case of baptism), which may be employed in the service of any one of a number of different ends (for the purpose of washing, to continue the above example, yet with the aim of simple physical cleanliness), it is necessary to identify in what way and to what end the action in question is being performed. And this is achieved, according to Aquinas, through the declaration of the minister's "intention" (*intentio*).[2] But if we ask in what the minister's intention consists, the answer appears at first glance to be patently paradoxical. To the extent that the minister operates in the sacrament as a mere "instrument" of the principal agent (which is God alone), it would seem as if his intention would be strictly superfluous to the securing of its salutary effect. And this would indeed be the case, Aquinas contends (employing a distinction that, as we shall see, again comes directly from Aristotle himself), were the minister but a simple "inanimate" instrument, which experienced movement only on account of having been moved by the principal agent. But insofar as he is, instead, an "animate" instrument, who is not only moved but who also moves himself in turn, his intention becomes absolutely necessary: "For it is by this," Aquinas writes, "that he subjects himself to the principal agent [*se subjiciat principali agenti*], namely, by intending to do what Christ and the Church do [*intendat facere quod facit Christus et Ecclesia*]."[3] Intention, in this context, is thus an essentially circular concept. And, as is often the case with concepts of this nature, it remains perfectly empty. The only content of the intention is the ministry, and the only content of the ministry is the intention. And yet, it is nothing other than this circle that defines the minister in his being, nothing other than this circle that makes him what he is: an intelligent, animate instrument.

Intention, in this sense, is thus an expressly ontological category. It names nothing subjective, and admits of no qualification whatsoever. Neither can it be considered right nor wrong. This is what the seemingly extreme thesis, which holds that even a perversity of intention on the part of the minister ultimately remains insufficient to render the sacrament invalid, demonstrates with great clarity. A priest, for example, may baptize a woman with the sole intention of abusing her, or else, he may consecrate the body of Christ only in order to use it as poison; but since what is prior does not in any sense depend on what is subsequent, even in these limit cases—in which the priest, to be sure, grievously sins—the sacrament itself retains all its validity.[4] A perverse intention perverts the *opus intendentis*, but not the *opus alterius*; it perverts the minister's "own work," but not the "work of Christ," whose minister he is.[5] Ministerial intention thus denotes something like a "zero degree"[6] of intentionality, a kind of pure intention that necessarily insists above and beyond any determinate intending.[7]

The only way, then, in which one may actively contribute to producing the sacramental effect, according to Aquinas, is to act *per modum ministerii*; but to act *per modum ministerii* means precisely to act as the mere instrument of the principal agent and hence to contribute nothing of what is truly one's own. It follows, as a direct corollary of this, Aquinas observes, "that the effect of the sacrament is not better conferred when it is conferred by a better minister [*effectus sacramenti non datur melior per meliorum ministrum*]."[8] Indeed, according to one of the most fundamental tenets of the Catholic Church, the sacraments maintain a strictly *ex opere operato* efficacy. That is, they remain objectively valid, and hence efficacious, absolutely independently of the personal worthiness of the agent who concretely confers them. They owe their efficacy solely to the *opus operatum* (the work done), and not in any sense to the *opus operantis* (the working of the worker). In spite of the apparent obscurity of this doctrine, we should be careful not to underestimate its profound significance, whose enduring influence extends well beyond the strictly theological sphere. For in it is formulated that seemingly exemplary modern notion that asserts the independence of the institution from the persons who represent it, or again—to put it in a key at once more expressly theological and yet more ostensibly secular—of the corporation from the members who compose it. In the minister, the efficacy of the action that is performed must be considered apart from the actual individual who performs it. If we are to properly situate its figure, in both its "religious" and its "political" guises, it can thus only be against the backdrop of the formation of this doctrine.

2.

That the Church would be able to secure objective validity for its praxis only at the cost of endorsing the extreme ethical indeterminacy of its own agents can thus hardly be considered a mere concomitant effect of this process. Indeed, as Agamben has observed, the formal definition of the minister as a "living instrument" (*instrumentum animatum*) of an operation whose principal agent is Christ—which we find in Aquinas, and whose philosophical history we shall seek to reconstruct in what follows—was aimed squarely at neutralizing the problem of the *opus operantis* once and for all.[9] If the minister indeed contributes to the production of sacramental efficacy, according to Aquinas, it is only insofar as he acts as its "instrumental cause" (*causa instrumentalis*). But what is an instrumental cause? How should we understand this apparently paradoxical formulation?

It has long been assumed that the introduction of the figure of the instrumental cause marked an important contribution with respect to Aristotle's theory of causation. In a well-known sequence both of his *Physics* and of his *Metaphysics*, the philosopher had distinguished four distinct causes in the determination of things: the material, the formal, the efficient, and the final. To begin with, he argued, one must presuppose the existence of some matter from which the process of generation will depart (the material cause). In Aristotle's own example, the bronze from which the statue will be formed. Next, this matter must receive the form that, as he writes, "brings it within the definition of the thing we say it is, whether specifically or generically" (the formal cause). In other words, the statue into which the bronze is shaped. But there must also be something or someone that initiates this transformation, an agent that produces an effect in a thing, thereby setting in train the process that changes it from what it was—the bronze—into what it will become—the statue (the efficient cause). Finally, there is the end or purpose for the sake of which the entire process was engendered in the first place (the final cause). Hence, for example, the act of memorialization on account of which the statue is erected.[10] With respect to Aristotle's fourfold partition, the instrumental cause would thus represent the addition of a fifth dimension—or rather, the introduction of a division internal to the sphere of the efficient cause itself. There would be, not one agent, but two: the agent that moves the instrument (the principal cause), and the instrument itself through which that movement is conveyed (the instrumental cause). And while the principal cause would produce its effect by virtue of its own form (as, for example, fire warms on account of its own heat), the instrumental cause would instead produce its effect not by virtue of its own form, but solely by virtue of the impetus imparted to it by the principal cause.[11]

In truth, however, the relationship of the instrumental cause to the efficient cause is much more complicated. For the instrumental cause is itself but an effect of the principal cause. In this lies its specific difference with respect to the principal cause. As Aquinas writes, in an important addendum:

A principal cause cannot, in any proper sense, be called the sign of its effect [*signum effectus*], even when that effect is hidden, and even when it itself is manifest to the senses. An instrumental cause, on the other hand, provided it is manifest, can be called the sign of a hidden effect [*signum effectus occulti*] in virtue of the fact that it is not only a cause but in some sense an effect too [*non solum est causa, sed quodammodo effectus*], insofar as it is moved by the principal agent.[12]

The comparative analysis must therefore be carried further still. Far from representing a simple contribution to the Aristotelian theory of causality—a mere variation, as it were—the figure of the instrumental cause, as Agamben has underscored, in fact subverts the very distinction between cause and effect upon which the entire edifice of the Aristotelian theory rests. In its case, as he has astutely observed, "the cause is a cause insofar as it is an effect and the effect is an effect insofar as it is a cause [*la causa è causa in quanto è effetto e l'effetto è effetto in quanto è causa*]."[13] The theory of the instrumental cause thus marks the addition of a radically new dimension, which is irreducible to any of the elements that compose

Aristotle's fourfold schema. What is a cause, whose unique force would appear to rest on the fact that it is itself but the visible sign of a hidden effect?

Excursus: The Instrumental Cause and the Performative

The instrumental cause defines not only the minister but also the sacraments themselves. Indeed, it is only to the extent that the sacraments serve as instrumental causes that they can truly be said, in accordance with the celebrated formula that Aquinas employs in precisely this context, to *efficiunt quod figurant* (effect what they signify).[14] And in this sense the theory of the instrumental cause occupies an important place in the genealogy of that particular sphere of language that J. L. Austin sought to inscribe under the rubric of the performative utterance.[15] It is also the case, however, that restoring the position of the instrumental cause within the context of this genealogy enables us to shed a particular light on the actual character of the performative utterance itself.

Efficiunt quod figurant: In this curious formula of unknown authorship that circulated widely throughout the High Middle Ages, that which distinguishes the sacraments of the new dispensation from those of the old appears as if in condensed form. The foundation for the distinction was the singular position accorded to the sacraments within the broader medieval doctrine of signs. It was Augustine who was responsible not only for furnishing the most perspicacious definition of the sign ("A sign is a thing which of itself makes some other thing come to mind, besides the impression that it presents to the senses"[16]), but also for inscribing the theory of the sacraments within the discrete framework of a "sacred semiology."[17] Like the other classes of sign, the sacrament too, he argued, is a reality that is at once sensible and intelligible. It is itself a tangible, material thing (water, for example, in the case of baptism), yet one that in turn refers to something else beyond itself, which is signified (the ablution and cleansing of the soul). In it, according to his characteristic formulation, "one thing is seen, another is understood [*aliud videtur, aliud intelligitur*]."[18] To the sensible/intelligible double, however, he would also add another. As a sign, the sacrament is the material and visible face of an invisible and spiritual event; the water of the baptismal rite the visible symbol of the invisible cleansing. It is here that we touch upon the dimension that constitutes the specificity of the sacrament with respect to the other classes of sign: Between what is seen and what is understood, between what is visible and what is invisible, according to Augustine, there must be a certain degree of "similitude" (*similitudinem*). Where there is no likeness between signifier and signified, there can be no sacrament. For him, the sacraments thus constitute a very particular species of sign, which owe their singular and privileged position within the larger hierarchy of signs to the fact that, in them, the signifier truly resembles the signified.

With respect to this definition, the scholastic theologians of the twelfth and thirteenth centuries would nonetheless seek to add a further dimension. The sacrament, they argued, is not a mere sign. More specifically, it is an *efficacious* sign. It is a sign that is itself effective of the reality that it signifies. If Hugh of St. Victor is rightly credited with orienting the comprehension of the sacrament in this direction, it was a widely disseminated twelfth-century *Summa sententiarum*—long thought to be one of Hugh's genuine works, but in truth only a paraphrase of him—that provided its clearest formulation. The sacrament, the unknown author of the *Summa* writes, is the sign of a sacred thing because it is the visible form of the invisible grace that is contained in it. But it is not only this. "Not only is it the sign of a sacred thing," we read,

> but it is also its efficacy [*Non enim solummodo sacrae rei signum, sed etiam efficacia*]. And this is the difference between the sacrament and the sign: for, in order for there to be a sign, nothing more is required than that it signify that of which it is said to be the sign; it need not confer it. The sacrament, on the other hand, not only signifies, but it also confers that of which it is the sign or signification [*Non solum significat, sed etiam confert illud cujus est signum vel significatio*].[19]

What distinguishes the sacrament from the sign is thus not only that it resembles what it signifies, but that it also confers it. According to the author of the *Summa*, the sacrament is, at one and the same time, significative and effective of the grace that it confers: it signifies what it effects and effects what it signifies. It was Peter Lombard, however, who was responsible finally for explicitly introducing the philosophical theme of causality into the theory of the sacraments and hence for formalizing the teachings of the Victorine School.[20] The sacrament, he argued, once again following Augustine, is a special kind of sign because it resembles the thing whose sign it is. But it is the sign of God's grace, he added, not only because it "bears its image" (*imaginem gerat*), but also because it "is its cause" (*causa existat*). The sacraments, according to his account, were thus instituted not only for the sake of signifying (*significandi*), but also for the sake of sanctifying (*sanctificandi*).[21]

After Peter—whose contribution perhaps coincides, not incidentally, with the first appearance of the formula itself (even though he believed himself to be citing Augustine)[22]—the debate is now concentrated on the precise species of cause to which the sacraments belong. And yet—crucially, from our perspective—the resolution of this debate does not proceed through an elision of the sacraments' semiotic character, but through a renewed emphasis on it. According to Aquinas, it is only to the extent that the sacraments are first taken as signs that they can in turn function as causes. In other words, qua sign they must themselves be the effect of a cause that transcends them, and only in this way may a properly causal status be ascribed to them. But this means that the *performative* character of these signs is indexed to their very instrumental causality. In accordance with the circular structure that we have already encountered previously, it is only to the extent that the sacraments act as instrumental causes that they can truly be said to *efficiunt quod figurant*; conversely, it is only to the extent that the sacraments *efficiunt quod figurant* that they may be defined as instrumental causes. Only an instrumental cause, and not a principal cause, can meet the apparently paradoxical requirement of being both a sign and a cause at the same time.[23] And in this sense the particular force that it incarnates perfectly reproduces the vicarious structure of the Trinitarian economy. It is here, however, that the intention of the animate instrument again shows its importance. It is only the minimal addition of the minister's intention to the sacrament (which, in the case of baptism, for example, receives expression in the words "I baptize you in the name of the Father, the Son, and the Holy Spirit"[24]) that in effect secures its performative "felicity." It is this minimal addition alone that, by transforming the sacrament into a sign, suspends its immediate reference to the world; yet solely in order to make it the instrument of a superior agent who in turn realizes an effect immanent to its own most proper operation.

3.

Scholars have often wondered from where in the philosophical tradition Aquinas derived his theory of instrumental causality, which appears nowhere in the seemingly exhaustive inventory of the modes of efficient causality enumerated in his own commentaries on Aristotle's aetiology. There, he had followed the authority of Avicenna in distinguishing, in addition to the four classes of cause (material, formal, efficient, and final), a further four modes of efficient causality. The first two are strictly correlated. An efficient cause is said to be "perfective" (*perficiens*) when it alone brings about the ultimate perfection of a thing (as, for example, when the builder builds a house). Yet it is said to be merely "dispositive" (*disponens*) when it does not itself perfect the thing but simply prepares the matter that will eventually lead to its perfection (as in the case of the laborer who hews the timber and stones with which the house will be built). Closest in spirit perhaps to the instrumental cause, yet still nonetheless clearly distinct from it, is the cause that Aquinas here calls the "auxiliary" (*adiuvans*), which does not operate in view of its own end, but which is instead itself disposed toward the end of a principal efficient cause (as in the case of a strategist, who assists the king in a military campaign not in view of his own end, but solely in view of that of the king himself). Finally, there is the cause he terms "advisory" (*consilians*), which differs from the principal efficient cause in that it specifies the end and form through which a subordinate agent must act (as when the naval architect gives to the shipwright the end and form of his activity).[25]

It was, to be sure, with the aid of the first two of these modes that the early Aquinas, in concert with the vast majority of scholastic theologians both before and after him, had sought to account for the singular operation of the sacraments in his commentary on the *Sententia* of Peter Lombard. *Causa disponens praeparat materiam, causa perficiens influit formam*: Adopting to the letter this formula couched in the vocabulary of the Avicennian physics that was then in vogue, the early thirteenth-century theologians easily grafted this apparently limpid schema onto the sacramental apparatus in order to account for its functioning. *Sacramenta disponunt anima ad gratiam, Deus influit gratiam in anima*: Like the principle of motion in the larger context of Avicenna's account of the physical world, the sacraments were understood to operate as a "dispositive" cause, which prepared the soul for the reception of grace; but it was the transcendental God alone (Avicenna's Agent Intelligence), who, qua "perfective" cause, was thought to be responsible for actually dispensing it and, thereby, for articulating the transition *de potentia ad effectum*.[26] And yet, as H.-F. Dondaine has shown in an influential essay, the commensurability between the Avicennian model and its sacramental application was ultimately only apparent. For, such was the extent of form's transcendence with respect to matter in Avicenna's system, that the two parallel stages of efficient causality, although linked in a necessary concordance, remained almost without any communication between them. Obviously, the same could not in any sense be said of the sacraments. The introduction of the theory of the instrumental cause—such is the implication of Dondaine's exposition— would be the element, added only later in the course of Aquinas's career, that would allow the two stages of the sacramental action to communicate with one another, while at the same time investing the sacraments themselves with a genuine efficient causality.

As the subtitle of his study would suggest, it is Dondaine's contention that the Avicennian model of dispositive causality would gradually be replaced in Aquinas's system by a model of instrumental causality much closer in inspiration to the genuine teaching of Aristotle himself (even if in accordance with strictly theological motivations). As he writes, summarizing the arc of his own argument, "Aquinas abandons an Avicennian schema of causality, substituting it with that of Aristotle and Averroes."[27] Such an interpretation, however, can be at best only partially correct. In the first place, because, as we have already intimated above, there is—and can be—no Aristotelian theory of instrumental causality in the strict sense.[28] It is true that instruments, such as the surgical implements employed by a physician, do appear in the context of Aristotle's discussion of the four causes (specifically, in relation to the final cause); but, being placed wholly in the service of a principal agent, they are presented either as means or as ends and never as causes in their own right.[29] It is also the case, moreover, as Dondaine himself concedes, that a conception of the instrumental cause (replete with references to Aristotle, however such references may ultimately be understood) is already clearly articulated, a propos of the sacraments, in Aquinas's own commentary on the *Sententia*. But here the instrumental cause is itself placed in the service of the dispositive cause, such that one can speak without contradiction of a genuine theory of instrumental dispositive causality. That there is a shift in Aquinas's sacramental theory, of this there can be no doubt. But it cannot simply assume the form of the neat arc such as Dondaine and others have presented it. It is as much a question of a shift in his theory of instrumental causality, as it is of a shift from dispositive causality to instrumental causality.[30]

4.

In a certain attenuated sense, however, the reference to Aristotle is indeed instructive. For even if it is true that there is—and can be—no strictly Aristotelian theory of instrumental causality, it is no doubt the case that Aquinas did, at least in part, derive his own theory from him. As his own citations clearly attest, however, it is neither in the *Physics* nor in the *Metaphysics* that we find Aristotle's most sustained discussion of instrumentality, but in the sequence of the *Politics* dedicated to the prepolitical art of household management (*oikonomikē*).[31] As is well known, Aristotle divides household management into three sets of heterogeneous relations: the "despotic" relation between the master and the slave; the "gamic" relation between the husband and the wife; and the "progenitive" relation between the father and the children.[32] It is in the context of the first of these that his discussion of instrumentality is concentrated. Against Plato, who in his *Statesman* had famously sought to construct a "science of the master" (an *epistēmē epitaktikē*, literally a "science of commandment"), Aristotle starts from the supposition that household management is, instead, merely an "art," a *technē*.[33] And, like the other "arts"—the model of the "craftsman," the *technitēs*, is evident here—it too, he suggests, should possess its own "instruments" (*organa*). Among instruments, however, some are "inanimate" (*apsycha*), while others instead are "animate" (*empsycha*). With respect to the art of navigation, for example, the ship's rudder would be, for its pilot, an "inanimate" instrument; his lookout man, by contrast, an "animate" instrument. And so, within the household: Among the many "possessions" (*ktēma*) that comprise the household—possessions that serve as instruments, Aristotle writes, for the maintenance of "life" (*zōē*)—there are some that are "inanimate," others instead that are "animate." It is to the latter category that the slave belongs.[34] Hence the first preliminary definition: "The slave is a living possession [*ktēma ti empsychon*]."[35] But because a *technē* may be oriented either toward *poiēsis* or *praxis*, and because the

slave is concerned solely with the latter, it will be necessary to add the further specification: the slave is "a subordinate agent of action [*hypēretes tōn
tēn praxis*]."³⁶

A living possession in the service of the master's action, the slave, then,
is in one sense part of the master and in another sense separate from him.
On the one hand, he belongs wholly to the master. According to one of
the more controversial (but perhaps least understood) claims of Aristotle's
theory, "a human being who belongs, by nature [*physei*], not to himself,
but to another, is by nature [*physei*] a slave."³⁷ In this sense, the slave forms
part of the master (although, as Aristotle notes, the inverse is not true: The
master is not part of the slave).³⁸ On the other hand, however, he is also
a part of the master that is somehow separable from him, which can be
employed as the instrument of the master's action. Separate and yet conjoined, the relationship between the master and the slave is such that when
the slave acts it is also the case that the master acts, but that when slave
suffers it is not the case that the master suffers. Indeed, as a remarkable
sequence of the *Eudemian Ethics* suggests, between the master and the slave
no genuine "community" (*koinonia*) can be formed: "for they are not two,
but the former is one and the latter a part of that one." In this sense, not
even the good is divisible between them, "but that of both belongs to the
one for whose sake the pair exist."³⁹ It is nonetheless the case that here, as in
any of the other innumerable instances in which there is "ruling" (*archein*)
and "being ruled" (*archesthai*)—and this includes even the living being
itself, where the soul rules over the body—that the two more often than
not function harmoniously together, in view of a common work that is
mutually advantageous to both.⁴⁰

For Aristotle, the existence of slavery is in accordance with the order
of nature. But this does not mean that his theory amounts to a justification of the existing institution of slavery. In a brilliant article, Victor Goldschmidt has shown that the singular methodological procedure that Aristotle employs here effectively inverts his usual order of exposition. If the
latter typically proceeds from "existence" toward "essence," here instead
it moves from "essence" toward "existence." If, in other words, it is Aristotle's characteristic manner to inquire first of all whether a thing exists
and only secondarily to ask what that thing is, here instead the procedure
is completely reversed: Starting from the definition of the thing, only secondarily does he proceed to investigate whether there is in existence any

entity that would correspond to such a definition.[41] As is well known, he answers in the affirmative, yet not without a certain degree of equivocation for which the singular methodological procedure alone provides. And this, in itself, according to Goldschmidt, is sufficient to charge his account with a critical force rarely recognized as such by commentators. "Nature," we read, "would like to distinguish between the bodies of freemen and slaves, making the one strong for necessary use, the other upright, and although useless for such work, useful for political life. . . . But the opposite often happens—that some have the souls and others have the bodies of freemen."[42] For Aristotle, the decisive question is thus whether or not the institution of slavery corresponds to the intention of nature as such. To which he answers: sometimes yes, sometimes no. In the case of the former, it must be praised as expedient and just; in the case of the latter, it must be criticized as inexpedient and unjust.[43] Far from constituting a defense of the existing institution of slavery, the Aristotelian inquiry into the *physis* and *dynamis* of the slave in fact provides the grounds for a sharp critique of those very instances where nature and convention do not coincide.[44] But this in itself already points to something fundamental. The Aristotelian theory of slavery, and of the particular mode of instrumentality that is embodied in it, is thus grounded uniquely and unequivocally in his theory of nature, which is to say, in his "physics."

5.

The theoretical paradigm for what Aquinas will call the instrumental cause is to be found in the eighth and final book of Aristotle's *Physics*. More specifically, it is to be found in the context of the philosopher's demonstration of the necessary supposition of an unmoved prime mover that would be the source and the cause of all motion. It thus forms an important part not only of his physics, but also of his metaphysics, which is to say, of his "theology" (*theologikē*).[45] As David Ross has elegantly summarized it, the argument of Book 8 charts a path that leads "from the eternal existence of change to the existence of an unmoved mover that causes it."[46] At the very outset of the treatise, then, Aristotle seeks first of all to demonstrate that the existence of motion in the cosmos is eternal. Never did it begin to be and never will it cease to be. Such a claim, he suggests, may be inferred starting from his own definition of motion. In order for motion to take place, it is necessary that not one but two capacities be present—a *dynamis tou poiein* and a *dynamis tou pathein* (what the medieval commentators, Aquinas included, will call *potentia activa* and *potentia passiva*). There must be an agent that is capable of producing motion in a patient, and there must be a patient that is in turn capable of receiving that motion.[47] Hence the following striking definition, which is formulated as such as early as Book 3: "Motion is the actualization of a potentiality qua potentiality."[48] Or, as he will reformulate it more precisely again at the beginning of Book 8: "The actualization of the movable qua movable [*entelecheian tou kinētou ē kinēton*]."[49] Given, then, that motion exists—something that no "physicist" denies—if one were to posit a period of rest prior to the commencement of motion, not only would motion itself have had to have occurred in order for the transition from the one (rest) to the other (motion) to have taken place, but one would also have to suppose the prior existence both of an agent capable of effectuating this transition and of a patient of being so effectuated. And these, too, would have to have either always existed (in which case, they would be the cause of a motion prior to that posited as first), or to have themselves come into being at some point (which would imply a motion even further prior again). Therefore, there can be no time in which there was not motion.[50] But nor, on the same grounds, can there be any time in which motion will cease to be. For any motion that is purported to be the last, Aristotle argues, must necessarily suppose a motion that can only take place subsequent to it.[51] Motion, then, is eternal. But a second thesis also immediately follows from this demonstration. Where there is motion, there must necessarily be a mover. In other words: Qua movable, the movable must either move itself, or else it must be moved by some external agent. But since, as Aristotle observes, even in the case where there is evidently self-movement (such as, for example, in the instance of animate beings), it is necessary that some part should serve as the agent with respect to the whole, he can conclude that all things that are in motion are of necessity moved by some agent, whether they be external or internal.[52]

It is in the context of his discussion of the cause of motion—and hence, in the course of his proof of the existence of an unmoved prime mover—that Aristotle comes the closest to articulating a genuine theory of instrumental causality. And it is starting from precisely this discussion, which informs his own account of slavery, that its theoretical paradigm will be transmitted to the philosophy of the Middle Ages. According to Aristotle, motion may be initiated in one of two ways. Either the subject of motion is moved immediately by a principal agent, or else it is moved by an intermediate agent (or, indeed, by the last in a chain of intermediate agents), which is itself moved by the principal agent and which only in turn acts directly upon it.[53] In other words, either A acts on B, or else A acts on B, which in turns acts on C.[54] It is his illustration of the operation particular to the latter that especially concerns us here. Taking up an example that will become something of a commonplace in scholastic philosophy (as we shall see, Aquinas himself will assume it almost identically in his treatise on the sacraments, while nonetheless bringing a decisive new inflection to it), he writes: "Thus the staff moves the stone and is moved by the hand, which again is moved by the man; in the man, however, we have reached a mover that is not so in virtue of being moved by something else."[55] On the one hand, then, Aristotle comments, we say that the last in the chain of movers (the staff) moves the stone, since only it comes into direct contact with it. On the other hand, however, we say that it is the first in the chain of movers (the man) that moves the stone, for it is he alone who initiates the movement that takes place only mediately through the staff. In reality, however, according to Aristotle, only the latter is true, it is only the man who actually moves the stone; for while the staff depends upon the man for its movement, the man does not in any way depend upon it: "The first moves the last, but the last does not move the first, and the first will move the thing without the last, but the last will not move it without the first."[56] Clearly it is the philosopher's intention here to demonstrate the impossibility of an infinite chain of movers, each drawing its impetus from the one immediately preceding it in the chain and each in turn imparting its motion to the one immediately following it: At the limit, there must be a primary agent that is not moved by anything else, but that either is unmoved or that moves itself. And it is starting from this last distinction that he will ultimately argue that, if the agent and the patient are not to coincide in the same being, it is necessary that the prime mover be itself unmoving. But it is in the course of this demonstration that something like an instrumental causality becomes thinkable. As he writes: "But if there were any need to consider which of the two, that which moves itself or that which is moved by something else, is the cause [aition] and principle [archē] of motion, everyone would decide for the former; for that which is itself a cause is always prior to that which is so in virtue of something else [*to gar auto kath'auto on aition aei proteron tou kath'eteron kai autou ontos*]."[57]

An instrumental causality is at best implied by Aristotle, but it is never directly articulated as such. This can be proven by the simple lexicographical observation that, in spite of its celebrated example, the vocabulary of instrumentality is nowhere in evidence in Book 8. *Causa principalis movet, causa instrumentalis movet mota*: If this elegant formula cited by Dondaine is certainly useful in pointing to the theory of instrumental causality's undisputed origin in Book 8 of the *Physics*, it nonetheless cannot be accurately described as the genuine "schema of Aristotle, restored by Averroes."[58] Rather, it can at best be described as a curious interpolation of the great Andalusian philosopher—or perhaps, more accurately, of his Latin translator—which, in passing into the hands of the scholastic masters (and above all, Aquinas himself), would enjoy a spectacular, if often surreptitious afterlife in the history of the Christian West. To be sure, Aristotle provides the theoretical framework for conceptualizing the action of a subordinate agent. But as the example of the slave eloquently attests, such an agent ultimately remains too subordinate for one to be able speak of a genuine efficient causality in its case, whether instrumental or otherwise. In Aristotle, effects are never causally attributed to the instruments. The master is not only utterly transcendent with respect to the slave; he is also the one for whose sake, and in whose name, both of them act. The action of the slave is the action of the master: They are not two, but one. In itself, then, the Aristotelian reference ultimately remains insufficient to ground Aquinas's theory. But it is nonetheless significant in its own right—for two distinct, yet interrelated reasons that perhaps already indicate the manner in which such a transition may ultimately be explained. In the first instance, because its emblematic figure appears solely in the context of the philosopher's discussion of "household management." In the second instance, because, as we have shown, its theoretical paradigm emerges out of his "theology." In Aristotle, there is already a clear link between the discourse of *oikonomia*, on the one hand, and the discourse of *theologia*, on the other. And that link is furnished by the account of the slave's living instrumentality.

6.

As has often been observed, however, there is another no less important source for Aquinas's theory of the instrumental cause. Around 1259, shortly after completing a three-year term as master of theology in Paris, Aquinas returned to Italy where he was briefly assigned to the Dominican priory in Orvieto. There he had access to the papal palace and library and hence to a vast collection of Greek patristic and conciliar texts with which very few of his contemporaries would have been familiar. It was starting from this encounter, it has been suggested, and above all with the writings of Athanasius and Cyril of Alexandria and with the proceedings of the great ecumenical councils of Ephesus and Chalcedon, that Aquinas would come to assign an increasing importance (as his citations thereafter indeed clearly attest) to a doctrine that he first encountered in the last of the Greek Fathers but that he now understood to condense an entire theological tradition in its economic formula. According to St. John of Damascus, as Aquinas often had occasion to repeat, Christ's humanity was an instrument of his divinity (*humanitas instrumentum divinitatis*). The shift in his theory of instrumental causality was thus precipitated by a shift in his Christology:[59] Just as the body was held to be the instrument of the soul, he would argue in the *Summa contra gentiles*—a notion that appears many times in Aristotle himself—so Christ's humanity was held to be the instrument of his divinity.[60] We must not underestimate the extraordinary significance of this analogy. It was owing to this thesis that Aquinas was able to account for the orthodox teaching of the Catholic faith regarding the Incarnation, which had received its most philosophically rigorous expression in the fifth of Boethius's theological tractates. If, contra the heretical teachings of Nestorius, on the one hand, who maintained that Christ had two distinct natures—the one divine, the other human—as well as two distinct persons corresponding to them, and those of Eutyches, on the other, who instead argued that he had only one nature and only one person, the orthodox Catholic position promulgated the "middle" view between the two extremes that, in Christ, two distinct natures were united in a single person (*ex distantibus naturis una fierit copulatione persona*), it was the suggestion that his humanity served as the instrument of his divinity that was responsible for securing this unification.[61] To employ the language of the Greek Fathers themselves, the "hypostatic union" (*henōsis kath'hypostasin*) was secured by the thesis concerning Christ's humanity's living instrumentality.

But the hypostatic union was also responsible for imparting a real efficient causality to the instrument as such. No longer would Christ's humanity be identified with a merely dispositive or moral causality, which was itself dependent upon the exemplary and meritorious character of his action; owing to its full participation in the action of the triune principal cause, it was now understood to function as a genuinely instrumental efficient cause, which truly cooperated in the administration of the saving power of the principal cause qua *instrumentum*. By the same token, however, it was hardly figured as a mere instrument here. Like the hand in Aristotle, Christ's humanity was understood to constitute something like the instrument of instruments.[62] It was a "conjoined instrument" (*instrumentum coniunctum*), which was connected to the principal cause as the hand is connected to the body. In this sense, it differed from other instruments—including, above all, the ministers themselves—for which it nonetheless furnished the model, which were instead designated as "separate instruments" (*instrumenta separata*). It was in this context that Aquinas would take up and critically redeploy, with respect to the sacraments, the very example that Aristotle had employed in order to illustrate the manner in which motion is imparted to its subject by way of an intermediate agent. The way in which a sacrament operates, he wrote, is to cause grace in its recipient by acting as an instrument. But there are two distinct kinds of instrument:

> One a separate instrument, such as a staff, the other a conjoined instrument such as a hand. And it is by the conjoined instrument that the separate instrument is moved, as a staff is moved by the hand. Moreover, the principal efficient cause of grace is God himself, and the humanity of Christ stands to him in the relation of a conjoined instrument, whereas a sacrament stands in the relation of a separate one. Thus it is right that the power to bestow salvation should flow from the divinity of Christ through his humanity into the sacraments themselves.[63]

With this the complete subordination of Aristotle's figuration of the instrument (whose cipher was the slave), which had prevented him from articulating a genuine theory of instrumental causality, is finally overcome, thereby once again confirming, in Aquinas's view, theology's superiority with respect to philosophy.[64] It was the participation of Christ's humanity in the salutary action of his divinity alone that allowed for the elaboration of a genuinely efficient conception of instrumental causality. At the same time, however, it was also equally what precluded the articulation of singularly disquieting thesis: namely, that Christ's humanity was the slave of his divinity.

7.

Let us attempt, then, to measure the shift that the elaboration of this notion accomplishes with respect to its classical model and to register the unexpected consequences that follow from it. For, as we shall see, what is at stake here is nothing less than a critical redefinition of one of the central categories of Aristotle's entire philosophy: the concept of *dynamis*. In Aristotle's demonstration, as we have seen, there could be no ambiguity in assigning the cause and the principle of motion. Every moved mover—every entity that, even while itself moving, is nonetheless moved by another again—preserves a reference to that on account of which it moves. Every *dynamis tou pathein*, every *potentia passiva*, that is to say, preserves a reference to the *dynamis tou poiein*, to the *potentia activa*, which is coextensive with its very being. It is only of the active power, however, that one can say that it is the cause and the principle of motion, in the sense that it alone produces the effect of movement in that which is moved (whether this be the first or the last in a chain of movers). And yet, as Martin Heidegger has argued in his important commentary on Book Theta of the *Metaphysics*,[65] considered in its totality the ontological definition of *dynamis*, which is what is implicit in this demonstration, necessitates the copresence of both of these two distinct elements. It is at once *dynamis tou poiein* and *dynamis tou pathein*, at once *potentia activa* and *potentia passiva*. Neither strictly cause nor strictly effect, the being of *dynamis* coincides with the relationship between them. And for the apparently simple but in truth very profound reason that, even if that which imparts motion (the *dynamis tou poiein*) is both structurally and chronologically prior, it is only on account of that which receives the movement (the *dynamis tou pathein*)—which, crucially, can receive but also resist it—that *dynamis* retains its heterogeneity, and hence its integrity, with respect to its conspicuous double in the Aristotelian system: *energeia*. It is above all in that which resists and thereby refuses movement that we encounter *dynamis* as such, which is to say, in its independence with respect to *energeia*.⁶⁶ According to the formula that Agamben, in Heidegger's wake, has described as the "cardinal point"⁶⁷ upon which Aristotle's entire doctrine of *dynamis* turns: "Every potentiality is impotentiality of the same and with respect to the same [*tou autou kai kata to auto pasa dynamis adynamia*]."⁶⁸ Only because every potentiality is also an impotentiality, only because every potentiality is constitutively bound to its own privation (*sterēsis*), can it exist as such, which is to say, in the absence of the concrete enactment of that of which it is the potentiality. Thus, to take up Aristotle's own well-known examples, the builder retains the capacity to build even when he is not building, the shoemaker the capacity to make shoes even when he is not making them, the kithara player the capacity to play even when he is not playing it.

As we have seen, it is the discernibility of cause and effect—and hence, the necessary copresence of *dynamis tou poiein* and *dynamis tou pathein*, of *potentia activa* and *potentia activa*—that the instrumental cause calls radically into question. Such that what results from its elaboration—this is the surprising thesis we would like to advance—is nothing less than a complete redefinition of the concept of *dynamis* (which we can now translate simply as "power," since, as we shall see, it is its very potential character that has been completely nullified). The instrumental cause is a cause that owes its unique force to the fact that it is itself but the sign of a hidden effect (*signum effectus occulti*). In this sense, the articulation of its concept constitutes nothing less than a neutralization of the very distinction between cause and effect, between active power and passive power (and, we might add, between governor and governed). Or rather, perhaps more precisely, it constitutes a complete redefinition of the sense of one of these two poles through that of the other. For since the incomparable efficacy of its action pertains to it only vicariously (that is to say, only insofar as it is itself the sign of a hidden effect), if the instrumental cause is to retain this unique force, then the motion imparted to it by the principal cause must be, in a very determinate sense, *irresistible*. Qua instrumental cause, it cannot not receive it; even more emphatically again, it cannot not transmit it in turn. Indeed, one could say that the condition of possibility for its reception lies solely in its ulterior transmission. In this way, a purely passive power, a capacity for receiving motion and of being affected by it, is reconfigured as an absolutely active power, as a capacity for transmitting that motion and of affecting another being in turn. A being of pure mediality, in short, is transformed into a being of absolute instrumentality.[69]

If every *dynamis*, according to Aristotle, is always constitutively an *adynamia* of the same and with respect to the same, then what defines it in its being is its capacity *not* to pass into actuality. And what gives reality and consistency to this capacity not to pass into actuality is what Aristotle calls *hexis*. To "have" (*echein*) a *dynamis*—for building, for making shoes, for playing the kithara—means precisely being able to not enact it. As Heidegger once again has observed, it is the specification of the sense of this "having," of this character of "possession" that pertains to the actuality of *dynamis* as such, which guides Aristotle in his well-known debate with the Megarians in Book Theta of the *Metaphysics*. "According to Aristotle," he writes, "*dynamis* is there, is actual [*wirklich*] if it is possessed [*gehabt*]; according to the Megarians, *dynamis* is actual if it is enacted [*vollzügen*]."[70] The instrumental cause, by contrast, is the very incarnation of a power that can never be "possessed," but only "enacted." As we have seen, what it receives, the motion imparted to it by the principal agent, is not something that can in any way be possessed, but only transmitted, only conveyed. In a sense no doubt very different to what this obscure group of Socratic thinkers had in mind, it thus represents the perverse confirmation of the Megarian thesis. Power, for the instrumental cause (and for those very particular beings and entities for whom it furnishes the definition), resides wholly and integrally in its exercise. But since *dynamis* and *energeia* are, as the philosopher often has occasion to repeat, but two of the many ways in which being is said, what follows from this rearticulation of power, this redefinition of *dynamis* in terms of *energeia*, is a subjacent thesis concerning being itself. The instrumental cause not only furnishes the paradigm for a form of power that cannot be possessed but only enacted, it also yields the no less ubiquitous example of a being that *is* only to the extent to which it *acts*.

8.

It is certainly significant, in this sense, that the very place in which John of Damascus's theorem was first formulated was the chapter in the *De fide orthodoxa* dedicated to a consideration of Christ's *energeiōn*, his "activities." The plural is obviously significant here: Just as there are two natures in Christ—the one divine, the other human—so, according to John (who here simply epitomizes the orthodox teachings of the Greek Fathers regarding the Incarnation), there are two activities. There is the divine activity that is consubstantial with the Father (*patri homoousios*), and there is the human activity that is consubstantial with us (*hēmin homoousios*).[71] On the one hand, the two activities are thus clearly distinct. It was not the human nature, he writes, that was responsible for raising Lazarus from the dead; but nor was it the divine nature that wept, together with the mourners, before his grave.[72] At the same time, however, to the extent that they are united in one and the same person, each one of them, he writes, is somehow "common" (*koinos*) to both natures. "For Christ is one," he continues, in a very important passage, which appears almost to present the symmetrical inverse to the sequence from the *Eudemian Ethics* that we have cited above,

> and one is his person, or hypostasis. Nevertheless, he has two natures: that of his divinity and that of his humanity. Consequently, the glory which proceeds naturally from the divinity became common to both by reason of the identity of person, while the humble things proceeding from the flesh became common to both. For he is one and the same who is both one thing and the other, that is, God and man; and to the same belong both what is proper to the divinity and what is proper to the humanity. Thus, while the divinity worked the miracles but not separately from the flesh, the flesh did the humble things but not apart from the divinity.[73]

In contrast to Aristotle's examples of the soul and the body, the craftsman and the tool, and the master and the slave, between the two natures of Christ—and hence between his two activities—there is thus genuine "community" (*koinonia*). It is nonetheless the case, however, that this relationship too is characterized by a fundamental asymmetry. For while the divinity "acts" (*enērgei*) by means of the flesh, this does not also mean that divinity also "suffers" (*epaschen*) through the flesh. And this is because, as the Damascene writes, "the flesh is indeed employed as an instrument of the divinity [*organon gar ē sarx tēs theotētos echrematisen*]."[74] Once again the parallel with Aristotle is instructive here. Whereas for the latter it was distinctly the slave who performed, and who thereby suffered, the master's action, here by contrast it is the divinity that, while remaining itself "impassive" (*apathēs*), in effect unites itself to the "suffering flesh" in order to "make the suffering salutary [*pathē ektelousa sōteria*]."[75] Rather than the slave being joined to the master (as we saw in Aristotle), here it is the "slave" who is, as it were, promoted to the point of participating in the master's glory. It nonetheless follows, as a direct corollary of this, that there is not, on the one hand, a divine action, and on the other, a human passion, but rather, that there are two distinct, yet complementary actions cooperating together to produce the same unprecedented and incomparable effect.[76] Christ acts simultaneously according to both natures, the one in concert with the other (and vice-versa). Hence, as John Chrysostom astutely observes in the quotation that initiates the Damascene's discussion: "It would not be wrong to call his passion [*pathos*] an action [*praxin*]. For in suffering all he did that great and wonderful work [*ergon*] of destroying death and working all the rest."[77]

It is in Christ's Passion that we find the paradigm not only of the instrumental cause but indeed of all ministerial action (the minister being, with respect to the *instrumentum coniunctum* of Christ's humanity, precisely an *instrumentum separatum*).[78] What characterizes this paradigm is the confluence of two distinct agents, both of whom act, but each according to a different modality: the one principally (but not exclusively) through an instrument, the other principally (but not exclusively) as an instrument. Perhaps the place in which the singular relationship between these two agents (or causes) is expressed with the most perspicacity is the only text in which Aquinas, at the risk of a grave equivocation, expressly adopts the Aristotelian definition of the slave to describe the activity of Christ's humanity. "The humanity of Christ," he writes, "is the instrument of his divinity: not, however, as an inanimate instrument, which in no way acts but is only acted upon [*quod nullo modo agit sed solum agitur*], but as an animate instrument, which is so acted upon that it itself acts [*quod ita agit quod etiam agitur*]."[79] But this passage also once again makes manifest the difference that separates the Thomistic paraphrase from its Aristotelian source. In a sense, it is Aquinas, and not Aristotle, who is able to resolve a fundamental aporia in the account of the slave's living instrumentality. In Aristotle, the slave's absolute passivity was indexed to the fact that his action was never his own but only ever that of his master. To the extent that the master and the slave are not two, but the former is one and the latter a part of that one, their action formed a single, undivided continuum. The action of the slave is the action of the master: nothing more, and nothing less. And yet, considered in and of itself, the slave remains a living, speaking, indeed acting being.[80] Among other things, the theory of the instrumental cause worked to neutralize this excess. In the paradigmatic instance, as we have seen, Christ's humanity is presented as an animate instrument that is so acted upon by his divinity that it itself acts. Here, then, by contrast, there are two distinct actions united in a single person: the action of the redeemer qua divine and the action of the redeemer qua human. The one-in-two of Aristotle thus passes over into the two-in-one of Aquinas. In a certain sense, one could say that the theory of the instrumental cause is premised upon the in-subordination of the instrument (the slave) with respect to the one who uses it (the master). Put otherwise: The minister is the *Aufhebung* of the slave. But this in-subordination necessarily proceeds hand in hand with its absolute denaturalization. With Christianity, the question is no longer, as it was for Aristotle, whether the institution of slavery corresponds to the order of nature or not. The existence of a distinct category of persons who, in one way or another, have freely chosen their own servitude is sufficient to demonstrate the fundamental divergence of its concept with respect to the Aristotelian model. To the extent that it receives its fundamental expression in the theory of the instrumental cause, Christianity is, then, in a much more precise sense than Nietzsche could have possibly ever imagined, a slave religion.[81] But it is precisely in this that its significant contribution to the history of philosophy consists.

Whereas critiques of instrumentalization, whether of reason or otherwise, have generally emphasized the manner in which the means, in being instrumentalized, is made subservient to the end that is thereby pursued,[82] we have shown here that there is a particular modality of instrumentalization—that of the instrumental cause, precisely—that takes place internal to the means as such, and that, by contrast, coincides with a curious form of in-subordination. The price to be paid for this in-subordination—an in-subordination that, in any case, is not really such, but that is instead maintained at that "zero degree" that is the minister's intention—could nonetheless not be higher. For, as we have sought to demonstrate, what results from it is nothing less than an indetermination of the very distinction between cause and effect, between action and passion, between governor and governed; and, as a result of this, nothing less than a profound transformation in the very nature of power. Insofar as it is acted upon (*agitur*), the animate instrument in some way remains a *potentia passiva*; but insofar as it in turn acts (*agit*), it is reconfigured as a *potentia activa*. In the instrumental cause, a being of pure passivity (the slave) is redefined through its absolute activity (the minister).[83] The minister is not a being who only in turn acts (and who thus retains the potentiality not to act); he is the very being of a determinate action. Power, for him, is something that can only be exercised, that can only be enacted—and never possessed. Perhaps nowhere is this registered with more clarity than in a curious translation and accompanying gloss to be found in Aquinas's own commentary on the *Politics*. Where Aristotle had spoken of the *physis* and *dynamis* of the slave (with the former designating his subordinate *nature* and the latter his instrumental *capacity*), Aquinas—inevitably already with the ministerial paradigm of the instrumental cause in mind—now speaks, on the one hand, of his *natura* and, on the other, of his *officium*. And he glosses the translation of *virtus* (*dynamis*) into *officium* in the following manner: "Since *virtus* is referred to action, *officium* is thus the appropriate action of someone [*nam virtus ad actionem referetur, officium autem est congruus actus alicuius*]."[84] As the genealogy of the office confirms, the ascription of an *officium* marks the point in which what one can do (and hence, also, what one can not do) is converted into what one must do; the point, that is to say, in which a capacity, even while remaining strictly voluntary, is transformed into a duty.[85] The principal Latin translation of the Greek *leitourgia*, *officium* thus names precisely this point of indiscernibility between cause and effect, and between action and passion, with which we must now come to terms.

Excursus: Political Christology

In a sequence of magisterial pages, Peter Brown has shown that the stakes of the Christological dispute that pitted Cyril of Alexandria against Nestorius were not merely theological in nature but ultimately theological-political. According to Brown, the real error of Nestorius, who preached the absolute transcendence and remoteness of God and who thus allowed only an attenuated divinity to attach to the human person of Christ, was that his theological system too closely resembled the imperial order within which his thought had been nurtured. "If Nestorius made one, crucial mistake," Brown writes, "it was the mistake of any religious system that appeared to replicate a little too faithfully the styles of social and political relationships current in the world around it."[86] It was easy, for example, for his opponents to insinuate that "his" Jesus had begun his life a mere man and only subsequently had been elevated to the status of a God, in much the same manner in which the son of the emperor would one day be declared in his turn an Augustus.[87] But that was not all. The utter transcendence of Nestorius's God in fact replicated one of the least favored aspects of the imperial system. For an impoverished people, the notion of a creator who stood as far apart from his creation as the emperor from his subjects offered little succor. It was on these grounds that Cyril of Alexandria—"one of the most unattractive figures of the annals of the Church"[88]—would go on the offensive. Employing an image whose theological-political significance (such as it appears, for example, in the Pseudo-Aristotelian treatise on the *De mundo*) Erik Peterson has duly underscored, Cyril would thus compare Nestorius's God to a Persian king, securely cloistered in the innermost recesses of his magnificent palace. So jealously guarded was the supreme majesty of this divinity, Cyril and his followers thereby implied, and so sharply resistant to even the meekest of intercessions in the lives of men, that, among other things, it risked becoming largely irrelevant.[89]

It was against this backdrop, according to Brown, that Cyril advanced his "daring proposal."[90] In his version—which, although not itself entirely free from the taint of Monophysitism, would ultimately lead to his canonization (and which, as such, stands in the background of the later accounts both of John of Damascus and Thomas Aquinas)—a far less abstract, almost physical unity of the two natures was foisted upon the person of Jesus Christ. At once more human and more divine, Cyril's Jesus was the thaumaturgical figure who, according to numerous anecdotes preserved in the gospels, could miraculously heal the sick with the mere touch of his hand. His, then, was a God who, in Brown's words, mysteriously "condescended" to join himself to humanity, yet without thereby ceding any of his divinity:

> Just because it was veiled in mystery, Cyril's language spilled out onto every level of the Christian imagination. It became a master image of solidarity, in the first place between God and humanity, but also, by refraction, between the emperor and his subjects, the rich and the poor, the weak and the powerful. Christians of all classes, who sought to "imitate" God in their actions, must now imitate a God who had committed Himself (through the incarnation) to intimate and enduring solidarity with every aspect of the wretchedness of the human condition.[91]

The symbol of this solidarity was the figure of Mary, *Theotokos*, "the bearer of God," whose cult began to be celebrated at this time. And its vehicle was the very milk that, like every other late antique person, the infant Jesus was understood to have received at his mother's breast. "By suckling Jesus, Mary had made God human. She had instilled in him, through the process of taking in human milk, the capacity for fellow feeling for fellow bearers of human flesh that was regarded as the foundation of all human sentiments of compassion, of mercy and of fellowship."[92] It is no doubt a touching image. Through the imbibing of his mother's milk, the divine savior had affirmed his kinship with the human congregation assembled in his name, thereby mirroring the separateness and yet inextricability of the twin natures mediated in his person. And yet, even here, it is important not to lose sight of the clear strategic purpose that the remarkable rhetorical flourish of Cyril's language nonetheless invariably served. It was the mediating figure of Jesus's humanity that first secured, for a divinity otherwise incapable of being present in the world because it was its presupposition, the very possibility of acting in it. It was the mediating figure of Jesus's humanity, that is to say, that first made possible the divine government of the world.[93] If Christ's humanity was the one true mediator, and to the extent that it served as the *instrumentum coniunctum* of his divinity,[94] it is nonetheless also the case that it furnished the paradigm for the efficacious action of a whole host of mediatory figures (*instrumenta separata*), extending from the angels through the sacraments and down to the human ministers themselves. From there, as we have seen, it would be but a short step to the more general extension of this paradigm outside the strictly theological sphere. One of the central claims of the present book is thus not only that Cyril's "daring solution" more closely resembled the situation of the Persian king—whose seemingly inexhaustible retinue of courtiers and scouts, generals and satraps, ensured that he had eyes and ears everywhere throughout the kingdom—than his polemic would at first have led us to believe, but that, consolidating a tendency already present in the late antique world, it in effect contributed to licensing and legitimating an ulterior form of power, at first limited to the confines of the Church and under the cover of the redeemer's salvific action, potentially even more pernicious and devastating in its effects than the one it purported to replace.

5

ANTHROPOLOGY OF OFFICE

1.

In *Opus Dei*, the important companion study to *The Kingdom and the Glory*, Agamben has sought to document how, over the course of a centuries-long process, the ethical tradition of ancient philosophy was progressively absorbed by the liturgical tradition of Christian theology to the point that it is no longer possible to clearly distinguish them.[1] In this process—which for Agamben reaches its apex in Kant's ethics, in which the transmogrification of virtue into duty, which Aquinas had merely intimated, appears fully accomplished[2]—it is unsurprising that the elaboration of the theory of the instrumental cause should be assigned an integral role. By underscoring this aspect, however, Agamben's intention is not simply to detail the theoretical justification for the constitutive vicariousness of the minister's action; it serves also to emphasize the extreme ethical indeterminacy that results from this.[3] Two distinct, yet interrelated ethical theses issue from his brief consideration:

(1) To the extent that the minister acts always as an instrumental cause—to the extent, that is to say, that his is always a vicarious action, an action that is performed only in the place, and only on behalf of, another who would be its principal cause—the efficacy of the action itself must be considered absolutely independently of the moral qualities of the subject who would be its executor. In the seemingly drastic but in truth commonplace adjudication of Aquinas himself: "It makes no difference to the instrument qua instrument what form or power it has besides that which is essential to it

as an instrument. . . . Hence, the ministers of the Church can confer the sacraments even when they are evil."[4]

(2) To the extent that the minister is, with respect to the effect that his action thereby produces, no more than its instrumental cause, he is himself, in his individual person, absolutely indifferent to the ethical consistency of his action: If he acts—and should he wish to fulfill his *leitourgia*, act he must—he does so only ever as a minister and never as himself. It is not even strictly necessary, according to Aquinas, that he should possess true faith: "Since in the sacraments the minister functions as an instrument, he acts not in his own power, but in the power of Christ [*non agit in virtute propria, sed virtute Christi*]."[5]

An action whose irreducible efficacy is absolutely guaranteed, yet that is in no way imputable to the concrete subject who administers it: such, according to Agamben, is the paradoxical ethical regime implicit in the ministerial praxis of the instrumental cause.

It suffices to briefly consider the pages of the *Nicomachean Ethics* dedicated to the question of moral action to measure the great divergence that this marks with respect to the paradigm of classical ethics.[6] For if the sphere of human action in its totality, according to Aristotle, may be broadly divided into the "voluntary" (*hekousion*) and the "involuntary" (*akousion*)—with those pertaining to the former deserving either of praise or blame, but those pertaining to the latter necessarily excluded from such considerations—the vicarious action of the minister can at best be assigned to that hazy third class that the philosopher calls "mixed" (that is, partly voluntary, partly involuntary).[7] On the one hand, it must be considered as voluntary, and absolutely so: there is no sacrament, as we have seen, without the ambiguous seal of the minister's "intention." And yet, as we have also seen, this intention consists in nothing more than subjecting oneself to the principal agent (*se subjiciat principali agenti*). Intention, that is to say, names the preliminary movement whereby the animate instrument, even while itself still moving, freely allows itself to be moved by the prime mover. The minister himself is thus the subject of the principal cause's action.[8] In this sense, however, although not strictly involuntary his action should be considered as more or less obligatory: Qua minister he must perform it. If an action may be defined as involuntary when the principle of its motion is situated outside the agent (*archē exōthen*), such that the agent himself contributes nothing to it;[9] and if, by contrast, it may be defined as voluntary when the principle of its motion is situated within the agent (*archē en autō*), such that he alone is its cause,[10] then the action of the instrumental cause can be considered neither as strictly involuntary nor as strictly voluntary. Or rather, it is both. Paradoxically, the principle of its movement is situated at once inside and outside the agent: It is both moving and moved. It is in one sense voluntary, and in another, albeit attenuated sense, involuntary. In other words: It is in one sense worthy of praise, and in another sense immune from blame. As surprising as this might seem at first glance, it is a position of complete moral indifference that defines the ministerial paradigm of the instrumental cause as such.

In a sense, however, the elaboration of the theory of the instrumental cause merely consolidates, at the conceptual level, an inclination that had already been precipitated, many centuries earlier, at the level of terminology. And it is the lasting impact of this terminological transformation that will allow us, in conclusion, to project our conceptual history of liturgical power onto the perspective of its modern secular avatars. "A terminological transformation," Agamben writes, "if it expresses a change in ontology, can turn out to be just as effective and revolutionary as a material transformation."[11] When Cicero, under the cover of a simple translation from the Greek, introduces into the ethical sphere, with the express intention of making it its very basis, a concept (that of *officium*) that previously had been altogether extraneous to it; and when Ambrose, following Cicero's example, yet integrating it with biblical instruction, seeks to reserve this same concept for the exclusive prerogative of the Christian minister—with these twin gestures, according to Agamben, the ethical and moral tradition of Western thought experiences a dramatic transformation, whose consequences are yet to have been fully registered. For him, what is at issue is nothing less than a transformation in the prevailing conception of being, which comes in this way to be assailed by a distinctly normative dimension. Henceforth, what preeminently is, is only what ought to be. Being is not only inclined toward action; it is wholly determined by it.[12] Building further on our analysis of liturgical power, we shall argue instead that this incitation to action eventually comes to assume the shape of a paradoxical anthropological imperative.

2.

Indeed, it was for morally ambiguous actions, stationed in an intermediary grey zone between the voluntary and the involuntary, between choice and obligation, that Cicero would first seek to apply the term *officium*. According to him, an *officium* as such—which, in the pages of his *De finibus* dedicated to the Stoics, he advances as a simple translation of the Stoic technical term *kathēkon*—may be classified neither as good nor as bad (*officium nec in bonis ponamus nec in malis*).[13] It is, to be sure, a necessary precondition for virtuous action; but it should not in itself be considered as virtuous. Rather, being in the first instance an action that is undertaken in accordance with one's natural constitution (and hence that is applicable even to plants and animals[14]), it subsists on a morally indifferent level that is common to all and is shared by wise and unwise alike.[15] In this sense, it is to be sharply distinguished from a *recte factum* (his translation of the more elevated Stoic concept of *katorthōma*), which is defined instead as a *perfectum officium*. A "right" action is an *officium* that has been perfectly performed; conversely, a "wrong" action will be one that has been imperfectly performed. Both, however, pertain to the sphere of moral action from which the mere *officia* as such, in the absence of any qualification, have been excluded.

In order to illustrate the nature of this distinction, Cicero first draws upon an example taken from the economic sphere. If to restore a trust "justly" constitutes a *recte factum*, simply to restore a trust would instead constitute a mere *officium*. It is thus the addition of the simple qualification "justly", which, in this case, transforms the *officium* into a *perfectum officium*.[16] A later example, furnished directly by the author himself, is even more illuminating again. Here Cicero attempts to read the Stoics as it were against themselves. In seeking to explode the so-called Stoic paradox, which maintains that all wrongdoing is equal, no matter how grave or how slight, he considers the example of a ship that has run aground. According to the Stoics themselves, it makes no difference whether the ship was carrying a cargo of gold or straw; in each case, the wrongdoing remains the same. Now while that is certainly true, Cicero maintains, from the perspective of the art of navigation itself—whether a ship is carrying gold or straw, he rightly observes, obviously has no bearing on its being steered either well or not well—the same cannot be argued from the perspective of the *officium*. In that capacity, the difference absolutely does matter: "Hence the nature of the object upon which the offence is committed, which in navigation makes no difference, in conduct makes all the difference [*in officio plurimum interest*]."[17] *Recte factum* (*katorthōma*) thus refers to the particular manner in which an activity is performed, and is illustrative of the distinct moral character of its agent: It designates an action that is undertaken in strict accordance with virtue. Hence, as has been astutely observed, it is often expressed in an adverbial form in which the standing of the agent itself is clearly what is at issue: walking about prudently, to cite but one of Stobaeus's numerous examples.[18] It is thus an absolute measure. *Officium* (*kathēkon*), by contrast, refers solely to the consistency of the action considered in itself, regardless of the moral character of its agent. At issue here, instead, is precisely the "appropriateness" of a particular action in a given situation. Far from being absolute, then, from this perspective the particular circumstances can be genuinely determining: Whether the grounded ship was carrying a cargo of gold or straw in fact becomes the key factor. Not only need these actions not necessarily be virtuous; in the strict sense, as we have seen, they are expressly precluded from such a categorization. All *katorthōmata* are, in the first instance, *kathēkonta*; but the inverse is not true: not all *kathēkonta* are necessarily *katorthōmata*. The basic condition in the absence of which there can be no virtue, but nonetheless not yet in itself virtuous, that distinct sphere of action that the Stoics termed *kathēkon* (and for which Cicero himself reserved the name *officium*) is thus at once included and excluded from the ethical domain.

In the text of the *De officiis* itself—the treatise that Cicero would address to his own son Marcus, and in which, by his own admission, he would seek more intently than before to combine things Latin with things Greek—his concerns are somewhat different again. If the distinction between *kathēkon* and *katorthōma* is again very clearly articulated toward the beginning of the treatise,[19] there is nonetheless now a marked emphasis on the manner in which the sphere of the former is effectively oriented toward that of the latter. So pronounced, in fact, is this orientation that even in the lines in which the Roman statesman first announces his theme, the particular conception of *officium* that he articulates there already clearly exceeds the strict limits of its Stoic model. Not only is its practical application understood to encompass the whole of life; even all that is honorable in life is said to depend upon its proper exercise. Conversely, all that is dishonorable in life is thought to result from its neglect. "For no phase of life," he writes, "whether public or private, whether in business or in the home, whether one is working on what concerns oneself alone or dealing with another, can be without its *officium*; on the discharge of such *officia* depends all that is honorable [*honestas*], and on their neglect all that is dishonorable [*turpitudo*] in life."[20] Although not constitutive of the supreme good, the *officia* thus now clearly participate in it. Even if the relationship between the two remains obscure, the "precepts" into which they are translated, he writes, nonetheless strictly "pertain to the end of the supreme good [*pertinent ad finem bonorum*]."[21] As such, it is not with the supreme good in itself, but with these very precepts by which, in his striking phrase, "the use of life in all its aspects may be regulated [*in omnis partis usus vitae conformari possit*]," that his treatise will be concerned.[22]

It is human beings alone, for Cicero, that are concerned with the *usus vitae*. In this sense, one could say it is his intention here to articulate something like a specifically human *officium*. More specifically again, one could argue that it is his aim to assert the strict pertinence of the *officia* to the sphere of exclusively human action. The precepts by which these *officia* would be governed, then, would thus constitute something like the necessary burden that man must assume on account of his admission into *societas*. They would be, as it were, what "cements" the fellowship of human beings with one another (*devincere hominem inter homines societatem*).[23] It goes without saying that this, too, represents an evident rupture with the concept's Stoic origins, even as represented by his own earlier account. Where the Stoic philosophers, as we have seen, had sought to locate the *kathēkonta* in the natural world, in that shared sense of self-belonging (*oikeiōsis*) common to humans, animals, and plants alike, Cicero here instead expressly seeks to ground the institution of *officia* on exactly what, according to him, constitutes the maximum point of difference between humans and the other living beings. While all animals, he observes— plants, significantly enough, no longer even figure in his analysis here— have been equally endowed with the instinct for self-preservation and the capacity for reproduction, and while all exhibit a certain degree of care and tenderness toward their young, the mere beasts remain forever rooted in the present instant of their existence, whereas man, with his superior vantage point, is able to survey the whole course of life:

> The most marked point of difference between man and beast is this: the beast, just as far as it is moved by the senses and with very little

perception of past or future, adapts itself to that alone which is present at the moment; while man—because he is endowed with reason, by which he comprehends the chain of consequences, perceives the causes of things, understands the relation of cause to effect and effect to cause, draws analogies, and connects and associates the present and the future—easily surveys the course of his whole life and makes the necessary preparations for its conduct [*facile totius vitae cursum videt ad eamque degendam praeparat res necessarias*].[24]

For Cicero, it is this capacity that separates man from the rest of the natural world. At the same time, however, the former is itself only a reflection of the very particular nature of man. As Agamben has rightly underscored, Cicero here invests the sphere of the *officium* with a distinctly anthropological significance.[25] But he is able to do so only on account of "universalizing" and even "naturalizing" the particular customs and conventions of the Roman *res publica* itself.[26] The common fellowship of speech and life; the formation and participation in public assemblies; the search for truth; the feeling for order, propriety and moderation in word and in deed; the sense of beauty and harmony in the visible world—all of these specific elements out of which all that is honorable is "forged" and "fashioned" have their distinct origins, according to Cicero, in human nature itself.[27]

Already in the text of the *De officiis* itself, then, a curious process of simultaneous "horizontalization" and "verticalization" of its central theme with respect to the Stoic model begins to appear (a process that will become even more pronounced again with its integration into the Christian tradition). The first has often been remarked: With its emphasis on the so-called *media officia* and their connection with the end of the supreme good (and not on the supreme good in itself), there is a patent "democratization" of the conception of virtue with respect to its Stoic treatment. No longer will it be the province of the sage alone; but it will be potentially attainable, albeit in an attenuated sense, by each and everyone purely on account of their belonging to the human species. Rather than emphasizing the absoluteness of the *perfectum officium*, Cicero here focuses instead on the eminently practical activities by which the entire human race participates together in the promotion of the public good. The second is more obscure, but Agamben has again powerfully underlined it. It is through the regulation of the use of life in all its aspects, as we have seen, that the human raises itself above the other animals. It is thus through the institution of the *officia* that human life—as opposed to animal life—becomes, in a word, "governable": "If man does not simply live his life like the animals, but 'conducts' and 'governs' it [*ma la 'conduce' e 'governa'*], the *officium* is what makes life governable [*ciò che rende la vita governabile*], it is that by means of which the life of humans is 'instituted' and 'formed.'"[28] What separates human life from animal life is thus its governability. To be human, from this perspective, is to be governable; it is to be capable of governing and of being governed in turn. And the *officium* is that through which this government becomes possible. To the "horizontalization" of virtue there thus corresponds an equally clear "verticalization" of the *officium* as such. In this sense, according to Agamben, it is certainly significant that Cicero here demonstrably shifts his focus away from the evaluation of discrete individual actions and toward the consideration of the *usus vitae* in its totality. Seneca will go even further again, speaking in one of his letters of moral instruction of the specifically *humani officii* by which men are bound, together with their gods, as members of a single great organism (*membra sumus corporis magni*).[29] Human beings, according to this definition, Agamben writes, are thus distinctly "beings of *officium*."[30]

3.

One of the most significant consequences of this twin process is that where for the Stoics themselves *kathēkon* and virtue were kept clearly distinct, they are now in a certain sense identified with one another. The *officium* is a virtue, but only to the extent that virtue itself is an *officium*: Precisely this circle, according to Agamben, is the ambiguous ethical legacy of Cicero's *De officiis*. It is as such that it will be taken up by the Christian tradition.[31] It was St. Ambrose, the energetic fourth-century bishop of Milan, who was principally responsible for the introduction not only of its philosophical concept, but even (as we learn from Augustine[32]) of the distinctly secular term itself into the ecclesiastical context. It is important, however, to observe the double register through which this introduction takes place. For if Ambrose's own *De officiis* clearly represents an attempt to rewrite Cicero's treatise, whose thematic division into three books it directly reproduces, within an overtly Christian context, it is nonetheless also motivated by concerns absolutely external to its classical model. It is not sufficient, according to Ambrose, for the topic simply to have been suggested by the pagan philosophical tradition; in accordance with a hermeneutic imperative that traverses his entire treatise, it must be grounded in divine scripture as well. What in Cicero was presented as the translation of the Stoic technical term *kathēkon*, in Ambrose appears instead as the translation of another originally secular term but one with an already clearly defined place within the biblical lexicon: *leitourgia*. To this end, he relates the undoubtedly fanciful tale of having inadvertently stumbled across the term while reading the Gospel, leading him to speculate that it was as if the Holy Spirit himself had exhorted him to speak on this topic. "Well now, a wonderful thing happened just this day," he writes,

> while I was reading the Gospel. As if he were encouraging me to write on the subject, the Holy Spirit brought before me a reading which confirmed my view that we too are able to speak of *officium*: when Zacharias the priest had become dumb in the temple and was unable to speak, "it came to pass," Scripture says, "that the days of his *officium* were completed; he went away to his own house." From what we read here, then, it is clear that we too can speak of *officium*.[33]

The passage in question is Luke 1:23; and the Greek term that *officium* translates here is one of the very rare attestations of *leitourgia* to be found in the New Testament, and indeed the sole appearance of the term in the context of the gospels themselves. In itself, the Scriptural example thus provides far from emphatic evidence for the "appropriateness" of the theme to the ecclesiastical context. Its particular use here, moreover, is consistent with that of the Septuagint, referring as it does to the "services" rendered by a priest "according to the order of Aaron."[34] And yet, Ambrose's discursive strategy is nonetheless absolutely clear: He seeks not only to "Christianize" the Stoic concept, but also securely to identify its reference with the public praxis of the priest.[35] In a manner that is even more pronounced than Cicero himself, Ambrose thereby knowingly conflates the philosophical and functional senses of the Latin term in order to anchor his investigation scripturally: From the *officia* particular to the human race in its totality we thus pass to the *officia* particular to a strictly delimited class of human beings.[36]

Perhaps nowhere does the continuity, and yet disparity, between Ambrose's text and its Ciceronian model appear more clearly than in the forms of address adopted by the two authors. On the one hand, they are perfectly continuous: Just as Cicero had written to instruct his son, so Ambrose too writes to instruct his "sons," the clergy of Milan. "In the same way that Cicero wrote to instruct his son," he writes, in one of the rare instances in which Cicero is directly mentioned by name, "I too am writing to mold you, my sons; for I do not feel any less love for you as children whom I have begotten in the gospel [*in evangelio genui*] than I would if I had fathered you literally in marriage. Nature [*natura*] is no stronger than grace [*gratia*] when it comes to love." It is precisely here, however, that the disparity begins to become more apparent. Not only is nature no stronger than grace when it comes to love, but the bond is even greater again, Ambrose contends, with those with whom one shares, so to speak, an "elective affinity." "In fact," he immediately continues, "we ought to have all the greater love for those who, we trust, will be with us forever than we do for those who are with us in this world only. Here, people often have sons who turn out to be a disappointment, the kind who disgrace their father; but with you it is different: we have chosen you beforehand, to love you."[37]

Just as theology is superior to philosophy, so here spiritual paternity trumps natural paternity. For the former is grounded not only in nature, but also in grace.[38] The classic Pauline distinction, which would soon form the basis of Augustine's protracted debate with the British monk Pelagius and his followers, indeed constitutes something of a lynchpin in Ambrose's thought.[39] It is important, however, not to interpret this opposition in too antithetical a fashion. For Ambrose, as for many other Christian thinkers both before and after him, nature too is a work of God. Seemingly paradoxically, Ambrose's use of the word *natura* would thus appear to encompass both the "natural" and the "supernatural," both the "physical" and the "metaphysical." And yet, for precisely this reason, he is able to synthesize the Stoic insistence upon the bond that nature herself has established between men with the Christian belief in the operation of the divine will without any apparent difficulty.[40] According to Ambrose, the *lex natura* of the Stoics coincides, at least up to a certain point, with the *lex natura* of the Christians. In any case, for him, owing to a tenacious patristic commonplace that can be traced back as far as Philo of Alexandria, the Stoic philosophers had simply modeled their conception of nature on the writings of Moses himself. The two conceptions of nature—the natural and the supernatural, the physical and the metaphysical—are united, more-over, in their opposition to strictly supernatural grace. In an important later sequence, Ambrose will again stage this opposition by distinguishing the "natural" relationship that extends between the members of a fam-ily and the "spiritual" relationship that obtains between the members of the Church. The *benevolentia* that, according to Ambrose, starts out in the family, with sons and parents and brothers, before progressing through different levels of relationship, conjoining distant and distinct polities up to the point of encompassing the entire globe ("having set out from paradise," he writes, "it has now filled the whole world"),[41] is even fur-ther enhanced by assembly in the Church: "Goodwill is enhanced by the communal nature of the church [*coetu ecclesiae*], by our partnership in the faith [*fidei consortio*], by our kinship as recipients of grace [*percipiendae gratiae necessitudine*], and by our participation in the mysteries [*myste-riorum communione*]."[42] Perhaps nowhere is the specificity of Ambrose's intervention with respect to the pagan model more evident than here: The *officia* are determined not only by nature, but also and above all by grace.

4.

The *officia* of which Ambrose speaks are thus measured by a different stan-dard (*regula*) than those of which the philosophers speak. While the latter, being oriented exclusively toward the good of this world, are measured by the standard of the present, the former, being oriented instead toward that of the world to come, are measured by the standard of the future. "We regard nothing as beneficial [*utile*]," he writes, "except that which helps define the grace of eternal life [*ad vitae illius aeternae prosit gratiam defini-mus*]."[43] It is thus on the basis of the *natura/gratia* opposition that Ambrose is able to advance a striking redeployment of the Stoic distinction between the *kathēkonta* and the *katorthōmata* (in Cicero's terms, between the *media officia* and the *perfecta officia*). In Cicero's treatment, as we have seen, there is a considerable softening of the ascetic rigor of the genuine Stoic ethics—what we have described as a "democratization of the virtues." Far from being excluded from participating in it, the *media officia*, in his account, are presented as contributing to the promotion of the *summum bonum*. Ambrose, by contrast, will seek to reassert the extreme vision of the Stoics, yet while grounding it on the authority of the divine scripture—indeed, of the Gospel itself. In the parable of the rich young man (Mt. 19:16–22), a young man is represented as asking the Messiah what good deed might secure for him the eventuality of eternal life. Should he wish to attain eternal life, Jesus informs him, the first thing he ought to do is keep the commandments. He must not commit murder; he must not commit adultery; he must not steal; he must not bear false testimony; he must honor his mother and father; he must love his neighbor as if he were himself. These, according to Ambrose, are the *media officia*.[44] But since he has faithfully observed all of these, the young man immediately proceeds to inquire if there is still more that he can do. "If you wish to be perfect," Jesus responds, "go, sell your possessions and give the money to the poor, and you will have treasure in heaven; then come, follow me."[45] This, instead, Ambrose writes, is the *perfectum officium*, what the Greeks called *katorthōma*.[46] The significance of this grounding of the distinction between the *media* and *perfecta officia* on the parable of the rich young man should not be underestimated. Through it, he was able not only to assert the superiority of the New Law with respect to the Old; but also, as Ivor Davidson has astutely observed, to begin to articulate, in strict accordance with the animating intention of the work as a whole, a patently "two-tiered model of spiritual calling."[47]

The exigencies to which the *media* and *perfecta officia* respectively respond indeed coincide exactly with the fundamental distinction between *praeceptum* and *consilium*, which Ambrose had adopted from Roman law elsewhere in his work and with respect to which the parable of the rich young man was invariably called upon as supporting evidence.[48] The latter distinction thus allows us to clarify with more precision exactly what was at stake in Ambrose's "Christianization" of the *officium*. In an important sequence of his *De viduis*, Ambrose had glossed the distinction such as it appeared in the translation of 1 Cor. 7:25 he had before him, in the following, striking manner:

> It is good that the Apostle said: "Concerning virgins, I have no commandment [*praeceptum*] of the Lord, I give counsel [*consilium*]." For a commandment is issued toward those subject, counsel is given to friends. Where there is a commandment, there is law [*lex*]; where there is counsel, there is grace [*gratia*]. The commandment calls back to nature [*ad naturam revocet*]; counsel calls forth to grace [*ad gratiam provocet*]. And therefore the law was given to the Jews, but grace was reserved for the elect.[49]

In this extraordinary passage, Ambrose follows the Apostle Paul in identifying the orders of nature and of law together in the figure of Jew, and he equates this identification with a particular type of normativity: that which corresponds to the juridical form of the commandment. At the same time, however, he also seeks to articulate the specificity of the Gospel in the addition of a supplementary element—namely, grace—which is superadded to the old dispensation and which calls the faithful forward toward the new. This is instead related to a different conception of normativity: that which corresponds to the more supple form of the counsel. It is not the case, however, that the latter merely represents the surpassing of the former. As the parable of the rich young man clearly demonstrates, the Gospel is not simply the end of the law; it is its perfection. The Messiah has not simply abolished the law; he has realized it in his very person. The commandments are not abrogated, but their rigorous observance may now be augmented by a form of moral action that, being strictly voluntary, responds not to the external law that is carved on tablets of stone but to the internal law that is inscribed on tablets of the human heart.[50] There is thus a specifically Christian form of law, but it is a *lex libertatis* as distinct from the *lex servitutis* of the Jews.[51] As Emanuele Coccia has shown,[52] it was in order to articulate this unprecedented juridical situation—amounting to nothing less than a normative revolution, irreducible both to classical civil law and medieval canon law—that the Latin fathers, beginning with Ambrose himself, had taken recourse to the extant legal distinction between *praeceptum* and *consilium* that they now nonetheless sought to refashion on a strictly scriptural basis:

> You will see the distance between commandment and counsel if you recall the case of him in the Gospel (Mt. 19:18–21) to whom it is first commanded not to murder, not to commit adultery, not to bear false testimony; for there is a commandment where there is punishment for sin. But when he related that the commandments of the law had been fulfilled, counsel is given to him that he should sell everything and follow the Lord; this is not what the commandment orders, but what the counsel conveys [*haec enim non praecepto imperantur, sed pro consilio deferuntur*]. For there are two forms of mandate [*mandati*]: one preceptive [*praeceptiva*], the other voluntary [*voluntaria*]. Hence the Lord in one way says: "Do not kill," which he commands; and in another

way: "If you want to be perfect, sell everything you have." Therefore, the one who is free from commandment is the one to whom free will [*arbitrium*] has been granted.[53]

The fraught history of what only much later will be termed *opera super-erogationis* begins here. That there is a form of human action—the "super-erogatory," precisely—that may be defined only in relation to the sphere of the *officium*, yet that, being voluntary (and not obligatory), by its very definition necessarily exceeds that *officium*: This is the paradoxical contribution of the specifically Christian form of normativity to the history of Western ethics.[54] In his *De officiis*, as we have seen, Ambrose would clearly seek to identify this division with the Stoic distinction between *kathēkonta* (*media officia*) and *katorthōmata* (*perfecta officia*). For him, it was very distinctly his "sons" who, on account of their spiritual closeness and devotion to the "true source of virtue," were expressly called upon to observe the latter: "Some *officia*, therefore, are of the first, and others of the middle rank: few participate in the first rank, many in the middle [*Alia igitur prima, alia media officia: prima cum paucis, media cum pluribus*]."[55] And yet here, importantly, the *officium* becomes "perfect" solely on account of its exclusive participation in the divine *virtus*, which is to say, with something that is absolutely external to it. According to Ambrose, the minister is thus the one whose particular *officium*—in parallel with that of the Messiah himself, on whose "eternal priesthood" his vocation is grounded and whose divine effectuality he conveys—consists in superabounding for the sake of the rest of humanity. In him, then, there takes place a further "verticalization" of the *officium*. No longer is it what distinguishes the sphere of humanity in its totality from the rest of the living beings (its governability); it is what articulates a division within the sphere of humanity itself (between those who govern and those who are governed).[56] The discreet introduction of a division between the human and the animal in Cicero thus results in the momentous introduction of a division within the human itself in Ambrose. Only in the case of the latter, however, may we speak of the birth of a hierarchy, of a sacred power, in the strict sense, to the extent that it alone marks the emergence of a division that transcends the order of nature as such: In this, the fundamental, and far from edifying, contribution of Christian theology to Western ethics essentially consists. And because it is the rule of hierarchy—which, as we have seen, has its paradigm in the instrumental cause—that one governs only insofar as one is governed, once instituted this division may be progressively extended up to the point that (as, much later, in Kant's ethics) it will eventually pass internally within each and every human being.

On the one hand, then, as has been acutely observed, Ambrose appears as more strictly Stoic than Cicero himself.[57] Through his mobilization of the distinction between the *media* and *perfecta officia*, he effectively reasceticizes, and thereby reethicizes, the entire sphere of the *officium* as such. The Stoic sage is reborn in the figure of the Christian minister. But unlike the sage, who is always an end in himself and who always acts in the strictest accordance with virtue, the minister is only the vehicle—the "instrument"—through whom the divine virtue must pass. He is not himself that virtue.[58] In this sense, perhaps despite Ambrose's best intentions to the contrary, he effectively voided the *officium* of any ethical character in and through the very gesture with which he invested it with it. We have said it already: Because he himself is never the author of his own actions, to be a minister is to be worthy of praise for an action for which one can receive no blame. In this sense, it is not so much the Stoic sage that is reborn in the Christian minister, but (as we have already seen Aquinas will clearly intuit many centuries later) Aristotle's household slave. Like the latter, he requires only the smallest amount of virtue—just enough, as Aristotle explains, to prevent him from failing in his function.[59]

5.

Minister, then, is the name of a function, and not of a substance. But is also the figure in which a function passes into being. The minister, then, is the cipher of the essential insubstantiality of being. He is not a being that only in turn acts, but the being of a very determinate type of action—that prescribed by his "office." As Agamben writes: "The priest must carry out his office insofar as he is a priest and he is a priest insofar as he carries out his office. The being prescribes the action, but the action wholly defines the being. . . . The priest is that entity whose being is immediately a task and a service—that is to say, a liturgy."[60] The minister is the being of a function, the being of a service, the being of a liturgy—in short, the being of an office. But precisely because of this, precisely because the minister is the being of an office, he is, like the angel, infinitely substitutable and eminently replaceable. This infinite substitutability, this eminent replace-ability, indeed this essential disposability of the priest, points to the second defining feature of the minister qua minister, which follows as a direct corollary from the first. His action is characterized not only by its constitutive vicariousness, but also, for this very reason, by its necessary industriousness. The minister—or, if you prefer, the "officer"—is the one who must act in order to be. For the minister, being means being "operative."[61] Because he can participate in the divine virtue only vicariously—which is to say, only on account of his office—virtue is, for him, irreducibly a figure of action and industry. He can be virtuous only to the extent that he acts virtuously, which is to say, only by exercising his office.[62] But since the office is what defines him in his being, his being is wholly circumscribed by what can only be described as a "virtuous" circle. In the most absolute sense, virtue has truly become for him a duty.

Contrary to what is popularly believed, an office is not something that can be held but something that can only be exercised. While it is true that, in the office, a function is, as it were, separated from its exercise and thereby granted a permanent institution, the "officer" is the one whose constitutive vicariousness necessitates that he must incessantly enact that function in order to be. Premised on the essential substitutability of the liturgical action of the priest, who must continually convey a virtue that is absolutely external to him and of which he can never be the master, the office is thus the very emblem of that power—which, today, we maintain, is more or less hegemonic across the globe—that must be executed in order to be possessed. At once constitutively vicarious and necessarily industrious, what, in a word, defines the paradigm of liturgical power is thus precisely its functionality. To the extent, however, to which, as we have seen, the theory of the office has been indissolubly conjoined, from its very beginnings, to a distinctly anthropological imperative, nothing less than a determinate shift in our understanding of what is human is betrayed by this hegemony. If, today, human beings are once again, as they were for Seneca and for Cicero, beings of the office, it is in a sense entirely different to what the Roman statesmen must have had in mind (even if they were among the first to precipitate this displacement). We have seen how, for Cicero, unlike the mere beasts, which simply "live" their lives, human beings—in this sense, unique throughout the animal kingdom—purposefully "conduct" and "govern" theirs. Being equally capable of acting honorably or dishonorably, expediently or inexpediently, theirs, then, is that life that is, by its very definition, eminently governable. Whence, according to Cicero, the intrinsic necessity of the office. Even if there is already at work in this account a tacit assumption of the primacy of acting over being, it is nonetheless clear that what defines the human is still very distinctly its capacity. Specifically human is that being that can act in a certain way—or else, can not. With the externalization of the office, that is no longer the case. The capacity not to has been withdrawn from it. The humanity of man has been indexed to a kind of performance. What defines the human can now only be its *efficiency*.

Much recent scholarship has sought to interrogate and to problematize the mobile threshold that both separates and conjoins the human and the animal.[63] We have argued, instead, that equally pressing—if not perhaps even more so—for the analysis of contemporary forms of life is the interrogation and problematization of the similarly mobile threshold that both separates and conjoins the human and the angel. Indeed, the two cannot be treated independently of one another: The increasing prestige into which that part of the human that would link it to the so-called higher species is elevated directly coincides with the increasing abjection into which that part that would link it to the lower species is plunged. That liturgy is what defines the angel in its being is, as we have seen, a metaphysical commonplace reflected throughout the Christian tradition, from the Letter to the Hebrews through to Erik Peterson himself.[64] Because what defines the essence of the angel is an "office" (and not a "nature"), they cannot not act without thereby ceasing to be. Their entire existence is thus deontologically circumscribed. The angel, in other words, presents the perfect emblem of that "operative" ontology whose gradual replacement of the classical ontological paradigm Agamben has sought to delineate in his most recent works. One of the central claims of the present book, however, is that this shift in ontology also entails a concurrent shift in anthropology, whose contours are yet to be fully described or even registered as such. The Christian heritage of secular modernity—one of whose defining features is the seemingly infinite proliferation of offices—entails a superabundant and supernumerary anthropology. According to an anthropological paradox that we have sought to explore in the preceding pages, it is only to the extent that one succeeds in becoming "like an angel" that one succeeds in becoming fully human.

CONCLUSION

In the concluding pages of his *Political Theology,* Carl Schmitt—crystallizing a sentiment common to all of his writings from this period—sought to summarize the basic tendency that, for him, characterized the spirit of the age. "Today," he announced,

> nothing is more modern than the onslaught against the political. American financiers, industrial technicians, Marxist socialists and anarchist-syndicalist revolutionaries unite in demanding that the biased rule of politics over the objectivity of economic life be done away with. There must no longer be political problems, only organizational-technical and economic-sociological tasks. The kind of economic-technical thinking that prevails today is no longer capable of perceiving a political idea. The modern state seems to have actually become what Max Weber envisaged: a giant business enterprise.[1]

According to Schmitt, the liberal "onslaught against the political," regarding which he was one of the earliest and most prescient witnesses, was being systematically carried out on twin fronts. In the economic-technical realm, on the one hand, the eminently political concept of battle gives way to the dynamic of perpetual competition; in the ethical-intellectual realm, instead, it finds itself transmogrified into endless conversation.[2] In these fields, as in many others, according to Schmitt, a principle of unlimited differentiation paradoxically results in the formation of an absolutely undifferentiated mass, in which no substantive political opposition is any longer possible.

As his important 1929 Barcelona lecture on "The Age of Neutralizations and Depoliticizations" makes clear, for Schmitt this dissolution of the political marks the final stage in a centuries-long process impelled by the progressive neutralization of each successive epoch's so-called central domain.[3] In Schmitt's novel account, the project of Western modernity can indeed be characterized by this uninterrupted pursuit for a coveted and achieved neutrality. The first and most important displacement, perhaps unsurprisingly, was the decentering of Christian theology. Following the disputes and struggles of the sixteenth and seventeenth centuries, according to Schmitt, theology lost its former centrality in favor of a purportedly more neutral domain: that of metaphysics. In ceasing to be central, the former domain thus found itself neutralized. Yet as Schmitt notes, the passage from a conflictual to a neutral domain always engenders new arenas of struggle, thereby necessitating an ever-renewed search for fresh sites of neutrality.[4] Thus the metaphysics of the seventeenth century is displaced by the "moralism" of the eighteenth century; and the moralism of the eighteenth century in turn by the "economism" of the nineteenth. Only with the reign of technology in the twentieth, finally, would the ultimate neutral ground be secured, beyond which no further neutralizations would be needed. Yet it is the very index of technology's neutrality—namely, its instrumentality—Schmitt continues, which also, and at the same time, reveals its specific limit. Precisely because technology serves all equally, everybody and every purpose (and that includes both war and peace), it can never truly be neutral. "No single decision can be derived from the immanence of technology, least of all for neutrality."[5] So perfectly indifferent to the ends that it pursues, according to Schmitt, is the so-called rationality of technology, that it serves one or another demand with always the same energy and vigor—whether it be, in his remarkable formulation, "for a silk blouse or poison gas"[6] or for anything else whatsoever.

It was against just this neutrality that Schmitt's "political theology" was directed. The counterrevolutionary force he sought to harness through the application of its concept was aimed squarely at arresting the inexorable drift toward depoliticization so characteristic of the modern state. We have seen that Schmitt did not merely vacillate between a "descriptive" and an "interventionist" political theology, as one authoritative interpretation would have it,[7] but, rather, that the former in fact served as the catalyst for the former. If it is true, on the one hand, as Schmitt famously asserts, that "the metaphysical image that a particular epoch forges of the world has the same structure as the form of political organization immediately evident to it"[8] (and thus that the modern constitutional state, for example, is grounded in a metaphysics and a theology—namely, deism—which consciously excludes any theistic and transcendent source of legitimacy), it is also the case, on the other, that the ruling metaphysical image and its corresponding form of political organization may be countered with the aid of weapons drawn from a different historical epoch. Thus, according to Schmitt, the conservative authors of the counterrevolution—Louis Gabriel Ambroise de Bonald, Joseph de Maistre, Juan Donoso Cortés—sought to locate a residual figure of transcendent authority using analogies borrowed from the ambit of the displaced theistic theology.[9] But the same holds in his time for the German jurist as well. It was against the prevailing neo-Kantian legal positivism for which Hans Kelsen was the exemplary theoretician (according to whom only the impersonal legal order itself, with its abstract system of norms, could be sovereign), and duly armed "with a clear and systematic analogy" derived from the theology of the Middle Ages, that Schmitt would in turn seek to furnish his notorious extralegal definition of sovereignty. The famous dictum according to which "all significant concepts of the modern theory of the state are secularized theological concepts" was thus intended not only to supply a hermeneutic matrix with which to gain access to the otherwise concealed origins of modernity,[10] but also, and indeed above all, to provide something like a fundamental principle with which to metaphysically reground a thoroughly deracinated concept of the political. With the term "political theology" Schmitt sought not just to assert a lasting continuity between theological and political concepts, which would survive even the trial of secularization; against the reigning rationality of economic-technical thinking, and the liberal constitutionalism in which the former found its juridical expression, it also denoted the attempt to reinject a figure of transcendence into a landscape mired in immanence.

The present book, by contrast, has advanced an alternative account by reconstructing, pace Schmitt, the theological origins of this very depoliticization. Far from being what arrests the course of depoliticization, Christian theology, in our rendering, appears as its very paradigm. As we have seen, this alternative account finds its point of departure in Erik Peterson's celebrated critique of Schmitt's political theology. For Peterson, who embeds his critique in a deep historical perspective, the two outstanding features of Schmitt's political theology—on the one hand, its championing of a form of political monotheism; on the other, its conscripting of theology for the ends of secular politics—had each been belied by the development of Christian dogma. In the first instance, by the nascent elaboration of the doctrine of the Trinity; in the second, by the pronounced disidentification of the earthly and heavenly realms. But Peterson's intervention was not limited simply to asserting the necessity of the latter starting from the concrete example of the former, as he more or less modestly claimed. As Agamben has rightly observed, at the same time in which Peterson strove to separate the higher concerns of theology from the politics of the world below, he also sought to establish the terms of what can only be described as an otherworldly politics. For Peterson, then, Christian theology is itself always already political, uniquely and eminently so; under no circumstances, then, may it pressed into the service of the politics of this world, because politics itself, according to his analysis, pertains strictly to the world to come—and to its unique earthly institution, the Church. "Christian politics," as far as the present world is concerned, thus coincides from this perspective with the administrative activities of the Church. It concerns not the transcendent legitimation of earthly sovereignty, but the immanent economy of the divine government itself.

Starting from the perspective thereby opened up, this book has sought to recover the unanticipated significance of liturgy for an understanding of the Christian underpinnings of contemporary political thought and forms. As we have seen, it is Peterson himself who argues that liturgy names the form of action particular to a specifically Christian politics. But the theologian concentrated his attention almost exclusively on the service that is rendered directly to God in the form of prayers and hymns. Politics, for him, thus assumes the form of doxology. This book has focused instead on the unexpected legacy of the service that is rendered in the first instance to man and only in a second instance to God as a concomitant effect of the first. It has thus argued that the political character that Peterson ascribes to the celestial liturgy must be viewed as epiphenomenal with respect to its this-worldly activity, which coincides with a paradigm of governance hitherto largely unstudied. The supposition of a Christian politics thus yields a missing chapter in the genealogy of what Foucault called "governmentality." It is elements toward this genealogy that the book has therefore sought to reconstruct.

What emerges from this reconstruction is the portrait of a distinct technology of power, which encompasses a number of highly specific features:

(1) To the extent that its principle is not domination but care, it is a form of power that is defined by its *beneficence* and even its *philanthropy* (which is of course not to say that its effects cannot be pernicious). As Foucault himself had already observed a propos of what he called pastoral power, it is a power that takes as its fundamental objective nothing less than the ultimate salvation of those over whom it is exercised.

(2) As such, it emerges as an inherently paradoxical form of power, which manifests itself precisely through *service*. Service, however, of a double kind: not only to those for whose sake it is administered, but also to the one in whose name it is administered.

(3) It is thus a distinctly *hierarchical* form of power (indeed, as is well known, the term hierarchy itself appears for the first time in precisely this context). It is a form of power, that is to say, that is exercised not only *over* subordinates, but also, and above all, *through* subordinates.

(4) What articulates the hierarchy is nonetheless always only the liturgy that it is incumbent upon each of its specific ranks to perform. Hierarchy, in other words, is always articulated according to function, and never according to substance. It is thus a form of power that is extraneous to the *nature* of the one who exercises it.

(5) It is therefore a distinctly *mimetic* form of power, albeit in a very specific sense that effectively collapses the distinction between those who exercise it and those over whom it is exercised, those who govern and those who are governed. For it is the governed themselves who govern precisely by imitating God insofar as he governs.

(6) It follows that it is constitutively *vicarious*. It is a form of power that is always on behalf of, and for the sake of, someone or something else—and never for itself. But this must be understood in an absolute, and not merely in a relative, sense: Having its paradigm in the Trinitarian *oikonomia* itself, there is no point beyond which the vicariousness of this power could ever

be eliminated. It is always secondary, never originary. Which is to say: It is always *mediated.*

(7) This means, finally, that it is an essentially *ephemeral* form of power, whose tenure does not outlast its concrete performance. According to the refrain that has often been repeated in the preceding pages, it cannot be possessed but only enacted. Indeed, its very reception is predicated upon its ulterior transmission. Expressed in modal terms, what defines this power is thus no longer a capacity, but only a *duty.*

Against the theological-political tradition that extends from Hegel by way of Weber to Schmitt, and that in each instance emphasizes the reference to a transcendent personal dimension,[11] the present book, which attempts to open a new perspective on the theological legacy of political concepts for the history of the present, has instead sought to recompose the lineaments of an economic theology whose distinctive feature would be its extreme *impersonality.* In this way, it has sought to aid our capacity for coming to terms with what is arguably the prevailing mode of government in modernity. Alongside the four traditional forms of government known to political thought since Greek antiquity—monarchy (the rule of one), aristocracy (the rule of the best), oligarchy (the rule of the few), and democracy (the rule of the many)—Hannah Arendt famously sought to inscribe a fifth, whose emergence she argued was specific to the modern age: bureaucracy, which she astutely defined as the rule of no one.[12] In Arendt's account, however, the advent of this new form of government is presented not as wholly unprecedented, but as the uniquely modern transposition, brought about by the rise of the civil society and the accompanying science of political economy, of the organizational device of the ancient household—monarchy—into the realm of the modern public sphere. One-man rule, the rule of the despot over his household, she argues, is transformed in society into "a kind of no-man rule."[13] The limit-form of rule,[14] no-man rule, for Arendt, thus marks the point in which the former passes into "pure administration." As such, the registration of this new form of government serves less as the addition of an alternative model of political organization than as a sign of the ultimate eclipse of politics and its consequent transmogrification into a mass housekeeping exercise.

According to Arendt, it was Christian otherworldliness that, by positing a higher realm that transcended worldly politics, in effect instrumentalized the latter, thereby transforming it into a mere means to that higher end. Even in the wake of the Reformation when this higher realm retreated into the domain of private experience, politics, she argues, nonetheless retained this instrumental character, even in the absence of a higher justification. It is not that politics then recovered the dignity that would be particular to it, but rather that what had been previously excluded from politics in the strict sense acquired a new dignity formerly refused it—precisely in being identified with it.[15] We have argued, instead, that the recoding of Christian antipolitics as a kind of otherworldly politics had already marked, at least at the level of theology itself, the manner in which the Church conceived its activities in the world below: It posited them as prepolitical, "economic" in the sense in which the Greeks understood this term. It follows from our analysis that a conceptual vocabulary that would be specific to the sphere of civil society in its disaggregation from the state had already been furnished for that proto-society that is the Church.[16] In this way, the economic theology that is only the instrument of a Christian politics in the sense that we have seen emerges as the hidden motor for the very depoliticization that Schmitt's political theology had sought to arrest. And because it has its condition of possibility in the heterogeneity of the domain to which it is applied with respect to that of politics, such a conceptual vocabulary could easily survive the evacuation of the transcendental horizon that had originally given it its sense and its direction. In today's "rule of no one," we are confronted with an economy that is no longer tethered to a monarchical principle,[17] but in which—as is well captured by the ambiguity of the ubiquitous phrase "economic governance"—a hypostasized economy has come to occupy the place thus vacated. According to what is only apparently a paradox, the economy is now subject not to a monarchy but to the economy itself. It is the conceptual history behind this transformation that we have sought to understand.

ACKNOWLEDGMENTS

This book was first drafted between 2011 and 2014 at the School of Culture and Communication at the University Melbourne, and completed between 2015 and 2016 at the Institute for Advanced Studies in the Humanities at the University of Queensland. I'd like to express my profound gratitude to Justin Clemens and John Frow, who were responsible for overseeing its first iteration, and to Peter Harrison and my colleagues at IASH for providing such an ideal environment in which to complete it. At various stages of its drafting, the manuscript was read either in whole or in part by several wonderful friends and by a couple of strangers as well. I'd like to thank Adam Bartlett, Bryan Cooke, Colby Dickinson, Simon During, Ian Hunter, Daniel McLoughlin, Kenneth Reinhard, Alison Ross, Dimitris Vardoulakis, Miguel Vatter, and Jess Whyte for their generous input and encouragement in this regard. Simon, Alison, and Miguel are also to be singled out for their invaluable guidance and mentoring as I negotiated the transition from manuscript to book.

I have had the great fortune to work with an incredibly attentive and patient editor in Tom Lay, who pushed me hard to produce the best possible book. I'm especially grateful to him and the team at Fordham University Press. Tim Campbell has also generously supported this project over the course of many years now, and I'm honored to have my work included in his Commonalities series. I'd also like to acknowledge Helen Tartar, who first showed an interest in my proposal. Thanks also to Tim Roberts at the Modern Language Initiative, who guided the book through its production stage, and to Edward Batchelder for his meticulous copyediting.

The ideas behind this book were first developed, and excerpts from it first read, in the context of reading groups, workshops, and conferences variously held at the University of Melbourne, the University of

Queensland, the University of New South Wales, the University of Western Sydney, the Australian Catholic University, and Monash University. I'd like to express my gratitude to all the participants and interlocutors in each of those venues. Numerous other friends and colleagues have provided encouragement and stimulated my thinking over the years, including especially the following: Tom Apperley, Andrew Benjamin, Brandon Chua, Marion Campbell, Alistair Duncan, Dannielle Evans, Tom Ford, Ian Hesketh, Peter Holbrook, Alex Murray, Connal Parsley, Knox Peden, Leigh Penman, Megan Quinlan, Janice Richardson, Jon Roffe, Anton Schütz, Joel Stern, Ian Weeks, Bianca Yianni, and Thanos Zartaloudis. A special thank you to Helen Johnson for her brilliant advice on the cover image.

I want to single out Justin Clemens, Emmett Stinson, and Jess Whyte for their incomparable friendship over the course of many years. I also want to acknowledge the extraordinary support of my extended family, with a special mention to my grandmother Jo Austin, my aunt Donna Gates, my sister Nat Wheeler and her husband Dan, and especially my parents John and Leanne Heron, who made everything possible. Finally, I owe an incalculable debt to my immediate family. To Jackie and Ollie, who were there from the beginning, and to Alice and Ned, who arrived at different stages of its composition: This book is dedicated to you.

An earlier, and shorter, version of Chapter 4 was published as "What Is a Minister? Toward a Theory of the Instrumental Cause" in *CR: The New Centennial Review* 15, 3 (2015): 135–65.

NOTES

Introduction

1. A number of major edited collections published in the past decade have contributed significantly to consolidating this standing. See *Political Theologies: Public Religions in a Post-Secular World*, ed. Hent de Vries and Lawrence E. Sullivan (New York: Fordham University Press, 2006); *Crediting God: Sovereignty and Religion in the Age of Global Capitalism*, ed. Miguel Vatter (New York: Fordham University Press, 2011); and *The Power of Religion in the Public Sphere*, ed. Eduardo Mendieta and Jonathan VanAntwerpen (New York: Columbia University Press, 2011).

2. Carl Schmitt, *Political Theology: Four Chapters on the Concept of Sovereignty*, trans. George Schwab (Chicago: University of Chicago Press, 2005), 36.

3. For a discussion of the tension between these two competing conceptions in Schmitt, see Jean-François Courtine, "A propos du problème théologico-politique," *Droits* 18 (1993): 109–18.

4. While the use of the term "political theology" obviously predates the twentieth century—most famously, of course, it appears in the title of Spinoza's *Tractatus Theologico-Politicus* (1670)—the significance of its reemergence during in the interwar period was stressed by Schmitt's contemporary, Erik Peterson, in the final footnote to his treatise on "Monotheism as a Political Problem," to which we shall shortly turn. See "Monotheism as a Political Problem," in *Theological Tractates*, trans. Michael J. Hollerich (Stanford, Calif.: Stanford University Press, 2011), 233n168. A deeper history, which would trace its use back to the Roman rhetor Varro's discussion of the Stoic conception of a *theologia tripertita* (which distinguishes a *theologia politikē* from a *theologia mythikē* and a *theologia kosmikē*) has often been proposed; but it is unclear to what extent this helps to illuminate the phenomenon in question. See, for example, Jan Assmann, *Politische Theologie zwischen Ägypten und Israel* (Munich: Carl Friedrich von Siemens Stiftung, 1992), 24. For the suggestion of a more proximate source, cf. Heinrich Meier, "What Is Political Theology?" *Interpretation* 30, no. 1 (2002): 79–92; and *The Lesson of Carl Schmitt: Four Chapters*

on the *Distinction between Political Theology and Political Philosophy*, trans. Marcus Brainard (Chicago: University of Chicago Press, 1998).

5. This is the fundamental interpretation of Carlo Galli. See *Genealogia della politica: Carl Schmitt e la crisi del pensiero politico moderno* (Bologna: Mulino, 1996), 333–459; and "Le teologie politiche di Carl Schmitt," in *Lo sguardo di Giano: Saggi di Carl Schmitt* (Bologna: Mulino, 2008), 52–84.

6. For the key terms "depoliticization" and "neutralization," see the important 1929 essay "The Age of Neutralizations and Depoliticizations," trans. Matthias Konzett and John P. McCormick, in *The Concept of the Political*, trans. George Schwab (Chicago: University of Chicago Press, 2007), 80–96. For the triumph of "economic-technical thinking," see above all *Roman Catholicism and Political Form*, trans. G. L. Ulmen (Westport, Conn.: Greenwood Press, 1995); and, for extended discussion, John P. McCormick, *Carl Schmitt's Critique of Liberalism: Against Politics as Technology* (Cambridge: Cambridge University Press, 1997).

7. See Giorgio Agamben, *The Kingdom and the Glory: For a Theological Genealogy of Economy and Government*, trans. Lorenzo Chiesa and Matteo Mandarini (Stanford, Calif.: Stanford University Press, 2011).

8. Peterson, "Monotheism as a Political Problem," *Theological Tractates*, 67–105.

9. Carl Schmitt, *Political Theology II: The Myth of the Closure of Any Political Theology*, trans. Michael Hoelzl and Graham Ward (Cambridge: Polity Press, 2008).

10. See, for example, Théodore Paléologue, *Sous l'œil du Grand Inquisiteur: Carl Schmitt et l'héritage de la théologie politique* (Paris: Cerf, 2004); Peter Hohendahl, "Political Theology Revisited: Carl Schmitt's Postwar Reassessment," *Konturen* 1 (2008), 1–28; and Michael Hoelzl and Graham Ward, introduction to Schmitt, *Political Theology II*, 1–29.

11. For the theological reception, see above all Jürgen Moltmann, *The Trinity and the Kingdom: The Doctrine of God*, trans. Margaret Kohl (Minneapolis: Fortress Press, 1993).

12. An important exception to this rule is György Geréby, "Political Theology versus Theological Politics: Erik Peterson and Carl Schmitt," *New German Critique* 35, no. 3; issue 105 (Fall 2008): 7–33.

13. See Peterson, "Monotheism as a Political Problem," 103–4. Although Peterson here curiously references *De civitate Dei* 3, 30, the theological justification in fact appears much later in the same work. See Augustine, *De civitate Dei* 19, 17; *Concerning the City of God against the Pagans*, trans. Henry Bettenson (London: Penguin, 2003), 878. Cf. also 19, 27; 892–93. For a discussion of Peterson's reference to 3, 30, see Jacob Taubes's 1979 letter to Schmitt, in *To Carl Schmitt: Letters and Reflections*, trans. Keith Tribe (New York: Columbia University Press, 2013), 27–31.

14. The thesis is first outlined is Peterson's important 1929 essay on "The Church" (see Peterson, *Theological Tractates*, 30–39), which precipitated his own

conversion to Catholicism; but it receives its most emphatic expression, as we shall see, in the "Book on the Angels" (Peterson, *Theological Tractates*, 106–42), which was published in the same year as his study on monotheism.

15. In this sense, it is no exaggeration to suggest that much of the major subsequent research conducted in this field—including that of Jacob Taubes and Jan Assmann, but also, closer to his own time, that of Eric Voegelin and Ernst Kantorowicz—follows, albeit in very different ways, the path opened by Peterson rather than Schmitt. The relevant works are Jacob Taubes, *The Political Theology of Paul*, trans. Dana Hollander (Stanford, Calif.: Stanford University Press, 2004); Jan Assmann, *The Price of Monotheism*, trans. Robert Savage (Stanford, Calif.: Stanford University Press, 2010); Eric Voegelin, *The New Science of Politics: An Introduction* (Chicago: University of Chicago Press, 1952); and Ernst Kantorowicz, *The King's Two Bodies: A Study in Mediaeval Political Theology* (Princeton: Princeton University Press, 1957). In the instance of Kantorowicz's earlier work, *Laudes Regiae: A Study in Liturgical Acclamations and Mediaeval Ruler Worship* (Berkeley: University of California Press, 1958), this is explicitly the case.

16. For Aristotle's distinction between the form of "rule" specific to the *polis*, on the one hand, and that particular to the *oikos*, on the other—which of course forms the basis of Hannah Arendt's political theory—see Aristotle, *Politics* 1255b19; *CW* 2:1992 and (Pseudo-)Aristotle, *Economics* 1343a3-4; *CW* 2:2130.

17. See Agamben, *The Kingdom and the Glory*, esp. 35–44, and, for an abbreviated account, "What Is an Apparatus?" in *What Is an Apparatus? and Other Essays*, trans. David Kishik and Stefan Pedatella (Stanford, Calif.: Stanford University Press, 2009), 9–10. There have been numerous recent attempts, starting from the fundamental theses of Max Weber, to describe the theological structure of the economy, emphasizing above all the crucial nexus between credit and debt. See, for example, the contributions of Samuel Weber, *Geld ist Zeit: Gedanken zu Kredit und Krise* (Zurich: Diaphanes Verlag, 2009); Elettra Stimilli, *Il debito del vivente: Ascesi e capitalismo* (Macerata: Quodlibet, 2011); and Joseph Vogl, *The Specter of Capital*, trans. Joachim Redner and Robert Savage (Stanford, Calif.: Stanford University Press, 2015). What distinguishes Agamben's approach, however, is that he is the first to have emphasized the economic structure of theology itself. Cf., however, Marie-José Mondzain, *Image, Icon, Economy: The Byzantine Origins of the Contemporary Imaginary*, trans. Rico Franses (Stanford, Calif.: Stanford University Press, 2005), which had already stressed the significance of the concept of *oikonomia* in the delimited instance, albeit insufficiently treated in Agamben's account, of the theology of the image.

18. See Peterson, "Monotheism as a Political Problem," 71.

19. For the history of this formula, see Schmitt, *Political Theology II*, 66–70. In seizing upon this maxim, Agamben now follows Schmitt, who not only sought to contextualize Peterson's use of it, but had also himself deployed it at numerous

points throughout his vast oeuvre—including in the 1934 preface he wrote for the second edition of *Political Theology*, which thereby sought to inscribe even the "neutral" power of the nineteenth century in its purview. See Schmitt, *Political Theology*, 1.

20. See Michel Foucault, *Security, Territory, Population: Lectures at the Collège de France, 1977–78*, trans. Graham Burchell (Houndmills, U.K.: Palgrave Macmillan, 2007), esp. 87–110.

21. See Foucault, *Security, Territory, Population*, 93–94.

22. Cf. Michel Foucault, *The History of Sexuality, Volume 1: The Will to Knowledge*, trans. Robert Hurley (London: Penguin Books, 1998), 90.

23. See Foucault, *Security, Territory, Population*, 94–95.

24. See Foucault, *Security, Territory, Population*, 76 (trans. modified). Cf. Agamben, *The Kingdom and the Glory*, 109–10.

25. In the latter context, the distinction between sovereignty and government is most immediately associated with the political writings of Rousseau and the theory of popular sovereignty. It is first articulated in the "Discourse on Political Economy" (1756) and then reprised at greater length in the Book III of *The Social Contract* (1762). See Jean-Jacques Rousseau, *The Social Contract and Other Later Political Writings*, ed. and trans. Victor Gourevitch (Cambridge: Cambridge University Press, 1997), 6 and 82–86. As Richard Tuck has established in a recent study, Rousseau himself did not invent the distinction, but rather adapted it from the "absolutist" tradition against which his own work was in many respects directed, where it had already received a highly sophisticated elaboration (above all, in the writings of Bodin and Hobbes). See Richard Tuck, *The Sleeping Sovereign: The Invention of Modern Democracy* (Cambridge: Cambridge University Press, 2016). Despite Bodin's claim to have invented the distinction, which Tuck substantially accepts, his own evidence at times indicates theological antecedents for it. See, for example, the citation from Hobbes's *De Cive* XIII.1, quoted on 94, in which the government of the commonwealth is compared to God's government of the world.

26. See Foucault, *Security, Territory, Population*, 106–7. Thus, for Foucault, the sequencing of Rousseau's two major treatments of the distinction between sovereignty and government is highly significant, in the sense that it is government (or what he terms "public economy" in this context) that is first defined in the "Discourse" and sovereignty only secondarily in *The Social Contract*.

27. Foucault, *Security, Territory, Population*, 103.

28. See Foucault, *Security, Territory, Population*, 192–93.

29. See Foucault, *Security, Territory, Population*, 122–85. For an attempt to situate this discussion in relation to the broader discussion of political theology, see Philippe Büttgen, "Théologie politique et pouvoir pastoral," *Annales HSS* 62, no. 5 (2007): 1129–54.

30. Roberto Esposito, *Living Thought: The Origins and Actuality of Italian Philosophy*, trans. Zakiya Hanafi (Stanford, Calif.: Stanford University Press, 2012), 250.

31. See, for example, Bruno Karsenti, "Agamben et le mystère du gouvernement," *Critique* 744 (2008): 355–75; Mitchell Dean, "Governmentality Meets Theology: 'The King Reigns, but He Does Not Govern," *Theory, Culture and Society*, 29, no. 3 (2012): 145–58; and Jessica Whyte, "'The King Reigns but He Doesn't Govern': Thinking Sovereignty and Government with Agamben, Foucault and Rousseau," *Giorgio Agamben: Legal, Political and Philosophical Perspectives*, ed. Tom Frost (London: Routledge, 2013), 143–61.

32. See Agamben, *The Kingdom and the Glory*, 104–6, but cf. also the important pages of *Homo Sacer: Sovereign Power and Bare Life*, trans. Daniel Heller-Roazen (Stanford, Calif.: Stanford University Press, 1998), 44–47, where he had established, on the basis of a close reading of Book Theta of Aristotle's *Metaphysics*, that the heterogeneity of potentiality (*dynamis*) with respect to actuality (*energeia*), is in fact predicated on the impotentiality (*adynamia*) of the same—that is, on the concurrent potentiality not to pass into actuality that necessarily insists within every potentiality: "The potentiality," he writes, "maintains itself in relation to actuality in the form of its suspension; it is capable of the act in not realizing it, it is sovereignly capable of its own impotentiality" (45). It is important to note that for Agamben the theme of divine impotentiality even encompasses the late Scholastic doctrine of God's *potentia absoluta*. For a different approach to this theme, which passes through the Jewish perspective of Hans Jonas ("The Concept of God after Auschwitz: A Jewish Voice," *Journal of Religion* 67, no. 1 [1987]: 1–13), see Gwenaëlle Aubry, "L'impuissance de Dieu," *Revue philosophique de la France et de l'étranger* 135, no. 2 (2010): 307–20.

33. It is true that Agamben speaks of two political paradigms in the broad sense that issue from Christian theology: "political theology, which founds the transcendence of sovereign power on a single God, and economic theology, which replaces this transcendence with the idea of an *oikonomia*, conceived as an immanent ordering—domestic and not political in a strict sense—of both human and divine life." Agamben, *The Kingdom and the Glory*, 1. It is my contention, however, that his analysis is oriented toward the reconstruction of a unitary matrix that would be anterior to their later partition. In order to arrive at an understanding at their historical separation, and hence at the appearance of the two paradigms, it is thus necessary first to grasp the sense of their originary structural interrelation.

34. While there is certainly a tradition that extends from Peterson himself to Ernst Kantorowicz and beyond that has argued for the political character of liturgy by stressing its acclamatory dimension (see, above all, Kantorowicz, *Laudes Regiae*), I have sought instead to position it instead as a technique of governance.

35. Cf. Heb. 8:1–7.

36. Ernst H. Kantorowicz, "Deus per Naturam, Deus per Gratiam: A Note on Mediaeval Political Theology," *The Harvard Theological Review*, 45, no. 4 (1952): 253–77.

37. Agamben, *The Kingdom and the Glory*, 138 (trans. slightly modified).

38. See Agamben, *The Kingdom and the Glory*, 138.

39. It is regrettable that Arendt never devoted a study exclusively to this theme, which is nonetheless present in almost all her writings. See, especially, Hannah Arendt, *The Human Condition* (Chicago: University of Chicago Press, 1958), 40, 45; *Eichmann in Jerusalem: A Report on the Banality of Evil* (London: Penguin Books, 1963), 289–90; and *On Violence* (New York: Harcourt, Brace, Jovanovich, 1970), 38–39, 81–82. Cf. also *The Origins of Totalitarianism*, 2nd ed. (London: Allen and Unwin, 1958), 213–16.

40. See Foucault, *Security, Territory, Population*, 192.

41. See Emanuele Coccia, "*Potestas dicitur multipliciter:* Le pouvoir et la nature," in *Un histoire du présent: Les historiens et Michel Foucault*, ed. Damien Bouquet, Blaise Dufal, and Pauline Labey (Paris: CNRS, 2013), 262–81.

1. THE ECONOMIC GOD

1. Augustine, *Confessiones*, 3, 6, 10; *Confessions*, trans. Henry Chadwick (Oxford: Oxford University Press, 1991), 41.

2. See Edward Peters, "What was God doing before He created the Heavens and the Earth?," *Augustiniana*, 34, 1–2 (1984); now in Peters, *Limits of Thought and Power in Medieval Europe* (Aldershot, U.K.: Ashgate, 2001), 54.

3. 1 Cor. 11:19. See, for example, *De Genesis contra Manichaeos*, 1, 2; *On Genesis: A Refutation of the Manichees*, in *The Works of Saint Augustine*, I/13, trans. Edmund Hill (New York: New City Press, 2002), 39.

4. See, above all, Daniel Boyarin, *Border Lines: The Partition of Judaeo-Christianity* (Philadelphia: University of Pennsylvania Press, 2004); but cf. also Alain Le Boulluec, *La notion d'hérésie dans le littérature grecque IIe-IIIe siècles* (Paris: Études Augustiniennes, 1985) and Karen L. King, *What Is Gnosticism?* (Cambridge, Mass.: The Belknap Press of Harvard University Press, 2003).

5. Peters, "What was God doing before He created the Heavens and the Earth?," 55.

6. Augustine, *Confessiones*, 11, 10, 12:152; 228.

7. Augustine, *De civitate Dei*, 11, 6; *Concerning the City of God against the Pagans*, trans. Henry Bettenson (London: Penguin, 2003), 436.

8. Augustine, *Confessiones*, 11, 14, 17; 231.

9. Ernst H. Kantorowicz, *The King's Two Bodies: A Study in Mediaeval Political Theology* (Princeton: Princeton University Press, 1957), 275.

10. Augustine, *De civitate Dei*, 12, 13; 486. On the idleness question more generally, see Richard Sorabji, *Time, Creation, and the Continuum: Theories in Antiquity and the Middle Ages* (Ithaca, N.Y.: Cornell University Press, 1983), 186–87; 249–52.

11. See Kantorowicz, *The King's Two Bodies*, 273–84.

12. Irenaeus, *Adversus haereses*, 2, 28, 3; *Contre les hérésies*, II, 2, ed. Adeline Rousseau and Louis Doutreleau (Paris: Cerf, 1982), 276–77.

13. Irenaeus, *Adversus haereses*, 2, 28, 3; 276–77.

14. Irenaeus, *Adversus haereses*, 2, 28, 2; 270–71. According to Peters's succinct summation: "Both Gnostics and Manichaeans knew very well what the divinity and its enemies were doing before the creation. . . . To ask the question 'What was God doing before He created the heavens and the earth', was to indict Genesis for failing to account, first, for the true nature of God in the 'Age Before' and, second, of failing to recognise creation as a flaw rather than as a significant and benevolent act." Peters, "What was God doing before He created the Heavens and the Earth?," 69–70.

15. Origen, *De principiis*, 3, 5, 1; *Traité des principes*, III, ed. Henri Crouzel and Manlio Simonetti (Paris: Cerf, 1980), 220–21.

16. Origen, *De principiis*, 3, 5, 3; 222–23. Aside from the fragments patiently collected by philologists (often, but not exclusively, drawn from the writings of his many detractors), Origen's treatise survives in its entirety only in the Latin translation of his disciple Rufinus of Aquileia. It goes without saying that this text must be treated with great caution: Although less than a sixth of the original has been preserved, there is ample evidence to suggest, not only that Rufinus's version is considerably softer than the original (in that it often proceeds by euphemistic paraphrase), but that it made significant omissions and, perhaps even more alarmingly, introduced extensive additions.

17. Origen, *De principiis*, 1, 4, 3; 168–69.

18. Origen, *De principiis*, 3, 5, 3; 222–25.

19. See Augustine, *De civitate Dei*, 12, 14; 487–89.

20. Augustine, *De civitate Dei*, 12, 16; 490 (trans. slightly modified).

21. See Augustine, *De civitate Dei*, 12, 16; 490–93. Cf. Augustine, *Confessiones*, 11, 30, 40; 244.

22. Aristotle, *De caelo* 292b1–6; *On the Heavens*, trans. W. K. C. Guthrie (London: William Heinemann, 1960), 208–9.

23. Plato, *Laws* 902e–903a; *Laws*, trans. R. G. Bury (London: William Heinemann, 1968), II:360–63.

24. Cicero, *De natura deorum*, 1, 2; *De natura deorum; Academica*, trans. H. Rackham (London: William Heinemann, 1967), 4–5.

25. Cicero, *De natura deorum* 1, 51; 52–53.

26. Cicero, *De natura deorum*, 1, 52; 52–53. Epicurus himself is particularly clear in his opposition to this "business." Indeed, one of the fundamental attributes of

the Epicurean deity is its absolute exemption from any public service, that is, its *a-leitourgia*: "The divine nature must not on any account be adduced to explain [the regularity of the orbits of the sun and the moon]," he writes in his Letter to Pythocles, "but must be kept free from the task [*aleitourgitos*] and in perfect bliss." See Diogenes Laertius, 10, 97; *Lives of Eminent Philosophers*, trans. R. D. Hicks (London: William Heinemann, 1926), II:624–25.

27. Cicero, *De natura deorum*, 2, 75; 194–97.

28. See Cicero, *De natura deorum*, 2, 76; 196–97.

29. Cicero, *De natura deorum*, 2, 59; 178–81.

30. Foucault, *Security, Territory, Population*, 192. Although, as Michel Senellart rightly notes (see Foucault, *Security, Territory, Population*, 217n1), the phrase *oikonomia psychōn* appears nowhere in the *Orations* of Gregory of Nazianzus to whom Foucault mistakenly attributes it, it does actually appear in the context of Basil of Caesarea's contemporaneous treatise on the Holy Spirit (13, 30), where such an activity is referred to those—including, above all, Basil himself, in his capacity as bishop of Caesarea—upon whom has been conferred "some ministry of the Word." See Basil of Caesarea, *Sur le Saint-Esprit*, ed. and trans. Benoît Pruche (Paris: Cerf, 1968), 352–53.

31. See Michel Foucault, *Security, Territory, Population: Lectures at the Collège de France, 1977–78*, trans. Graham Burchell (Houndmills, U.K.: Palgrave Macmillan, 2007), 192.

32. See Giorgio Agamben, *The Kingdom and the Glory: For a Theological Genealogy of Economy and Government*, trans. Lorenzo Chiesa and Matteo Mandarini (Stanford, Calif.: Stanford University Press, 2011). 17–52.

33. See, for example, Joseph Moingt, *Théologie trinitaire de Tertullien, III: Unité et processions* (Paris: Aubier, 1966), 892–93, who distinguishes between "organic monotheism," on the one hand, and "economic trinitarianism," on the other.

34. Eph. 3:8–9. Cf. also Eph. 1:8–10 and Col. 1:24–25.

35. See Agamben, *The Kingdom and the Glory*, 21–23, for examples from Paul; and, for a more extensive examination, J. Reumann, "*Oikonomia*-Terms in Paul in Comparison with Lucan *Heilgeschichte*," *New Testament Studies* 13 (1966): 147–67.

36. See Agamben, *The Kingdom and the Glory*, 20–21.

37. A use of the term that, significantly, is already attested prior to Paul, both in the Stoic sources as well as in those of Hellenistic Judaism. See Reumann, "*Oikonomia*-Terms in Paul," 150–53. It is important to note, moreover, that when Hippolytus and Tertullian come to speak of a "mystery of the economy," rather than an "economy of the mystery," even there the sense of the term remains largely unchanged. What has changed, however, is the sense of the activity in question, which, on account of its having been identified with what it must reveal, has now itself become mysterious and even inscrutable. And hence which must now be interpreted. See Agamben, *The Kingdom and the*

Glory, 38–39, and *Il mistero del male: Benedetto XVI a la fine dei tempi* (Bari: Laterza, 2013), 32.

38. The distinction between *epistēmē* and *technē* is of considerable importance in this context because it shows precisely why, in the wake of the proclamation of the orthodox dogma at Nicaea, the fact that the first elaboration of the Trinity was undertaken in strictly "economic" (and not "metaphysical") terms would constitute such an embarrassment for later theologians. It accounts, on the one hand, for the emergence of the clear separation of *theologia* and *oikonomia* in post-Nicene theology, where *oikonomia* now refers simply to the divine plan of salvation; and, on the other, for the necessary repression of every trace of the "reckless" ante-Nicene doctrines that had sought to elaborate the substance of the Trinity itself in economic terms. For the definition of *oikonomia* as nonepistemic, see Aristotle, *Politics* 1255b20–21; *CW* 2:1992. For the distinction between *epistēmē* and *technē*, see Aristotle, *Nicomachean Ethics* 1139b14–40a23, trans. W. D. Ross (rev. J. O. Urmson), in *CW* 2:1799–1800.

39. As Aristotle proceeds to observe in the *Politics*, even if there were a "science" of the master—a "despotics"—it would be of no particular significance or importance: for the master need only know how to "order" (*epitattein*) what the slaves in turn must "execute" (*poiein*). See Aristotle, *Politics* 1255b32–35; *CW* 2:1992.

40. Hippolytus of Rome, *Contra Noetum*, 3, 4; *Contra Noetum*, ed. and trans. Robert Butterworth (London: Heythrop Monographs, 1977), 48–49.

41. Hippolytus, *Contra Noetum*, 8, 2; 64–65 (trans. slightly modified).

42. See Agamben, *The Kingdom and the Glory*, 38–39.

43. See Hippolytus, *Contra Noetum* 14, 3; 74–75.

44. Hippolytus, *Contra Noetum* 14, 4–5; 74–75.

45. See Tertullian, *Adversus Praxean* 12, who speaks of one who "commands" and another who "does." In *Adversus Praxean*, ed. and trans. Ernest Evans (London: S. P. C. K., 1948), 146.

46. See Agamben, *The Kingdom and the Glory*, 39.

47. Roberto Esposito, *Categories of the Impolitical*, trans. Connal Parsley (New York: Fordham, 2015), 61.

48. See Hannah Arendt, *The Human Condition* (Chicago: University of Chicago Press, 1958), 222–25.

49. See, also, Hannah Arendt, "What Is Authority?" in *Between Past and Future: Eight Exercises in Political Thought* (New York: Viking Press, 1968), esp. 104–20.

50. See Agamben, *The Kingdom and the Glory*, 55.

51. Irenaeus, *Adversus haereses*, 3, 24, 2; 478–79.

52. Tertullian, *Adversus Marcionem* 1, 25, 3; *Adversus Marcionem*, ed. and trans. Ernest Jones (Oxford: Clarendon Press, 1972), 70–71. Cf. Diogenes Laertius 10, 139; II:662–63.

53. Cicero, *De natura deorum*, 1, 53; 52–53.

54. Lucretius, *De rerum natura*, 5, 156–65; *De rerum natura*, trans. W. H. D. Rouse; rev. Martin Ferguson Smith (London: William Heinemann, 1975), 390–91. Where possible, however, I have preferred to follow the more accurate translations of Tony Long and David Sedley in *The Hellenistic Philosophers*, ed. A. A. Long and D. N. Sedley (Cambridge: Cambridge University Press, 1987), 59.

55. Lactantius, *De ira Dei*, 8; *Lactantius: The Minor Works*, trans. Mary Francis McDonald (Washington, D. C.: Catholic University of American Press, 1965), 73.

56. Aristotle, *Nicomachean Ethics* 1097a30–32, in *CW* 2:1735.

57. Lucretius, *De rerum natura*, 4, 824–31; 340–43.

58. Lucretius, *De rerum natura*, 4, 833–42; 342–43/55–59.

59. Lucretius, *De rerum natura*, 4, 843–52; 342–43.

60. Lucretius, *De rerum natura*, 4, 857; 342–43.

61. See, among others, Arnaldo Momigliano, "The Disadvantages of Monotheism for a Universal State," *Classical Philology* 81, no. 4 (1986): 292–93, and Guy G. Stroumsa, "Moses the Lawgiver and the Idea of Civil Religion in Patristic Thought," in *Teologie politiche: Modelli a confronto*, ed. Giovanni Firolamo (Brescia: Morcelliana, 2005), 136–37.

62. Erik Peterson, "Monotheism as a Political Problem," in *Theological Tractates*, trans. Michael J. Hollerich (Stanford, Calif.: Stanford University Press, 2011), 233–34n168.

63. Jacob Taubes, letter to Schmitt, in *To Carl Schmitt: Letters and Reflections*, trans. Keith Tribe (New York: Columbia University Press, 2013), 28.

64. See Augustine, *De civitate Dei* 3, 30; 131–32.

65. Peterson, "Monotheism as a Political Problem," 104.

66. Agamben, *The Kingdom and the Glory*, 10 (trans. slightly modified).

67. See Peterson, "Monotheism as a Political Problem," 72–76.

68. See, for example, evidently on the basis of the same source material, Philo, *De specialibus legibus* 1, 18; *Philo in Ten Volumes*, 7:108–9: "For it is quite ridiculous to deny that if the mind in us, so exceedingly small and invisible, is yet ruler of the organs of sense, the mind of the universe, so transcendently great and perfect, must be the King of kings [*basileus basileōn*] who are seen by Him though He is not seen by them."

69. See Peterson, "Monotheism as a Political Problem," 70–72.

70. See Peterson, "Monotheism as a Political Problem," 71. For discussion of Peterson's appropriation of this formula, whose origins may indeed be older again, see Schmitt, *Political Theology II*, 66–70.

71. Peterson, "Monotheism as a Political Problem," 102.

72. Peterson, "Monotheism as a Political Problem," 103. Cf. Gregory of Nazianzus, *Oration* 29, 2; *Discours 27–31 (Discours théologiques)*, ed. and trans. Paul Gallay (Paris: Cerf, 1978), 178–79.

73. Gregory of Nazianzus, *Oration* 29, 2; 179.

74. See Peterson, "Monotheism as a Political Problem," 103–4.

75. See Peterson, "Monotheism as a Political Problem," 69.

76. "The rule of a household," we read in an important passage of the *Politics*, "is monarchical [*oikonomikē monarchia*]," See Aristotle, *Politics* 1255b19; *CW* 2:992. The pseudo-Aristotelian *Economics* is even more explicit again: "The science of politics involves a number of rulers, whereas the sphere of economics is a monarchy [*hē oikonomikē de monarchia*]." See (Pseudo-)Aristotle, *Economics* 1343a3–4; *CW* 2:2130.

77. See Agamben, *The Kingdom and the Glory*, 81.

78. Aristotle, *Metaphysics* 1075a11–19; *CW* 2:1699.

79. See Agamben, *The Kingdom and the Glory*, 14.

80. Agamben, *The Kingdom and the Glory*, 14.

81. See Agamben, *The Kingdom and the Glory*, 14.

82. Tertullian, *Adversus Praxean* 3, 133 (trans. slightly modified). Cf. Peterson, "Monotheism as a Political Problem," 81.

83. Tertullian, *Adversus Praxean* 3, 132.

84. See above, Section 5.

85. Tertullian, *Adversus Praxean* 3, 133 (trans. modified).

86. See Tertullian, *Adversus Praxean* 3, 133.

87. See Agamben, *The Kingdom and the Glory*, 43.

88. See Peterson, "Monotheism as a Political Problem," 82.

89. Tertullian, *Apologeticus* 24, 3; translation in Tertullian, *Apology; De Spectaculis*, trans. T. R. Glover (London: William Heinemann, 1966), 132–33.

90. Peterson, "Monotheism as a Political Problem," 83.

91. And yet, he was certainly aware that both the Jewish and Christian traditions would employ a similar idea in their curious doctrine of "the angels of the nations." See below, Chapter 2, Excursus: On the Angels of the Nations. Indeed, as we shall see, in 1951 Peterson would publish a significant article on precisely this theme. See Erik Peterson, "Das Problem des Nationalismus im alten Christentum," *Theologisches Zeitschrift* 7, no. 2 (1951): 81–91. In the context of the monotheism essay, however, it is important to note that he discusses this notion only very selectively, insofar as it pertains to Origen's theoretical rival, the pagan philosopher Celsus, and not to Origen himself, who not only devotes some very important pages of his *Contra Celsum* to its exposition in a Christian context, but who also clearly employs it as a justification for monotheism. If it is indeed true, as Celsus contends, Origen writes, that the different parts of the earth have been apportioned to different overseers, who, he asks, was responsible for the initial distribution? Who oversees the overseers? See Origen, *Contra Celsum* 5, 26, trans. Henry Chadwick (Cambridge: Cambridge University Press, 1965), 283–84. Cf. Peterson, "Monotheism as a Political Problem," 221–22n117.

92. Tertullian, *Apologeticus* 24, 4; 132–33. Cf. Philo, *De decalogo* 61; 7:36–37.

93. See, especially, Agamben, *The Kingdom and the Glory*, 53–55.

94. For a competing attempt to think the relation between anarchy and economy, cf. here the brilliant study by Reiner Schürmann, *Heidegger on Being and Acting: From Principles to Anarchy*, trans. Christine-Marie Gros (Bloomington: Indiana University Press, 1990).

95. For further discussion, see Nicholas Heron, "The Ungovernable," *Angelaki* 16, no. 2 (2011): 159–74.

2. LITURGICAL POWER

1. In the final analysis, this was the curious premise of Schmitt's belated response to Peterson in 1970, which ensured that his riposte completely missed the mark. To argue, as Schmitt does, that Peterson himself remained incapable of preserving the absolute purity of the theological against contamination by impure politics, and that he thereby inadvertently committed the very trespass that his treatise sought to argue against, is to singularly misconstrue the sense of Peterson's intervention.

2. Erik Peterson, "Monotheism as a Political Problem," in *Theological Tractates*, trans. Michael J. Hollerich (Stanford, Calif.: Stanford University Press, 2011), 68 (trans. modified).

3. See Giorgio Agamben, *The Kingdom and the Glory: For a Theological Genealogy of Economy and Government*, trans. Lorenzo Chiesa and Matteo Mandarini (Stanford, Calif.: Stanford University Press, 2011), 15.

4. See Jürgen Moltmann, *The Trinity and the Kingdom: The Doctrine of God*, trans. Margaret Kohl (Minneapolis: Fortress Press, 1993), 193–200.

5. See Erik Peterson, *Heis Theos. Epigraphische, formgeschichtliche und religionsgeschichtliche Untersuchungen* (Göttingen: Vandenhoeck und Ruprecht, 1926).

6. Peterson, "The Church," *Theological Tractates*, 38 (trans. slightly modified).

7. Peterson, "The Book on the Angels," *Theological Tractates*, 106–42. While the treatise on monotheism has received significant attention, including the publication of an edited collection dedicated entirely to its discussion—see *Monotheismus als politisches Problem? Erik Peterson und der Kritik der politischen Theologie*, ed. Alfred Schindler (Gütersloh: Gütersloher Verlagshaus Gerd Mohn, 1978)—the bibliography on this equally important text is comparatively scarce. See, however, Christoph Schmidt, "Apokalyptischer Strukturwandel der Öffentlichkeit: Von der politischen Theologie zur Theopolitik: Anmerkungen zu Erik Petersons 'Buch von den Engeln—Stellung und Bedeutung der heiligen Engel im Kultus' von 1935," in *Die theopolitische Stunde: Zwölf Perspektiven auf das eschatologische Problem der Moderne* (Munich: Wilhelm Fink Verlag, 2009), 113–42.

8. Peterson, "Book on the Angels," 107.

9. Peterson, "Book on the Angels," 108 (trans. modified).

10. Peterson, "The Church," 38.

11. See Peterson, "Book on the Angels," 108. Starting from the scriptural authority of Eph. 2:19, which speaks of the "fellow-citizens" (*sympolitai*) of the "household of God" (*oikeioi tou theou*), the notion that the angels are the citizens of the heavenly city forms something of a recurring topos in the political thought of St. Augustine. See, among many other possible examples, *Sermo* 341a, 11: *The Works of Saint Augustine, III:10: Sermons (341–400)*, trans. Edmund Hill (Hyde Park, New York: New City Press, 1995), 26; *Enarrationes in Psalmos* 36, 4: *The Works of Saint Augustine, III:16: Exposition of the Psalms, 33–50*, trans. Maria Boulding (Hyde Park, N.Y.: New City Press, 2000), 131; and, above all, *De civitate Dei*, 10, 25; *Concerning the City of God against the Pagans*, trans. Henry Bettenson (London: Penguin, 2003), 406–8. It should not be forgotten that the monotheism essay is dedicated to Augustine and opens with the supplication that he "whose impact has been felt in every the spiritual and political transformations of the West" should assist both the readers and the author of this book with his prayers. Peterson, "Monotheism as a Political Problem," 68.

12. See Peterson, "Book on the Angels," 235n12.

13. See Agamben, *The Kingdom and the Glory*, 144–48. Cf., also, *Opus Dei: An Archaeology of Duty*, trans. Adam Kotsko (Stanford, Calif.: Stanford University Press, 2013), 27.

14. Peterson, "Book on the Angels," 112.

15. Peterson, "Book on the Angels," 109 (trans. slightly modified).

16. See Peterson, "Book on the Angels," 109–11. The passage in question is Rev. 4:6–10. For the Old Testament parallel, cf. Ezek. 1:5–28.

17. Cf. Rev. 4:10.

18. Cf. Rev 4:10–11.

19. Peterson, "Book on the Angels," 112.

20. Cf. Rev. 5:9–10: "They sing a new song: 'You are worthy to take the scroll and to open its seals, / For you were slaughtered and by your blood you ransomed for God / From every tribe and language and people and nation [*ek pasēs phylēs kai glōssēs kai laou kai ethnous*]; / You have made them to be a kingdom and priests [*basileian kai hieris*] serving our God, / And they will reign on earth."

21. Peterson, "Book on the Angels," 113.

22. Peterson, "Book on the Angels," 114.

23. See Peterson, "Book on the Angels," 114. For Peterson's interpretation, it is of critical importance that, for their final intonation, the elders are joined first by the multitude of holy angels, who number "thousands upon thousands" (Rev. 5:11), and then by "every creature in heaven and on earth and under the earth and in the sea" (5:13). As he writes (116; trans. slightly modified): "The entire cosmos is drawn into its praise."

24. See Peterson, "Book on the Angels," 134.

25. On this particular point, which doubtless played a significant role in Peterson's conversion to Catholicism, it is possible to cite a genuine influence of Schmitt

over Peterson's thought. Cf. Carl Schmitt, *Roman Catholicism and Political Form*, trans. G. L. Ulmen (Westport, Conn.: Greenwood Press, 1995).

26. See Peterson, "Book on the Angels," 134–35. It is curious to note that when in the late 1950s Jürgen Habermas composed his celebrated *Habilitationsschrift* on the *Structural Transformation of the Public Sphere*, it was, at least in part, on the model of Peterson's "himmlische Öffentlichkeit"—as mediated by the theory of democracy sketched by Carl Schmitt in his *Constitutional Theory*, which is cited numerous times in the text—that the German philosopher conceived his "basic blueprint" of the bourgeois public sphere, famously defined as "the sphere of private persons come together as a public." See Habermas, *The Structural Transformation of the Public Sphere: An Inquiry into a Category of Bourgeois Society*, trans. Thomas Burger (Cambridge: Polity Press, 1989), 27. Cf. Carl Schmitt, *Constitutional Theory*, ed. and trans. Jeffrey Selzer (Durham, N.C.: Duke University Press, 2008), esp. 271–78, where the influence of Peterson's theory of acclamations is unmistakable. The theory of "communicative action," which is but the philosophical consequence of Habermas's earlier investigations, must in the final analysis be seen as a particular species of what we are calling "liturgical power." Even though it may contest how this power is exercised (by whom, with respect to whom and to what end), it fundamentally does not contest its paradigm, and in this way, surreptitiously contributes to reinforcing it.

27. On the honorific dimension of liturgies, see M. I. Finley, *The Ancient Economy*, updated ed. (Berkeley: University of California Press, 1999), 151–53. The liturgical system of course paved the way for the phenomenon of "euergetism," which Paul Veyne had studied in a now classic work. See Paul Veyne, *Bread and Circuses: Historical Sociology and Political Pluralism*, abr. trans. Brian Pearce (London: Allen Lane, 1990).

28. See J. K. Davies, *Athenian Propertied Families, 600–300 B.C.* (Oxford: Clarendon Press, 1971), xxi. The major textual evidence for this claim is to be found in Aristotle, *Politics*, 1291a33–34; *CW* 2:2049.

29. See Pseudo-Xenophon, *Constitution of the Athenians*, 1, 13, in *Scripta Minora*, trans. E. C. Marchant (London: William Heinemann, 1984), 481–83. Cf. also Xenophon, *Oeconomicus*, 2, 5–6; *Memorabilia and Oeconomicus*, trans. E. C. Marchant (Cambridge, Mass.: Harvard University Press, 1997), 375–77, in which Socrates suggests that the Athenians would punish Critobulus no less than if they had caught him stealing should he fail to acquit his liturgies adequately.

30. See Agamben, *Opus Dei*, 1. Thus, in a well-known sequence of his *Politics*, Aristotle recommended that in democracies "it is probably better to prevent men from undertaking costly but useless public services [*leitourgias*] like equipping choruses and torch-races and other similar services, even if they wish to." Aristotle, *Politics*, 1309a20–21; *CW* 2:2078.

31. See Aristotle, *Nicomachean Ethics*, 1122a18–1123a33; *CW* 2:1771–72. For commentary on this passage, see Veyne, *Bread and Circuses*, 13–18.

32. See Naphtali Lewis, *The Compulsory Public Services of Roman Egypt* (Florence: Edizioni Gonnelli, 1982). Cf., also, the discussion in Emanuele Coccia, introduction to *Angeli: Ebraismo Cristianesimo Islam*, ed. Giorgio Agamben and Emanuele Coccia (Vicenza: Neri Pozza, 2009), 490–94 (all translations of this text are my own).

33. See Naphtali Lewis, "*Leitourgia* and Related Terms," *Greek, Roman and Byzantine Studies* 3 (1960), 181–82.

34. Specifically in Aristotle, *Politics*, 1330a13; *CW* 2:2110. Of the common land, one portion, he advised, should be reserved for the "worship of the gods [*theous leitourgias*]."

35. See Agamben, *Opus Dei*, 3; and also, Peter Brown, *Poverty and Leadership in the Later Roman Empire* (Hanover, N.H.: University Press of New England, 2002), 29–31.

36. On the semantics of "immunity," see Esposito, *Immunitas: The Protection and Negation of Life*, translated by Zakiya Hanafi (Cambridge: Polity Press, 2011), 5–6. Here, significantly enough, it is the performance of a *munus* of a very particular kind that is itself the condition of *im-munitas*.

37. György Geréby, "Political Theology versus Theological Politics: Erik Peterson and Carl Schmitt," *New German Critique* 35, no. 3; issue 105 (Fall 2008): 7–33.

38. The abstract noun *leitourgia* is in fact specifically formed with *leitos*, which is a derivative of *laos*. For discussion, see Émile Benveniste, *Indo-European Language and Society*, trans. Elizabeth Palmer (London: Faber and Faber, 1973), 373–75.

39. Peterson, *Heis Theos*, 179.

40. Cicero, *De re publica*, 1, 25; *De re publica; De legibus*, trans. Clinton Walter Keyes (London: William Heinemann, 1970), 65 (trans. modified). Peterson conveniently elides the adjoining phrase *et utilitatis communione* from the definition that Cicero places in the mouth of Scipio to further emphasize his point.

41. See Augustine, *De civitate Dei*, 19, 21; 881–83. Cf. 2, 21; 75. For discussion of Augustine's reading of Cicero, see R. A. Markus, *Saeculum: History and Society in the Theology of St. Augustine* (Cambridge: Cambridge University Press, 1970), 64–66.

42. Augustine, *De civitate Dei*, 19, 21; 882.

43. It is true that in a later chapter Augustine offers a softer definition of the *populus* and that of the *res publica* that follows from this; but this definition, according to which a people would be a multitude assembled by "common agreement on the object of their love" (rather than by legal consensus) holds only for earthly polities and particularly for those of ancient Rome. See Augustine, *De civitate Dei*, 19, 24; 890–91.

44. Peterson, *Heis Theos*, 179.

45. It is precisely this aspect of Peterson's dissertation that Schmitt will take up in his *Constitutional Theory*. See Schmitt, *Constitutional Theory*, 272–74. As

should become apparent in what follows, the particular irony of his application of Peterson's theory of acclamations to the definition of direct democracy becomes especially clear when one considers that, in the strict sense, the "public" to which acclaiming people give rise is not "democratic."

46. See here the important pages of Ernst H. Kantorowicz's *Laudes Regiae: A Study in Liturgical Acclamations and Mediaeval Ruler Worship* (Berkeley: University of California Press, 1946), 78–84, which stage a clear polemic with Peterson.

47. See Michel Foucault, *Security, Territory, Population: Lectures at the Collège de France, 1977–78*, trans. Graham Burchell (Houndmills, U.K.: Palgrave Macmillan, 2007), 122–226.

48. See Foucault, *Security, Territory, Population*, 122.

49. See Foucault, *Security, Territory, Population*, 123–24. For an important sampling of relevant texts, see *Ancient Near Eastern Texts Relating to the Old Testament*, ed. James B. Pritchard (Princeton: Princeton University Press, 1969).

50. Oswyn Murray, "The Idea of the Shepherd King from Cyrus to Charlemagne," in *Latin Poetry and the Classical Tradition: Essays in Medieval and Renaissance Literature*, ed. Peter Goodman and Oswyn Murray (Oxford: Clarendon Press, 1990), 4–5. The most well-known use of the shepherd image to refer to Yahweh is Ps. 23:1–4. For an example of it being referred to the Messiah, cf. instead Ezek. 34:23–24.

51. There are, by contrast, many examples of it being employed politically in a strictly negative form, as in the "shepherds" of Jer. 2:8, who have transgressed against the Lord. Cf. Jer. 10:21; 23:1–2; Isa. 56:11; Ezek. 34:1–10; Zech. 10:3.

52. Gen. 49:24.

53. Jer. 50:19.

54. Foucault, *Security, Territory, Population*, 124–25 (trans. modified).

55. See especially Michel Foucault, "*Omnes et singulatim*: Toward a Critique of Political Reason," in *Essential Works of Foucault, 1954–1984, Volume Three: Power*, ed. James D. Faubion (London: Penguin, 2000), 301–3; but also *Security, Territory, Population*, 124–25.

56. Foucault, *Security, Territory, Population*, 125 (trans. modified).

57. Heb. 13:20.

58. Cf. Jn. 10:11–18.

59. Lk. 15:4. Cf. Mt. 18:12–13.

60. While there is not a single instance of a negative portrayal of the shepherd to be found in the New Testament, it is striking to observe that, within Rabbinic Judaism, it comes increasingly to be figured in exclusively negative terms. The Rabbis (*Midrash Tehillim*, 23, 2) even go as far as to question how, given the despicable nature of shepherds, Psalm 23 could present Yahweh himself as a shepherd: "R. Jose bar Hanina taught: In the whole world you will find no occupation more despised than that of the shepherd, who all his days walks about with his staff and

his pouch. Yet David presumed to call the Holy One, blessed be He, a shepherd!" In *The Midrash on Psalms*, I, trans. William G. Braude (New Haven, Conn.: Yale University Press, 1959). On this contrast, see Joachim Jeremias, s.v. *poimen*, in *Theological Dictionary of the New Testament*, vol. 6, ed. Georg Friedrich, trans. Geoffrey Bromiley (Grand Rapids, Mich.: Eerdmans, 1968), 488–89.

61. Foucault, *Security, Territory, Population*, 164.

62. Foucault, *Security, Territory, Population*, 148.

63. See Foucault, *Security, Territory, Population*, 152–53.

64. See Foucault, *Security, Territory, Population*, 153.

65. Foucault, *Security, Territory, Population*, 147–48.

66. See Foucault, *Security, Territory, Population*, 140–47. For Plato, see *The Statesman*, 261d–276d; translation in *The Statesman; Philebus*, trans. W. R. M. Lamb (Cambridge, Mass.: Harvard University Press, 1975), 22–75.

67. Foucault, *Security, Territory, Population*, 147.

68. See, for example, Xenophon, *Memorabilia*, 3, 2, 1; *Memorabilia and Oeconomicus*, 174–75; and Aristotle, *Nicomachean Ethics*, 1161a15; *CW* 2:1835.

69. See Foucault, *Security, Territory, Population*, 136. Regarding Homer, Foucault himself cites *The Iliad*, 2, 254; but many further examples could be suitably furnished. For a comprehensive inventory of all the appearances of *poimena/poimeni laōn* formula in Homer, whether in reference to Agamemnon or otherwise, see Johannes Haubold, *Homer's People: Epic Poetry and Social Formation* (Cambridge: Cambridge University Press, 2000), 197.

70. Cf., above all, LXX Ex. 19:5–6 and Deut. 7:6, but the references could be multiplied many times.

71. Haubold, *Homer's People*, ix.

72. This would seem all the more apposite given that the point of departure for Foucault's investigation is, of course, the apparently modern concept of the "population."

73. Giorgio Agamben, *The Time That Remains: A Commentary on the Letter to the Romans*, trans. Patricia Dailey (Stanford, Calif.: Stanford University Press, 2005), 47.

74. One contemporary political thinker to have been attentive to the differing historical valences of the multiple Greek terms for "people" is Étienne Balibar. See, for example, Étienne Balibar, s.v *demos/ethnos/laos*, in *Dictionary of Untranslatables: A Philosophical Lexicon*, ed. Barbara Cassin (Princeton: Princeton University Press, 2014), 201–3.

75. For details, see Hermann Strathmann, s.v. *laos*, in *The Theological Dictionary of the New Testament*, vol. 4, ed. Gerhard Kittel, trans. Geoffrey Bromiley (Grand Rapids, Mich.: Eerdmans, 1967), 30–32.

76. Strathmann, *laos*, 29.

77. Strathmann, *laos*, 32.

78. See Benveniste, *Indo-European Language and Society*, 371.

79. See *The Iliad*, II, 87; *The Iliad, I: Books 1–12*, trans. A. T. Murray; rev. William F. Wyatt (Cambridge, Mass.: Harvard University Press, 1999), 66–67.

80. Benveniste, *Indo-European Language and Society*, 371–72. See also, for a more detailed account, Henri Jeanmaire, *Couroi et Courètes. Essai sur l'éducation spartiate et sur les rites d'adolescence hellénique* (Lille: Bibliothèque Universitaire, 1939), 43–54.

81. See Jeanmaire, *Couroi et Courètes*, 54.

82. Benveniste, *Indo-European Language and Society*, 372 (trans. slightly modified).

83. For the celebrated distinction between the three types of authority—legal, traditional and charismatic—see Max Weber, *Economy and Society, Economy and Society: An Outline of Interpretive Sociology*, ed. Guenther Roth and Claus Wittich (Berkeley: University of California Press, 1978), 1:215–16. For further discussion of charismatic authority, see 1:241–54 and 2:1111–57.

84. Benveniste, *Indo-European Language and Society*, 372. Indicative passages include *The Iliad*, I, 54; 1:16–17; II, 280; 1:82–83 and XI, 189; 1:506–7, in which *laon* is employed as a simple synonym for the army; more often not, however, it appears in conjunction with the specification of a particular people, as in the characteristic expression *laos Achaiōn*, "the people (or army) of the Achaeans." See, for example, *The Iliad*, VI, 223; 1:290–91. In one particularly telling passage, Aeneas is seen to gather other Trojan leaders behind him in preparation for the battle with the Cretans, after whom the *laoi* are presented as marching "as sheep follow after the ram to water from the place of feeding." This is said to cause the "shepherd" to rejoice in his heart. See *The Iliad*, XIII, 489–94; *The Iliad, II: Books 13–24*, trans. A. T. Murray; rev. William F. Wyatt (Cambridge, Mass.: Harvard University Press, 1999), 38–39.

85. See Jeanmaire, *Couroi et Courètes*, 58.

86. For the use of *orchame laōn*, see, among others, *The Iliad*, XVII, 13; 2:228–29; for *koirane laōn*, 7, 234; 1:330–31; for *kosmētore laōn*, 1, 16; 1:12–13.

87. Foucault, *Security, Territory, Population*, 122.

88. Strathmann, *laos*, 30 and 32. Cf., also, Hans Bietenhard, s.v. people, in the *New International Dictionary of the New Testament Theology*, ed. Colin Brown (Exeter, U.K.: Paternoster Press, 1976), 796, who speaks, almost identically, of "a new meaning which brought it new life."

89. Orsolina Montevecchi, "Laos. Linee di una ricerca storico-linguistica," in *Actes du XVe Congrès International de Papyrologie* 4, ed. Jean Bingen and Georges Nachtergael (Brussels: Fondation Égyptologique Reine Élisabeth, 1979), 51–67 (all translations from this are my own).

90. Montevecchi, "Laos," 58. A translation of the decree is available in *The Hellenistic World from Alexander to the Roman Conquest*, ed. M. M. Austin (Cambridge: Cambridge University Press, 2006), 491–96. The relevant sequence

reads: "King Ptolemy the ever-living, beloved of Ptah, God Manifest and Beneficent, born of King Ptolemy and Queen Arsinoe, Father-Loving Gods, has conferred many benefits on the temples and those who dwell in them and on all the subjects in his kingdom . . . and has sustained many expenses to bring Egypt to a state of prosperity and to establish the temples, and has given away freely from his own means, and of the revenues and dues he receives from Egypt some he has completely remitted and others he has reduced, so that the people and all others [*laos kai hoi alloi pantes*] might enjoy prosperity during his reign" (492).

91. Montevecchi, "Laos," 61.

92. See Montevecchi, "Laos," 62.

93. Just to cite examples from the Book of Genesis (cf. LXX 19:4, 26:11, 34:22, 41:40, 41:55 and 47:21, respectively), but many further examples could be furnished from the Pentateuch alone. See Montevecchi, "Laos," 63–64.

94. It is interesting to note that the oldest recorded appearances of the expression *'am YHWH* in the Hebrew Bible, Judg. 5:11 and 13, have a distinctly military connotation, thus mirroring that which we have seen characterizes the epic use of *laos*. See Bietenhard, s.v. people, 796.

95. Montevecchi, "Laos," 64.

96. *Lexicographia sacra* was the title of two lectures given by Gerhard Kittel, the editor of the *Theologisches Wörterbuch zum Neuen Testament*, at the University of Cambridge on October 20 and 21, 1937. An eminent specialist in Rabbinic Judaism, in 1946 Kittel was ordered to stand trial before the International War Crimes Tribunal in Nuremberg for crimes against the Jewish people.

97. LXX Deut. 7:6; translation in *La Bible d'Alexandrie, 5: Le Deutéronome*, trans. Cécile Doguiez and Marguerite Harl (Paris: Cerf, 1992), 161 (my translation from the French). It is important to note that here, as at Ex. 19:5, *laos periousias* translates the Hebrew *segullah*, which simply designates a precious possession, a treasure. There is thus no corresponding reference to the people in the Hebrew original. On this, see the translators' notes in *La Bible d'Alexandrie, 2: L'Exode*, trans. Alain Le Boulluec and Pierre Sandevoir (Paris: Cerf, 1989), 199–200. Montevecchi ("Laos," 64) also underscores this point.

98. LXX Lev. 19:2; translation in *La Bible d'Alexandrie, 3: Le Lévitique*, trans. Paul Harle and Didier Prator (Paris: Cerf, 1988), 164 (my translation from the French). Cf., also, Lev. 11:44–45, 20:7, 20:26; Nu. 15:4; Dt. 28:9.

99. LXX Ex. 33:12–13; translation in *La Bible d'Alexandrie, 2: L'Exode*, 332–33 (my translation from the French).

100. Montevecchi, "Laos," 65.

101. LXX Ex. 15:13; 174. This is one of the very passages that Foucault cites from the Hebrew Bible as evidence of the exercise of Yahweh's pastoral power with respect to his people. Even if it is not strictly the case that the Greek *kataluma*

preserves the sense of "pasture" present in the Hebrew *naweh*, the sense remains the same. See Foucault, *Security, Territory, Population*, 126.

102. Cf., for one example among many, Lk. 7:24. It is curious to note that of the 141 appearances of the term in the New Testament, 84 of them are to be found either in Luke's Gospel or in Acts. As Strathmann has observed: "One may thus conclude that it is a favorite word of Luke's." Strikingly, aside from one exception [Mk. 14:2 = Mt. 26:5 = Lk. 22:2], there are no *laos* passages common to the three gospels. In the fourth gospel, on the other hand, it barely figures at all. See Strathmann, *laos*, 50. In the Pauline Letters, by remarkable contrast, it only ever appears in direct citations from the Septuagint.

103. For an example of the former, cf. Lk. 2:32; for one of the latter, Acts 21:28.

104. Acts 15:14–17 (trans. slightly modified); cf. Amos 9:11–12.

105. 1 Pet. 2:9; cf., also, Tt. 2:14, which employs the exact expression *laon periousian*.

106. Rom. 9:25; cf. Hos. 2:23. For an example of this interpretation, see Strathmann, *laos*, 54.

107. Hebrews stops short of speaking of a "new" people of God, but it does speak, citing Jer. 31:31, of a "new covenant" (*diathēken kainēn*), which has made the first "grow old." Cf. Heb. 8:8–13. For the references to the Christian community as the "people of God," cf. Heb. 4:9 and, above all, 1 Pet. 2:10: "Once you were not a people [*ou laon*], but now you are God's people [*laos theou*]," which appears as a variation on Rom. 9:25.

108. See above, 75–78.

109. This development has been duly noted by Balibar, *demos/ethnos/laos*, 203: "If according to the general perspective, *laos* is the totality of the Christian people forming the church (*ekklēsia*, taken from the name of the 'assembly of the citizens' in the Greek political terminology), it is also more precisely the 'simple faithful' as opposed to the *klēros* (or the priests, who are the theological equivalent of magistrates)." It is this "important twist," which we shall theorize in what follows, that, as Balibar is doubtless well aware, will give rise to the specifically French notion of *laïcité*.

110. See Foucault, *Security, Territory, Population*, 202.

111. It is telling that Foucault's two brief yet crucial references to the clergy/laity "dimorphism" appear within the context of his account of the emergence of what he terms "counter-conducts"—but which have been more soberly termed "religious movements"—in the later Middle Ages (the most well known and successful of which is obviously the Protestant Reformation), but is only liminally present in his highly suggestive but ultimately unconvincing portrait of the Christian pastorate itself. Unconvincing to the extent that it largely abandons the question of its "institutionalization," choosing instead to focus on the far less significant development of individual techniques of

"spiritual direction" and the practices of unconditioned obedience that invariably accompanied them. As we will attempt to show in the pages that follow, the specificity of the Christian pastorate and its larger significance for the genealogy of governmentality hinges, above all, on the particular concept to which its institutionalization gives reality: the concept of hierarchy. For Foucault's account of the Christian pastorate, see the lecture of February 22 in *Security, Territory, Population*, 163–85. On the emergence of "religious movements," see the monograph of Herbert Grundmann, *Religious Movements in the Middle Ages: The Historical Links between Heresy, the Mendicant Orders, and the Women's Religious Movement in the Twelfth and Thirteenth Centuries, with the Historical Foundations of German Mysticism*, trans. Steven Rowan (Notre Dame, Ind.: University of Notre Dame Press, 1995).

112. It is important to note that what Foucault calls the "institutionalization of the pastorate" coincides with what Weber calls the "objectification of charisma": they name the very same phenomenon. See Weber, *Economy and Society*, 2:1135–41.

113. Foucault, *Security, Territory, Population*, 192.

114. LXX Deut. 32:8–9; 325–27 (trans. slightly modified).

115. See, above all, Origen, *Contra Celsum*, 5, 29–30; 286–87. In almost analogous terms, but with decidedly different emphasis, the fourth-century Roman nobleman Quintus Aurelius Symmachus will speak, in passionate defense of the diversity of religious customs and in supplication of the appropriate funding for public religion, of the various "guardians" (*custodes*) assigned by the divine mind to each of the different cities of the empire. Just as each man receives, at birth, a separate soul, so, in the same way, according to Symmachus, each people receives its own special "genius" to guide its destiny (*populi fatales genii dividuntur*). See Symmachus, *Relationes*, 3, 8; text and translation in *Prefect and Emperor: The Relations of Symmachus, AD 384*, ed. and trans. R. H. Barrow (Oxford: Clarendon Press, 1973), 38–39.

116. See Erik Peterson, "Das Problem des Nationalismus im alten Christentum," *Theologisches Zeitschrift 7*, no. 2 (1951): 81–91.

117. Erik Peterson, "Das Problem des Nationalismus im alten Christentum," 90. Of course, as Peterson duly records, there is a third option, for which Origen's disciple, Eusebius of Caesarea, is the spokesperson. For him, the national unification accomplished by the Roman Empire under Constantine would represent the eruption of the messianic kingdom on earth. Needless to say, it is precisely then, according to Peterson, that monotheism becomes a "political problem."

118. Cf. Peterson, "Book on the Angels," 125–26 and 138. On the doctrine of the angels of the nations more generally, see Jean Daniélou, "Les sources juives de la doctrine des anges des nations chez Origène," *Recherches de science religieuse 38* (1951): 132–37, and, especially, *Origen*, trans. Walter Mitchell (New York: Sheer and Ward, 1955), 224–37.

119. See 1 Clement 44, 3; 54, 2; 57, 2; *The Apostolic Fathers, I*, ed. and trans. Bart D. Ehrman (Cambridge, Mass.: Harvard University Press, 2003), 114–15, 130–31, and 136–37.

120. See 1 Clement 40, 5; 106–7.

121. See 1 Clement 1, 1–2; 34–37.

122. See 1 Clement 3, 1; 38–39. Cf. Deut. 32:15.

123. 1 Clement 3, 3; 38–41.

124. 1 Clement 29, 1–2; 86–87.

125. 1 Clement 30, 3; 88–89.

126. 1 Clement 33, 1; 92–93.

127. 1 Clement 34, 5, 94–95.

128. 1 Clement 34, 6–7; 94–97.

129. The theme, if not quite yet the term itself, which, as we shall see, would have to wait until the late fifth or even early sixth century for its first appearance in the writings of Pseudo-Dionysius the Areopagite. The designation of Christ as a "high priest" (*archiereus*)—in accordance with, yet also in distinction from, the gradation characteristic of the Levitical priesthood—in the Letter to the Hebrews nonetheless plays a decisive role in Clement's argumentative strategy. See, especially, 1 Clement 36, 1; 98–99.

130. 1 Clement 37, 3; 100–101.

131. 1 Clement 37, 4; 102–3.

132. 1 Clement 37, 5; 102–3.

133. 1 Clement 46, 6–7; 118–19.

134. 1 Clement 40, 1–5; 106–7.

135. 1 Clement 41, 1; 108–9.

136. See below, 148n4.

137. See 1 Clement 42–44; 108–15.

138. Cf. Gal. 3:29.

139. 1 Pet. 2:9. Cf. Ex. 19:6.

140. 1 Pet. 5:3.

141. Cf., especially, Heb. 7:11–22.

142. 1 Clement 44, 2–3; 112–15 (trans. slightly modified).

143. See Sigmund Freud, "The Antithetical Meaning of Primal Words," trans. Alan Tyson, in *The Standard Edition of the Complete Psychological Works of Sigmund Freud, Vol. XI (1910): Five Lectures on Psycho-Analysis, Leonardo Da Vinci and Other Works*, ed. James Strachey (London: The Hogarth Press, 1957), 155–161. For commentary, see Émile Benveniste, "Remarks on the Function of Language in the Freudian Discovery," in *Problems in General Linguistics*, trans. Mark Elizabeth Meek (Coral Gables: University of Miami Press, 1971), 75–87.

144. See Ignace de La Potterie, "The Origin and Basic Meaning of the Word 'Lay,'" in La Potterie and Stanislaus Lyonnet, *The Christian Lives by the Spirit*, trans. John Morriss (Staten Island, N.Y.: Alba House, 1971), 267–84.

145. See La Potterie, "The Origin and Basic Meaning of the Word 'Lay,'" 268–69.

146. La Potterie, "The Origin and Basic Meaning of the Word 'Lay,'" 272.

147. See La Potterie, "The Origin and Basic Meaning of the Word 'Lay,'" 272.

148. La Potterie, "The Origin and Basic Meaning of the Word 'Lay,'" 272. Cf. LXX Ex. 19:24; 204.

149. See La Potterie, "The Origin and Basic Meaning of the Word 'Lay,'" 273–76.

150. See La Potterie, "The Origin and Basic Meaning of the Word 'Lay,'" 279.

151. For details, including the above quote, see Christine Mohrmann, "Les origines de la latinité chrétienne," in *Études sur la latin des chrétiens, III: Latin chrétien et liturgique* (Roma: Edizioni di Storia e Letteratura, 1965), 78–82.

152. See La Potterie, "The Origin and Basic Meaning of the Word 'Lay,'" 279.

153. It suffices to recall the following definition from the more or less contemporary *Institutiones* of Gaius, 1, 3: "Plebeians and people differ in that the people is the whole citizen body, including the patricians; but the plebeians are the citizens without the patricians [*plebs autem a populo eo distat, quod populi apellatione universi cives significantur, connumeratis etiam patriciis; plebis autem apellatione sine patriciis ceteri cives significantur*]"; Gaius, *The Institutes of Gaius*, ed. and trans. W. M. Gordon and D. F. Robinson (London: Duckworth, 1988), 20–21.

154. La Potterie, "The Origin and Basic Meaning of the Word 'Lay,'" 283.

155. See the remarkable conclusion to his essay (La Potterie, "The Origin and Basic Meaning of the Word 'Lay,'" 284), in which he appears clearly to retreat from the implications of his own thesis. Noting that it is important to distinguish carefully between the study of terminology and that of theology, he continues: "Everything we have said so far may give the impression that the role of lay people was conceived in a very negative way. This is not so. The complete meaning of a function in the Church cannot be drawn from an analysis of the term that designates it. . . . *Theologically speaking, it remains entirely true that lay people are members of the people of God*. We have simply wished to show that this teaching is not part of the formal meaning of the word 'lay'" (emphasis mine).

156. If Balibar has rightly stressed the "eschatological" character of the first signification—whose secularized form he sees determining the modern conception of emphatic nationhood (see Balibar, *demos/ethnos/laos*, 202–3)—our analysis has instead sought to emphasise the "economic" character of the second signification. On the tension between the "eschatological" and "economic" orientations of the Church—a tension that, extending Balibar, we could suggest is transferred in its totality to the modern nation qua *laos*—see Giorgio Agamben, *Il mistero del male: Benedetto XVI e la fine dei tempi* (Bari: Laterza, 2013), 17.

157. See Giorgio Agamben, "What Is a People?" in *Means without End: Notes on Politics*, trans. Vincenzo Binetti and Cesare Casarino (Minneapolis: University of Minnesota Press, 2000), 29–35. See also the pertinent remarks of Reinhart Koselleck in "Volk, Nation, Nationalismus, Masse," in *Geschichtliche Grundbegriffe:*

Historisches Lexikon zur politisch-sozialen Sprache in Deutschland, VII, edited by Otto Brunner, Werner Conze, and Reinhart Koselleck (Stuttgart: Klett-Cotta, 1992), 145, which possibly served as the point of departure for Agamben's reflections. For Koselleck—who expressly frames this distinction in terms of the opposition between ruler and ruled—the division that separates the "multitude" from the "citizens" is perfectly continuous with that which separates the "congregation" (*das Kirchenvolk*) from the "Church's ministers" (*die kirchlichen Amtsträger*).

3. THE PRACTICE OF HIERARCHY

1. Thomas Aquinas, *Summa theologiae*, 1, q. 108, a. 1; *Summa theologiae, Volume 14: Divine Government (1a2ae. 103–9)*, trans. T. C. O'Brien (London: Blackfriars, 1975), 122.

2. See above, Chapter 1, Section 7.

3. Thomas Aquinas, *Summa theologiae*, 1, q. 108, a.1, resp.; 122–23 (trans. modified). Following a grammatical ambiguity that has profoundly marked the vocabulary of order since its very inception, it is not always possible to distinguish the use of the substantive from that of the imperative. As René Roques has effectively shown, the "order-arrangement" is always also, and at the same time, an "order-commandment" (and vice-versa). See René Roques, *L'Univers Dionysien: Structure hiérarchique du monde selon Pseudo-Denys* (Paris: Aubier, 1954), 36–39.

4. Cf. Acts 17:34.

5. Ronald H. Hathaway, *Hierarchy and the Definition of Order in the "Letters" of Pseudo-Dionysius: A Study in the Form and Meaning of the Pseudo-Dionysian Writings* (The Hague: Martinus Nijhoff, 1969), xxi.

6. The most emphatic statement of this identity, and of this difference, comes again from Hathaway: "The metaphysics of Pseudo-Dionysius is, in one sense, equivalent in all its parts to the metaphysics of Neoplatonism after Proclus. In another sense, it is that same metaphysics as it affects and is affected by the idea of hierarchy." See Hathaway, *Hierarchy and the Definition of Order in the "Letters" of Pseudo-Dionysius*, 37. For details, see Roques, *L'univers dionysien*, 68–81. It was this very dependence that would ultimately precipitate the belated unmasking of the author's fictitious identity by Lorenzo Valla in the fifteenth century. To this day, however, and despite much speculation, the author's actual identity remains completely unknown.

7. PG 4, 29; translation in Paul Rorem and John C. Lamoreaux, *John of Scythopolis and the Dionysian Corpus* (Oxford: Claredon Press, 1998), 149 (trans. slightly modified).

8. Pseudo-Dionysius, *De coelesti hierarchia*, 2, 5; Denys L'Aréopagite, *La hiérarchie céleste*, trans. Maurice de Gandillac (Paris: Cerf, 1970), 87–88 (all translations of this text are my own).

9. Pseudo-Dionysius, *De coelesti hierarchia*, 3, 1; 87.

10. See Proclus, *The Elements of Theology*, ed. and trans. E. R. Dodds (Oxford: Clarendon Press, 1971), 38–39: "Every effect remains [*menei*] in its cause, proceeds [*proeisin*] from it, and reverts [*epistrephei*] to it."

11. Pseudo-Dionysius, *De coelesti hierarchia*, 3, 2; 87–88. Cf. Proclus, *Elements of Theology*, 36–37: "All reversion is accomplished through the likeness [*homoiotētos*] of the reverting terms to the goal of reversion." The apparently unlikely significance of this notion of assimilation to God, that is, of divinization—a notion that the Neoplatonists themselves traced back a well-known sequence of the *Theaetetus* ("We ought," Socrates suggests, "to try to escape from earth to the dwelling of the gods as quickly as we can; and to escape is to become like God, so far as this is possible [*homoiōsis theō kata to dynaton*]")—for a specifically Neoplatonic "political philosophy" has been recently considered by Dominic J. O'Meara in *Platonopolis: Platonic Political Philosophy in Late Antiquity* (Oxford: Clarendon Press, 2003). Not unsurprisingly, an important place in O'Meara's reflection (159–71) is reserved for what he terms the "Neoplatonic ecclesiology" of Pseudo-Dionysius—Pseudo-Dionysius being the first author to furnish a definition for this important and pervasive philosophical concept: "Divinization [*theosis*]," he writes, "is the assimilation [*aphomoiōsis*] and unification [*henōsis*], as far as is possible, to God." See Pseudo-Dionysius, *De ecclesiastica hierarchia*, 1, 3; 376. For Plato, see *Theaetetus*, 176b; *Theaetetus; Sophist*, trans. Harold North Fowler (London: William Heinemann, 1967), 128–29. Our suggestion here will be somewhat different with respect to O'Meara's: divinization, not so much as the acquisition of "political virtue," but as a technique of "governance."

12. Pseudo-Dionysius, *De coelesti hierarchia*, 3, 2; 88.

13. Pseudo-Dionysius, *De coelesti hierarchia*, 3, 2; 89–90.

14. Pseudo-Dionysius, *De ecclesiastica hierarchia*, 1, 4, in *PG* 3, 376.

15. Pseudo-Dionysius, *De ecclesiastica hierarchia*, 1, 3; 376.

16. Emanuele Coccia, introduction to *Angeli: Ebraismo Cristianesimo Islam*, ed. Giorgio Agamben and Emanuele Coccia (Vicenza: Neri Pozza, 2009), 476.

17. Pseudo-Dionysius, *De coelesti hierarchia*, 3, 2; 90.

18. Pseudo-Dionysius, *De coelesti hierarchia*, 3, 3; 92.

19. It is significant that René Roques should preface his inquiry into "the hierarchical structure of the world according to Pseudo-Dionysius" with the following remark: "To employ a terminology that is perhaps not entirely adequate, the present study sought to retain the *oikonomia* of Pseudo-Dionysius, rather than his *theologia*, at its center." See Roques, *L'univers dionysien*, 29–30. Although the term *oikonomia* appears nowhere in the Dionysian corpus, Ysabel de Andia has advanced the curious suggestion that its place is expressly taken up by another at first glance distant term: *philanthropia*. The "divinization of the saved" is thus effectuated through the activity of divine *philanthropia*. See Ysabel de Andia, *Henosis: L'Union*

à *Dieu chez Denys l'Aréopagite* (Leiden: Brill, 1996), 288–92. On the uneasy finitude of the theological economy—whose negotiation in the Christian tradition coincides with the explication of 1 Cor. 15: 24: "Then comes the end, when [Christ] hands the kingdom over to God the Father, after he has evacuated [*katargēsē*] every ruler and every authority and power"—see Giorgio Agamben, *The Kingdom and the Glory: For a Theological Genealogy of Economy and Government*, trans. Lorenzo Chiesa and Matteo Mandarini (Stanford, Calif.: Stanford University Press, 2011), 159–164.

20. Gregory the Great, *Homiliae in Evangelium* 34, 8; *Forty Gospel Homilies*, trans. David Hurst (Kalamazoo, Mich.: Cistercian Publications, 1990), 286.

21. Gregory the Great, *Homiliae in Evangelium* 34, 8; 287.

22. See Gregory the Great, *Homiliae in Evangelium* 34, 8–9; 287. In the celestial city, by contrast, in which they are "citizens," they have no need for names.

23. See Coccia, *Angeli*, esp. 455–78.

24. This is the ultimate sense of the celebrated Thomistic dictum according to which God is that being whose essence is his existence.

25. Coccia, *Angeli*, 457.

26. Again, following the genial formulation of Coccia, *Angeli*, 473: "Hierarchy, then, would be that form of power that one possesses only to the extent that one is capable of receiving it from others and transmitting it to others."

27. According to Gregory the Great, who is here glossing Pseudo-Dionysius, the higher bands of angels never actually withdraw from God. "Those which are pre-eminent," he observes, "never have any external function [*exterioris ministerii nequaquam habent*]." Once again, it is only those angels that receive names that are indicative of such that are sent to minister to us: "The lesser ranks are sent, the greater ones do the sending." Hierarchy of function thus clearly characterizes the celestial hierarchy as well. See Gregory the Great, *Homiliae in Evangelium* 34, 12–13; 292–93.

28. Far from being emblematic of an exquisite moral superiority as they are so often represented, supplemented by a glorious halo, in the religious iconography of the Middle Ages, angels are thus, at best, morally ambiguous, and at worst, morally repugnant. Whether they are interceding on behalf of their maker to provide spiritual direction to expectant pilgrims or to mete out acts of gruesome punishment to unrepentant sinners, they carry out their duties with equal vigor and in a state of almost studied indifference. Even worse than that, they form, together with God, a two-tiered model for the operation of power—a model whose application would, of course, extend well beyond the strictly celestial sphere—in which an unparalleled efficiency coincides, not unsurprisingly, with the complete abdication of any form of moral or ethical responsibility. As one of the greatest novelists of the twentieth century would have his "man *with* qualities" presciently observe, such arrangements—which one finds "everywhere these days"—allow for the almost

automatic functioning of power: "Wherever you find two such forces, a person who really gives the orders and an administrative body that executes them, what automatically happens is that every possible means . . . is used, whether or not it is aesthetically or morally attractive. When I say automatically I mean just that, because the way in which it works is to a high degree independent of any personal factor. The person who really wields the power takes no hand in carrying out his directives, while the managers are covered by the fact that they are acting not on their own behalf but as functionaries." See Robert Musil, *The Man without Qualities*, trans. Sophie Wilkins (New York: Vintage International, 1995), 1:696.

29. Coccia, *Angeli*, 465.

30. Cf. Gen. 2:2–3.

31. According to a fascinating chapter in the history of medieval philosophy, the "intermediary" character of angels necessitated the addition of two further categories to the prevailing Aristotelian definition of time. Not only was a distinct "measure" required for angelic being (what the Scholastics denominated *aevum*, after the Greek *aiōn*), but one was required for angelic operations as well. This they termed *tempus discretum* or, alternatively, simply *tempus angelorum*. While the former sought to account for a form of nonsuccessive duration distinct from divine *aeternitas* (in other words, for the idea of a "created eternity"), the latter—which is of particular interest here—was instead employed to refer to the notion of a noncontinuous succession independent of physical extension. The angels, it was argued, especially in their dealings with humans (in their "external function," to evoke the terminology of Gregory the Great), certainly must be said to move from one place to another; but, being incorporeal, they need not necessarily traverse the intervening space between them in order to do so. To avoid positing a single angel in two distinct places at one and the same time, and thereby threatening the principle of noncontradiction, however, it would be necessary to suppose a particular "measure" which would account for such a noncontinuous succession: that which would proceed by discrete instants. On this, see Pasquale Porro, "Angelic Measures: *Aevum* and Discrete Time," in *The Medieval Concept of Time: Studies on the Scholastic Debate and its Reception in Early Modern Philosophy*, ed. Pasquale Porro (Leiden: Brill, 2001), 131–59.

32. *Leitourgika pneumata* is, of course, the singular definition of the angels advanced in the Letter to the Hebrews. Cf. Heb. 1:14: "Are not all angels," we read, "spirits in the divine service [*leitourgika pneumata*], sent to serve for the sake of those who are to inherit salvation?"

33. See Philo, *De somnis*, 1, 135–42; 5:369–73. On this passage, see Harry Austryn Wolfson, *Philo* (Cambridge, Mass.: Harvard University Press, 1947), 1:375–76

34. Plato, *Symposium*, 203a; *Lysis; Symposium; Gorgias*, trans. W. R. M. Lamb (London: William Heinemann, 1925), 179.

35. Plutarch, *Moralia*, 416d; *Plutarch's* Moralia, trans. Frank Cole Babbitt (London: William Heinemann, 1936), 5:387 (trans. slightly modified).

36. Plutarch, *Moralia*, 416e-f; 5:389–91.

37. Plutarch, *Moralia*, 417a; 5:389.

38. Thomas Aquinas, *Summa contra gentiles*, lib. 3, cap. 77, n. 1; *Summa Contra Gentiles, Book Three: Providence*, trans. Vernon J. Bourke (Notre Dame, Ind.: University of Notre Dame Press, 1975), 258–59.

39. Thomas Aquinas, *Summa contra gentiles*, lib. 3, cap. 77, n. 3; 259 (trans. modified).

40. Régis Debray has rightly observed that Christian angelology constitutes a "proto-mediology." See Régis Debray, *Transmitting Culture*, trans. Eric Rauth (New York: Columbia University Press, 2000), 31–44.

41. Thomas Aquinas, *Summa contra gentiles*, lib. 3, cap. 77, n. 6; 3:260.

42. Thomas Aquinas, *Summa contra gentiles*, lib. 3, cap. 78., n. 2; 261. As we shall see in the next chapter, the seemingly paradoxical notion of an "instrumental cause" (*causa instrumentalis*), which begins to find expression here, will assume increasingly importance in the development of Aquinas's thought.

43. Thomas Aquinas, *Summa theologiae*, 1, q. 103, a. 6, resp.; 27.

44. It is important to note that q. 103 is broadly devoted to the reconciliation of the monarchical principle of Aristotle's "theology" with that form of divine activity that Aquinas here calls *gubernatio*. See, for example, *Summa theologiae*, 1, q. 103, a. 3, resp; 16–17, which concludes with the same Homeric citation that forms the point of departure for Peterson's treatise on monotheism.

45. See Thomas Aquinas, *Summa theologiae*, 1, q. 103, a. 6, resp.; 27.

46. Thomas Aquinas, *Summa theologiae*, 1, q. 103, q. 4, resp; 18–19.

47. See Agamben, *The Kingdom and the Glory*, 159–259.

48. Thomas Aquinas, *Summa theologiae*, 1, q. 103, a. 6, ad. 3; 27 (trans. modified).

49. Thomas Aquinas, *Summa contra Gentiles*, lib. 3, cap. 77, n. 4; 259.

50. I employ the term "noneconomic" in the sense that Max Weber uses it in his account of charismatic authority: "Charismatic authority is basically an extraordinary [*außertägliche*] and hence necessarily non-economic [*außerwirtschaftliche*] power, and its vitality is immediately endangered when everyday economic interests become predominant, as it threatens to happen everywhere." Max Weber, *Economy and Society: An Outline of Interpretive Sociology*, ed. Guenther Roth and Claus Wittich, trans. Ephraim Fischoff, et al (Berkeley: University of California Press, 1978), 2: 1120. Significantly, however, in our exposition the "economic" and the "noneconomic" are no longer opposed to one another, as they are in the Weberian account, but continuous—albeit in a very particular sense.

51. It was Carl Schmitt who was responsible for introducing the Pauline figure of the *katechon* into political theory. See Carl Schmitt, *The Nomos of the Earth in the International Law of the* Jus Publicum Europaeum, trans. G. L. Ulmen (New York: Telos Press, 2006), 59–62. It is important to note, however, that Schmitt's treatment of the enigmatic entity or person that the Second Letter to the Thessalonians

presents as restraining the "mystery of lawlessness" (but also thereby of forestalling the second coming of Christ and the advent of the Kingdom of God) was preceded, by more than two decades, by a discussion to be found in Peterson's important essay on "The Church." See Erik Peterson, "The Church," in *Theological Tractates*, trans. Michael J. Hollerich (Stanford, Calif.: Stanford University Press, 2011), 32–33. And while Schmitt sought to renew an antique tradition that extends as far back as Tertullian and Lactantius by identifying the *katechon* with the empire, Peterson, by contrast, engages another tradition with a competing claim to patristic authority that identifies it instead with the Church. On these two interpretations, see Augustine, *De civitate Dei* 20, 19; *Concerning the City of God against the Pagans*, trans. Henry Bettenson (London: Penguin, 2003), 931–35. For Peterson, as we have seen, it is the suspension of the concrete eschatological that founds the historical existence of the Church; it follows that its continued existence is premised on the non-imminence of the Kingdom, with which it nonetheless communicates— precisely through its liturgy. Already for Peterson, liturgy is thus the vehicle in which a "katechontic" function is identified with the Church.

52. Karl Marx, *Critique of Hegel's 'Philosophy of Right,'* trans. Annette Jolin and Joseph O'Malley (Cambridge: Cambridge University Press), 45.

53. Marx, *Critique of Hegel's 'Philosophy of Right,'* 46.

54. Marx, *Critique of Hegel's 'Philosophy of Right,'* 46.

55. Marx, *Critique of Hegel's 'Philosophy of Right,'* 47 (trans. slightly modified).

56. Marx, *Critique of Hegel's 'Philosophy of Right,'* 47.

57. See Marx, *Critique of Hegel's 'Philosophy of Right,'* 50.

58. Marx, *Critique of Hegel's 'Philosophy of Right,'* 49.

59. See Marx, *Critique of Hegel's 'Philosophy of Right,'* 51.

60. Marx, *Critique of Hegel's 'Philosophy of Right,'* 50 (trans. slightly modified).

61. Cf. Karl Marx, "A Contribution to the Critique of Hegel's 'Philosophy of Right': Introduction," in *Critique of Hegel's 'Philosophy of Right'*, 141.

4. Instrumental Cause

1. Thomas Aquinas, *Summa theologiae*, 1, q. 112, a. 1, resp.; *Summa theologiae, Volume 15: The World Order (1a. 110–19)*, trans. M. J. Charlesworth (London: Black-friars, 1970), 34–35.

2. Thomas Aquinas, *Summa theologiae*, 3, q. 64, a. 8, resp.; *Summa theologiae, Volume 56: The Sacraments (3a. 60–5)*, trans. David Bourke (London: Blackfriars, 1974), 126–27.

3. Thomas Aquinas, *Summa theologiae*, 3, q. 64, a. 8, ad. 2; 126–27 (trans. slightly modified).

4. Thomas Aquinas, *Summa theologiae*, 3, q. 64, a. 10, resp.; 134–35. Curiously enough, there is one instance, according to Aquinas, in which the intention is

sufficient to vitiate the sacramental efficacy: when the minister intends to joke or mime (*intentio ludicra vel jocosa*). From the perspective of sacramental theology, a jocular intention is thus more grievous than a perverse one. See *Summa theologiae*, 3, q. 64, a. 10, ad. 2; 134–35.

5. Thomas Aquinas, *Summa theologiae*, 3, q. 64, a. 10, ad. 3; 134–37.

6. On this notion, see above all the important 1937 study of Jakobson, "Signe zéro," in *Selected Writings*, II, (The Hague: Mouton, 1971), 211–19. For a brief history of its transposition from the relatively restricted sphere of structural linguistics to its much broader application across the whole breadth of the human sciences, see Giorgio Agamben, *The Time That Remains: A Commentary on the Letter to the Romans*, trans. Patricia Dailey (Stanford, Calif.: Stanford University Press, 2005), 101–4.

7. In this sense, Ivan Illich's striking definition of the *causa instrumentalis* as a "cause without intention" can be only partially correct. Illich nonetheless remains one of the only modern thinkers to have insisted on the significance of this important development in the theory of causation, with which we shall soon be concerned, whose emergence he locates in the twelfth century and which for him coincides with the invention of technology as such. See Ivan Illich and David Cayley, *The Rivers North of the Future: The Testament of Ivan Illich* (Toronto: House of Anasi Press, 2005), 71–79.

8. Thomas Aquinas, *Summa theologiae*, 3, q. 64, a. 1, ad. 2; 104–5 (trans. slightly modified).

9. See Giorgio Agamben, *Opus Dei: An Archaeology of Duty*, trans. Adam Kotsko, 21–22. For the definition, see *Summa theologiae*, 3, q. 64, a. 8, ad. 1; 126–27.

10. Aristotle, *Physics*, 194b25–194a3; *CW* 1:332–33. Cf. Aristotle, *Metaphysics*, 1013a25–1013b4; *CW* 2:1600.

11. See Thomas Aquinas, *Summa theologiae*, 3, q. 62, a. 1, resp; 52–53.

12. Thomas Aquinas, *Summa theologiae*, 3, q. 62, a.1, ad. 1; 54–55.

13. Agamben, *Opus Dei*, 53 (trans. slightly modified).

14. See Thomas Aquinas, *Summa theologiae*, 3, q. 62, a.1, ad. 1; 54–55.

15. J. L. Austin, *How to Do Things with Words*, ed. J. O. Urmson (Oxford: Clarendon Press, 1962). For a vastly amplified sense of this category with respect that outlined by Austin himself, see also the important book of Oswald Ducrot, *Dire et ne pas dire: Principes de sémantique linguistique*, 2nd ed. (Paris: Hermann, 1991).

16. Augustine, *De doctrina christiana*, 2, 1, 1; *De Doctrina Christiana*, ed. and trans. R. P. H. Green (Oxford: Clarendon Press, 1995), 56–57.

17. Augustine, *De civitate Dei*, 10, 5; *Concerning the City of God against the Pagans*, trans. Henry Bettenson (London: Penguin, 2003), 377.

18. Augustine, *Sermo 272*, 2; *The Works of Saint Augustine, III:7: Sermons (230–272a)*, trans. Edmund Hill (New York: New City Press, 1993), 300 (trans. slightly modified).

19. *Summa sententiarum*, 4, 1; *PL* 176, 117b.

20. See, among others, M.-D. Chenu, *La théologie au douzième siècle* (Paris: Vrin, 1976), 309–10, who asserts that Peter is responsible for introducing the term *causa* not only to sacramental theology, but also—through this—to theology *tout court*.

21. Peter Lombard, *IV Sententiarum* 1, 2; Peter Lombard, *The Sentences*, trans. Giulio Silano (Toronto: Pontifical Institute of Medieval Studies, 2010), 4:4.

22. See Peter Lombard, *IV Sententiarum* 4, 1; 4:18.

23. See Thomas Aquinas, *Summa theologiae*, 3, q. 62, a.1, ad. 1; 54–55.

24. See Thomas Aquinas, *Summa theologiae*, 3, q. 64, a.8, ad. 1; 126–27.

25. See Thomas Aquinas, *Commentaria in octo libros Physicorum*, lib. 2, lect. 5, n. 5: *Commentary on Aristotle's "Physics,"* trans. Richard J. Blackwell, Richard J. Spath and W. Edmund Thirlkel (London: Routledge and Kegan Paul, 1963), 88; and *Sententia libri Metaphysicae*, lib. 5, lect. 2, n. 4–7; *Commentary of Aristotle's "Metaphysics,"* trans. John P. Rowan (Notre Dame, Ind.: Dumb Ox Books, 1995), 283. I have principally followed the latter, which is far richer in terms of detail.

26. See H.-F. Dondaine, "A propos d'Avicenne et de Saint Thomas: de la causalité dispositive à la causalité instrumentale," *Revue Thomiste* 51 (1951), 441–43 (all translations of this text are my own).

27. Dondaine, "A propos d'Avicenne et de Saint Thomas," 441.

28. It is highly likely that the addition of the instrumental cause (*aitiōn organikon*) appeared for the first time, together with the paradigmatic cause (*aitiōn paradeigmatikon*), within the ambit of Neoplatonism. See, for example, Proclus, *Commentaire sur le Timée*, trans. A. J. Festugière (Paris: Vrin, 1967), 2:104: "The causes of the world are counted as follows: final cause, paradigmatic cause, efficient cause, instrumental cause, formal cause, material cause." That it should appear together with the paradigmatic cause ought to come as no surprise. For one of the effects of the introduction of the paradigmatic cause is the concurrent introduction of a hierarchy into the theory of causes. Following Plato's own distinction (cf. *Timaeus*, 46d), the instrumental, the formal, and the material are thus designated as merely "accessory causes" (*synaitiōn*), in contrast with the causes *tout court*: the final, the paradigmatic and the efficient. As Proclus himself continues: "[Plato] will see the instrumental, the material and formal causes as a *consequence* of the fundamental principles set forth initially" (emphasis mine). As we shall see, however, the "authentic" origin of this concept may be said to have had only an indirect influence over the formation of its scholastic counterpart.

29. See Aristotle, *Physics*, 194b35–195a3; *CW* 1:333; *Metaphysics*, 1013b1–4; *CW* 2:1600.

30. Indeed, given the importance that the instrument qua instrument plays in the elaboration of Aquinas's theory, it might perhaps be more accurate to speak of a shift from an instrumental dispositive causality to a dispositive instrumental

causality. See here the important gloss on the instrumental cause to be found much earlier sequence of the *Summa*: "A secondary instrumental cause does not enter into a superior cause's action unless because of something proper to itself it acts dispositively to the effect of the principal agent [*nisi inquantum per aliquid proprium dispositive operetur ad effectum principalis agentis*]." Thomas Aquinas, *Summa theologiae*, 1, q. 45, a. 5, resp.; *Summa theologiae, Volume 8: Creation, Variety and Evil (1a. 44–49)*, trans. Thomas Gilby (London: Blackfriars, 1967), 44–5.

31. See, for example, Thomas Aquinas, *Summa theologiae*, 3, q. 63, a.2, resp.; 82–83.

32. See Aristotle, *Politics*, 1253b2–11; *CW* 2:1988.

33. See Aristotle, *Politics*, 1255b21–22; *CW* 2:1992. Cf. Plato, *Statesman*, 260b-c, 14–17.

34. See Aristotle, *Politics*, 1253b24–33; *CW* 2:1989. In accordance with the semantic sphere to which the Latin term *minister* indubitably belongs, the phrase *instrumentum animatum* itself, which we have seen Aquinas applies to the minister, thus directly translates Aristotle's *organon empsychon*, which refers directly to the slave.

35. Aristotle, *Politics*, 1253b33; *CW* 2:1989.

36. Aristotle, *Politics*, 1254a8; *CW* 2:1989 (trans. modified).

37. Aristotle, *Politics*, 1254a15–16; *CW* 2:1989 (trans. modified).

38. See Aristotle, *Politics*, 1254a9–14; *CW* 2:1989.

39. Aristotle, *Eudemian Ethics*, 1241b18–22; *CW* 2:1967

40. See, especially, Aristotle, *Politics*, 1254b5–20; *CW* 2:1990.

41. See Victor Goldschmidt, "La théorie aristotélicienne de l'esclavage et sa méthode," in *Zetesis: album amicorum door vrienden en collega's aangeboden aan Prof. Dr. E. de Strycker ter gelegenheid van zijn 65e verjaardag* (Antwerp: Der Nederlandsche Boekhandel, 1973), 151 (all translations of this text are my own).

42. Aristotle, *Politics* 1254b28–34; *CW* 2:1990–91 (trans. slightly modified).

43. See Aristotle, *Politics*, 1255a1–2; *CW* 2:1991.

44. See Goldschmidt, "La théorie aristotélicienne de l'esclavage et sa méthode," 158–59.

45. For Aristotle's express nomination of the theoretical science that deals with things that are both separable and immovable—as opposed to that which deals with things that are separable but not immovable (physics) and that which deals with things that are immovable but not separable (mathematics)—as "theology," see *Metaphysics*, 1026a13–20; *CW* 2:1620. On Aristotle's "theology," the remarks of Werner Jaeger, *Aristotle: Fundamentals on the History of His Development*, trans. Richard Robinson (Oxford: Clarendon Press, 1934), 217–27, are still pertinent. On the contribution of the "physics" to the "theology," see furthermore, W. D. Ross, *Aristotle's Physics* (Oxford: Clarendon Press, 1936), 94–102.

46. Ross, *Aristotle's Physics*, 85.

47. See Aristotle, *Physics*, 202a13–22; *CW* 1:344–45.

48. Aristotle, *Physics*, 201a10; *CW* 1:343 (trans. modified).

49. Aristotle, *Physics*, 251a9; *CW* 1:419 (trans. slightly modified).

50. See Aristotle, *Physics*, 251a9–29; *CW* 1:419.

51. See Aristotle, *Physics*, 251b29–252a5; *CW* 1:420.

52. See Aristotle, *Physics*, 255b31–256a3; *CW* 1:427.

53. See Aristotle, *Physics*, 256a4–6; *CW* 1:427.

54. See Aristotle, *Physics*, 256a4–6; *CW* 1:427.

55. Aristotle, *Physics*, 256a7–9; *CW* 1:427 (trans. slightly modified).

56. Aristotle, *Physics*, 256a10–12; *CW* 1:428.

57. Aristotle, *Physics*, 257a28–31; *CW* 1:430.

58. See Dondaine, "A propos d'Avicenne et de Saint Thomas," 448.

59. On all of the above, see Bernard Blankenhorn, "The Instrumental Causality of the Sacraments: Thomas Aquinas and Louis-Marie Chauvet." *Nova et Vetera* (English edition) 4, 2 (2006), 275–77 and 283–84, who thus locates the *Summa contra Gentiles*, which was conceived and written during his stay in Orvieto, as the decisive turning point.

60. See Thomas Aquinas, *Summa contra Gentiles*, lib. 4, cap. 41, n. 11; translation in *Summa Contra Gentiles, Book Four: Salvation*, trans. Charles J. O'Neil (Notre Dame, Ind.: University of Notre Dame Press, 1975), 196. The claim that Christ's humanity is the instrument of his divinity is repeated throughout the *Summa theologiae* too, including in the treatise on the sacraments itself. See *Summa theologiae*, 3, q. 64, a. 3, resp.; 110–11. For Aristotle, see *Nicomachean Ethics*, 1161b1–5; *CW* II:1835; and, more explicitly again, *Eudemian Ethics*, 1241b22–23; *CW* II:1967–68.

61. Cf. Boethius, *Contra Eutychen et Nestorium*, esp. cap. 7; text and translation in *The Theological Tractates and the Consolation of Philosophy*, esp. 114–21. With its insistence that the Latin *persona* here translates the Greek *hypostasis* and not *prosōpon* (as is usually the case), Boethius's fifth tractate remains one of the most important texts in the history of the construction of the "person." For discussion, see Alain Boureau, "Droit et théologie au XIIIe siècle," *Annales HSS* 47, no. 6 (1992): 1118–19; and, for its significance within the broader history of law, Yan Thomas, "Le sujet concret et sa personne: Essai d'histoire juridique rétrospective," in Olivier Cayla and Yan Thomas, *Du droit de ne pas naître: À propos de l'affaire Perruche* (Paris: Gallimard, 2002), 124–35.

62. Cf. Aristotle, *De anima*, 432a1–2; *On the Soul*, trans. J. A. Smith, in *CW* I:686.

63. Thomas Aquinas, *Summa theologiae*, 3, q. 62, a. 5, resp.; 66–67 (trans. slightly modified). Cf. *Summa theologiae*, 3, q. 64, a. 5, resp.; 110–11: "Since [Christ's humanity] is an instrument that is conjoined to his divinity in person it possesses a certain priority and causality in relation to the separated instruments [*instrumentum extrinsecorum*], which are the ministers of the Church and the sacraments themselves."

64. See Mark D. Jordan, *Rewritten Theology: Aquinas after His Readers* (Oxford: Blackwell Publishing, 2006), 167.

65. See Martin Heidegger, *Aristotle's "Metaphysics" 1–3: On the Essence and Actuality of Force*, trans. Walter Brogan and Peter Warnek (Bloomington: Indiana University Press, 1999), 73–91.

66. See Heidegger, *Aristotle's "Metaphysics," 76.*

67. Giorgio Agamben, *Homo Sacer: Sovereign Power and Bare Life*, trans. Daniel Heller-Roazen (Stanford, Calif.: Stanford University Press, 1998), 45. Following Heidegger, Agamben has devoted significant attention to the *dynamis/energeia* opposition both in Aristotle and beyond. In addition to *Homo Sacer*, 44–48, see especially the important title essay of his collection *La potenza del pensiero: Saggi e conferenze* (Vincenza: Neri Pozza, 2005), 273–87.

68. Aristotle, *Metaphysics*, 1046a30–31, observing Heidegger's important correction of the manuscript. See Heidegger, *Aristotle's "Metaphysics," 91.*

69. It is certainly significant that the "instruments" which Aristotle discusses in the context of his articulation of the fourfold aetiology should be described as *kinēsantos metaxy* (see Aristotle, *Physics*, 194b35); *metaxy* being the very term through which the concept of the "medium" first entered the philosophical lexicon. In his treatise on the soul, Aristotle had sought to affirm the necessity of a "medium" (*to metaxy*) for sense perception. Such a necessity, he argued, can be easily demonstrated in the case of vision. If that which has color is placed too close to the eyes, he writes, it cannot be seen. And hence it is not true, as Democritus maintains, that were the intervening space to be perfectly empty even an ant in the sky would be clearly visible: "For seeing is due to an affection [*paschontos*] of what has the perceptive faculty, and it cannot be affected by the seen color itself; it remains that it must be affected by what comes between [*tou metaxy*]. Hence it is indispensable that there be something in between [*ti einai metaxy*]—if there were nothing, so far from seeing with greater distinctness, we should see nothing at all." Aristotle, *On the Soul*, 419a17–21; *CW* 1:667. For a discussion of the particular *ontology* that is implicit in Aristotle's theory of sense perception, see Friedrich Kittler, "Toward an Ontology of Media," *Theory, Culture and Society*, 26, nos. 2–3 (2009): 23–31, and above all, Emanuele Coccia, *La vita sensibile* (Bologna: Mulino, 2011), 31–83. As Coccia shows (61–63), far from a theory of the instrumental cause, it is in fact the most radical theory of mediality—a theory of pure reception—that we owe to Averroes.

70. Heidegger, *Aristotle's "Metaphysics," 152.*

71. John of Damascus, *De fide orthodoxa*, 3, 15; *Writings*, trans. Frederick H. Chase Jr. (Washington, D. C.: Catholic University of America Press, 1958), 304.

72. John of Damascus, *De fide orthodoxa*, 3, 15; 310.

73. John of Damascus, *De fide orthodoxa*, 3, 15; 310.

74. John of Damascus, *De fide orthodoxa*, 3, 15; 311 (trans slightly modified).

75. John of Damascus, *De fide orthodoxa*, 3, 15; 311.

76. That John is aware of the transformation that is at issue here would appear to be attested by the discussion that immediately concludes the chapter. Here

John attempts—not all that convincingly—to dismiss the objection that since the human action, by way of contrast to the divine, is called passion, this amounts to concluding that there is only one action in Christ, the divine. What would follow from such reasoning in terms of comparison and contrast, he argues, would be the absurd conclusion that if the divine nature is good, then the human nature must necessarily be evil. Or even worse, that if the human nature is evil, the divine nature must necessarily be good. Nonetheless, there could be no clearer acknowledgement of the implicit redefinition of *dynamis* in terms of *energeia* that is effectively carried out here. See John of Damascus, *De fide orthodoxa*, 3, 15; 312–14.

77. John Chrysostom, *Homilia 1 in Acta*, 3; qtd. in John of Damascus, 3, 15; 310 (trans. slightly modified). It should be noted that John of Damascus directly links this reconfiguration of passion in terms of action with the discourse concerning Christ's *oikonomia*. In a truly remarkable sequence, he writes: "Now the body of itself has no inclination for physical suffering, nor yet did it avoid and refuse to accept what was painful. Neither was it affected by external influences; rather, it was moved in accordance with the order of its nature, with the Word willing and disposing it economically to suffer and do what is proper to it [*tou logou thelontos kai parachōrountos oikonomikōs paschein auto kai prattein ta idia*], so that through its work the truth of its nature might be guaranteed." See John of Damascus, *De fide orthodoxa*, 3, 15; 311–12 (trans. slightly modified). Curiously enough, the adverb "economically" is elided in the English translation.

78. That there might be a broader politico-theological application to the theory of the instrumental cause did not escape Ernst Kantorowicz, who has demonstrated its clear uptake as early as Baldus's *Consilia*. According to Baldus's often-repeated formulation, the king himself would serve as an instrument with respect to his dignity (*rex instrumentum dignitatis*). See Ernst H. Kantorowicz, *The King's Two Bodies: A Study in Mediaeval Political Theology* (Princeton: Princeton University Press, 1957), 437–46. It goes without saying that if the instrumentality of Christ's humanity furnishes the paradigm for an entire sequence of vicarious agents, acting as *instrumenta separata* with respect to his *instrumentum conjunctum*, the same could also be said of that of the sovereign himself (and, by extension, of any incorporated entity).

79. Thomas Aquinas, *Summa theologiae*, 3, q. 7, a. 1, ad. 3; *Summa theologiae, Volume 49: The Grace of Christ (3a 7–15)*, trans. Liam G. Walsh (London: Blackfriars, 1973), 8–9 (trans. modified).

80. In classical Athens, the speech of a slave could be admitted publicly (which is to say, as testimony in the context of a trial) only if forcefully extorted under conditions of torture. Indeed, as the ancient sources clearly attest, the vocabulary of Athenian law even reserved a particular term for this specific kind of "evidentiary" torture: *basanos*. Confronted with references to this "barbaric" practice, the historians of ancient Greece have typically reacted either with incredulity or with silence.

And yet, however cruel and ultimately unjustified it may have been, the motivation behind it nonetheless remains perspicuous. As Moses Finley has summarized the situation with typical acumen: "If a slave is a property with a soul, a non-person and yet indubitably a biological human being, institutional procedures are to be expected that will degrade and undermine his humanity and so distinguish him from human beings who are not property. Corporal punishment and torture constitute one such procedure." M. I. Finley, *Ancient Slavery and Modern Ideology* (London: Chatto and Windus, 1980), 95. As Page duBois has noted, moreover, torture, in this context, constitutes a "practice of the state, which carves the line between slave and free on the bodies of the unfree." Page duBois, *Torture and Truth* (New York: Routledge, 1991), 63. But the line thereby carved is not only between slave and master, unfree and free; it is also between the sphere of the *oikos*, on the one hand, and that of the *polis*, on the other. In the context of the genealogy that we have been tracing here, Christianity's repurposing of the slave in the guise of the minister would be further evidence of the eventual erasure of the sharp demarcating line that separated the *polis* from the *oikos* in the ancient world and that is among the most important legacies that the Christian tradition has bequeathed to modernity.

81. This is expressly underscored by Aquinas himself in a very important section of the *Summa* dedicated to the notion of *religio*. Asking whether religion can be truly considered a virtue when the very structure of the relationship that it demands implies a necessary servitude, Aquinas responds emphatically in the affirmative: "A slave can freely do what is owed to his master, and thus make a virtue of necessity [*facit de necessitate virtutem*], by doing his duty voluntarily [*debitum voluntarie reddens*]. Similarly, serving God can be a act of virtue when a man does it voluntarily." See *Summa theologiae*, 2–2, q. 81, a. 2, ad. 2; *Summa theologiae, Volume 39: Religion and Worship (2a2ae. 80–91)*, trans. Kevin D. O'Rourke (London: Blackfriars, 1964), 16–17 (trans. modified). On this passage, see Agamben, *Opus Dei*, 102–3, who discerns in it the origin of the Kantian concept of *Tugendpflicht*.

82. See, for example, Max Horkheimer, *The Eclipse of Reason* (New York: Oxford University Press, 1947). It would be easy enough to demonstrate that critiques of this type are also of Christian origin and can be traced back to the famous Augustinian distinction between *frui* and *uti*, that is, between things that are to be *enjoyed* only for their own sake and things that are to be *used* only for the sake of that which is to be enjoyed. Of course, it is this very same passage that is also responsible for strictly prohibiting the enjoyment of temporal things (which Augustine terms their "abuse"), and hence for sanctioning their mere use alone. "In this mortal life," he writes, "we are travellers away from our Lord: if we wish to return to our homeland where we can be happy we use this world, not enjoy it [*utendum est hoc mundo, non fruendum*]." See Augustine, *De Doctrina Christiana*, 1, 3, 3–4; 14–17. The very passage that would provide the grounds for the critique of instrumentalization thus makes the strongest possible case for its necessity.

83. Conversely, the incipient irony that this most apparently spiritual of beings (the minster) should be defined on the basis of that figure (the slave), whose ultimate *ergon*, according to Aristotle, is the "use of the body" (*sōmatis chrēsis*), ought not be lost from view. See Aristotle, *Politics*, 1254b18; *CW* 2:1990.

84. Thomas Aquinas, *Sententia libri Politicorum*, lib. 1, lect. 2, n. 14; *Commentary on Aristotle's* Politics, 24 (trans. modified).

85. See Agamben, *Opus Dei*, 65–88.

86. Brown, *Poverty and Leadership in the Later Roman Empire*, 102.

87. See Brown, *Poverty and Leadership in the Later Roman Empire*, 101.

88. D. S. Wallace-Hadrill, *Christian Antioch* (Cambridge: Cambridge University Press, 1982), 129, cited in Brown, *Poverty and Leadership in the Later Roman Empire*, 103.

89. See Brown, *Poverty and Leadership in the Later Roman Empire*, 103–4.

90. Brown, *Poverty and Leadership in the Later Roman Empire*, 104.

91. Brown, *Poverty and Leadership in the Later Roman Empire*, 104.

92. Brown, *Poverty and Leadership in the Later Roman Empire*, 106.

93. As Agamben has noted, the emergence of that modality of power that Foucault termed *le gouverner des hommes* was possible neither from the perspective of Judaism, in which an "angelic function" remains completely extraneous to God, nor from that of Islam, in which God himself directly intervenes in all events at all times. Among the Abrahamic religions, Christianity alone could set in train this eventuality. As he writes: "If the government of the world is still today in the hands of the Christian West (even if we do not know for how much longer), this is certainly not unrelated to the fact that Christianity, unique among the three monotheistic religions, had made the government of the world an internal articulation of the divinity and, in this way, had divinized angelic power." See Giorgio Agamben, introduction to *Angeli: Ebraismo Cristianesimo Islam*, ed. Giorgio Agamben and Emanuele Coccia (Vincenza: Neri Pozza, 2009), 19. It is important, moreover, to observe that this internal articulation of the divinity is in turn mirrored in the twin natures of the "person" of Christ himself.

94. According to Augustine, who here cites from Philippians 2:7, Jesus appeared "in the form of a slave [*in forma servi*]," precisely "in order that he would be the mediator [*ut mediator esset*]." See *De civitate Dei*, 9, 15; 361.

5. ANTHROPOLOGY OF OFFICE

1. Giorgio Agamben, *Opus Dei: An Archeology of Duty*, trans. Adam Kotsko (Stanford, Calif.: Stanford University Press, 2013). The intimate relationship between *Opus Dei* and *The Kingdom and the Glory* is clearly delineated in the former's preface.

2. As we have seen, according to Agamben this inheritance is marked even at the lexical level in Kant's placing of the doctrine of duties of virtue (*doctrina officiorum*

virtutis) at the center of his ethics. See Agamben, *Opus Dei*, 111–12. For Kant's defi-
nition of "duty of virtue" (*Tugendplicht*), see Immanuel Kant, *The Metaphysics of Morals*, in *Practical Philosophy*, ed. and trans. Mary J. Gregor (Cambridge: Cambridge University Press, 1996), 524–26.

3. See Agamben, *Opus Dei*, 52–54, 81–82.

4. Thomas Aquinas, *Summa theologiae*, 3, q. 64, a. 5, resp.; 116–17 (trans. slightly modified).

5. Thomas Aquinas, *Summa theologiae*, 3, q. 64, a. 9, resp.; 130–31 (trans. slightly modified).

6. For a detailed discussion of these pages, see the important essay of Jean-Pierre Vernant, "Intimations of the Will in Greek Tragedy," in Jean-Pierre Vernant and Pierre Vidal-Naquet, *Myth and Tragedy in Ancient Greece*, trans. Janet Lloyd (New York: Zone Books, 1988), above all 55–69.

7. Aristotle, *Nicomachean Ethics* 1110a11; *CW* II:1752.

8. Once again, important differences notwithstanding, the structural parallel that this presents with respect to Kant's notion of "self-constraint" (*Selbstzwang*), which performs the same role for the doctrine of virtue that external constraint performs for the doctrine of right, is striking. In attempting to disclose the apparent paradox of an end that is at the same time a duty, Kant writes: "To have an end that I have not myself made an end is self-contradictory, an act of freedom which is not yet free.—But it is no contradiction to set an end for myself that is also a duty, since I constrain myself to it [*ich da mich selbst zwinge*] and this is altogether consistent with freedom." Kant, *The Metaphysics of Morals*, 514. In this way, Kant's virtuous person becomes, as it were, the minister of himself. Self-constraint, that is to say, is the device that effects a stunning internalization of the ministerial paradigm, which makes Kant's virtuous person at one and the same time the principal and the instrumental cause of his own action.

9. See Aristotle, *Nicomachean Ethics* 1110a1; *CW* II:1752.

10. See Aristotle, *Nicomachean Ethics* 1111a23–24; *CW* II:1754.

11. Agamben, *Opus Dei*, 79.

12. See, especially, Agamben, *Opus Dei*, 87–88.

13. See Cicero, *De finibus bonorum et malorum* 3, 17, 58; *De finibus bonorum et malorum*, trans. H. Rackham (London: William Heinemann, 1931), 276–77.

14. See Cicero, *De finibus* 3, 6, 20; 236–39. Cf. Diogenes Laertius 7, 107; II:212–13: "For even in plants and animals . . . you may discern fitness of behaviour [*kathēkonta*]." The *kathēkonta* thus pertain more generally to the sphere of what the Stoics called *oikeiōsis*. On the latter, see above all S. G. Pembroke, "Oikeiōsis," in *Problems in Stoicism*, ed. A. A. Long (London: Athlone Press, 1971), 114–49, who goes as far as to transfer Diogenes's well-known assessment of Chrysippus to the concept of *oikeiōsis* itself: "If there had been no *oikeiōsis*," he writes, "there would have been no Stoa" (114–15).

15. See Cicero, *De finibus* 3, 18, 59; 276–79.

16. See Cicero, *De finibus* 3, 18, 59; 278–79.

17. Cicero, *De finibus* 4, 27, 76; 384–85.

18. See the editors' remarks in *The Hellenistic Philosophers,* 1:365.

19. See Cicero, *De officiis* 1, 3, 8; *De officiis,* trans. Walter Miller (London: William Heinemann, 1928), 10–11.

20. Cicero, *De officiis* 1, 2, 4; 6–7 (trans. slightly modified). It is perhaps indicative of the ambiguity of Cicero's treatment here that in Walter Miller's classic translation, *officium* is rendered with "moral duty," while, as we have seen, its Stoic counterpart, is strictly morally neutral.

21. Cicero, *De officiis* 1, 3, 7; 8–9.

22. Cicero, *De officiis* 1, 3, 7; 8–9 (trans. modified).

23. See Cicero, *De officiis* 1, 7, 22; 24–25.

24. Cicero, *De officiis* 1, 4, 11; 12–13.

25. See Agamben, *Opus Dei,* 74.

26. The significance of this last point has recently been underlined in Peter Brown, *Through the Eye of a Needle: Wealth, the Fall of Rome, and the Making of Christianity in the West, 350–500 AD* (Princeton: Princeton University Press, 2012), 130.

27. See Cicero, *De officiis* 1, 4, 12–14; 12–17.

28. Agamben, *Opus Dei,* 74–75 (trans. modified). That Agamben intends his analysis of the *officium* to be read in the context of the discussion of "philosophical anthropology" is attested by the fact that his language here distinctly recalls Arnold Gehlen's characterization of the human as a *Mängelwesen*. Cf. Arnold Gehlen, *Man: His Nature and Place in the World,* trans. Clare McMillan and Karl Pillemer (New York: Columbia University Press, 1988), 10: "To say that man is not 'firmly established' means that he draws on his own aptitudes and talents to survive; of necessity, he relates to himself in a way that no animal does. I would say that he does not so much *live* as *lead* [führt] his life." A study that would seek a rapprochement between the concept of *Führung* and Foucault's discussion of governmentality remains to be written. For indications, see Agamben, *The Kingdom and the Glory,* 74–77, and *Opus Dei,* 75–76.

29. See Seneca, *Epistula* 95, 52; text and translation in *Ad Lucilium Epistulae Morales,* III, trans. Richard M. Gummere (London: William Heinemann, 1925), 90–91, cited in Agamben, *Opus Dei,* 90.

30. Agamben, *Opus Dei,* 90.

31. See Agamben, *Opus Dei,* 76.

32. See Augustine, *Epistula* 82, 21; *Letters 1–99,* trans. Roland Teske (New York: New City Press, 2001), 326.

33. Ambrose, *De officiis* 1, 8, 25; Ivor J. Davidson, ed., *Ambrose: De officiis,* I (Oxford: Oxford University Press, 2001), 132–33.

34. Cf. Lk. 1:5; cf. 1 Chr. 24:1–19.

35. See Agamben, *Opus Dei*, 78.

36. See the commentary of Davidson in *Ambrose: De officiis*, II:470. It is telling, in this regard, that since the seventeenth century Ambrose's treatise has principally been known by the qualified title *De officiis ministrorum*.

37. Ambrose, *De officiis* 1, 7, 24; I:130–31.

38. It is worth noting that Agamben fails to stress the importance of the *natural gratia* opposition to Ambrose's intervention in the context of his own genealogy of the "office." Cf. Agamben, *Opus Dei*, 65–86, and 77–79 on the contribution of Ambrose in particular.

39. See, especially, Baziel Maes, *La loi naturelle selon Ambroise de Milan* (Rome: Presses de l'Université Grégorienne, 1967), 60–64.

40. See Ambrose, *De officiis* 1, 28, 132–35; I:193–97. Cf. Cicero, *De officiis* 1, 16, 50–51; 52–57.

41. Ambrose, *De officiis* 1, 32, 169; I:216–17.

42. Ambrose, *De officiis* 1, 33, 170; I:216–17.

43. Ambrose, *De officiis* 1, 9, 28; I:132–33 (trans. slightly modified).

44. See Ambrose, *De officiis* 1, 11, 36; I:136–39.

45. Mt. 19:21, quoted in Ambrose, *De officiis* 1, 11, 37; I:138–39.

46. Ambrose, *De officiis* 1, 11, 37; I:138–39.

47. See Davidson, in *Ambrose: De officiis*, II:481–82.

48. This holds all the way up to the seventeenth century and the very origins of modern political thought with Thomas Hobbes, who still gives the parable of the rich young man to illustrate the difference between "command" and "counsell"—two terms that, as he astutely observes, are seemingly indistinguishable at the level of grammar, both receiving their linguistic expression in the form of the imperative ("For the words *Doe this*, are the words not onely of him that Commandeth; but also of him that giveth Counsell")—in the chapter of his *Leviathan* dedicated to the specification of the latter. See Thomas Hobbes, *Leviathan*, ed. Richard Tuck (Cambridge: Cambridge University Press, 1996), 178–79.

49. Ambrose, *De viduis* 12, 72, in *PL* 16, 256b (all translations of this text are my own).

50. Cf. 2 Cor. 3:3.

51. See Thomas Aquinas, *Summa theologiae*, 1–2, q. 108, a. 4, resp.; *Summa theologiae, XXX: The Gospel of Grace (1a2ae. 106–114)*, trans. Cornelius Ernst (Oxford: Blackfriars, 1972), 60–61: "The difference between a counsel and a commandment lies in this, that a commandment implies necessity [*importat necessitatem*], while a counsel is left to the choice [*in optione*] of the one to whom it is given. And so it is fitting that in the new law, which is the law of freedom [*lex libertatis*], counsels should be provided as well as commandments, but not in the old law, which is the law of servitude [*lex servitutis*]" (trans. slightly modified).

52. Emanuele Coccia, "La legge della salvezza: Bernardo di Clairvaux e il diritto monastico," *Viator* (English and Multilingual Edition) 41 (2010): 127–46, esp. 131–36.

53. Ambrose, *De viduis* 12, 73, in *PL* 16, 256c. Cf. *Dig.* 17, 1, 2, 6: "The mandate is in your interests alone if, for example, I give you a mandate to invest your money in the purchase of land rather than lend it out at interest or, conversely, to lend it out at interest rather than invest in the purchase of land. A 'mandate' of this type is counsel rather than commandment [*cuius generis mandatum magis consilium est quam mandatum*] and, for this reason, it is not obligatory, as no one incurs an obligation as the result of counsel [*nemo ex consilio obligatur*], even if the counsel was not in the best interests of the person to whom it was given; for everyone is free to ascertain for himself whether counsel is to his advantage." Translation in *The Digest of Justinian*, I, trans. and ed. Alan Watson (Philadelphia: University of Pennsylvania Press, 1985) (trans. slightly modified). I owe this last reference to Coccia, "La legge della salvezza," 131. On the basis of this confluence, Coccia seeks to articulate the specificity of the concept of *consilium*, and thereby of Christian normativity more broadly, in the form a genuine juridical paradox—that of "a law which," as he writes, "purports not to be able to be a law [*una legge che pretende di poter non essere tale*]":

> In the concept of *consilium*, the entire Christian philosophy of law and the relationship of its messianism with respect to the law is condensed. Indeed, paraphrasing a well-known formula of the Franciscan Hugh of Digne who had formulated it in order to express the juridical paradox of Franciscan life, one could say that, from the perspective of the history of normative categories, Christianity is a normative system that purports to depart from the norm [*che pretende di uscire dalla norma*]; a Christian is thus whoever demands the right to have no right [*il diritto a non avere alcun diritto*], because it is life itself that must now be transformed into law. (135) (Translation mine)

The tension between the figure of the monk, on the one hand, which is the subject of Coccia's investigation, and that of the minister, on the other, which is the subject of our investigation, may be sought in their respective articulations with respect to this "juridical paradox."

54. See Coccia, "La legge della salvezza," 133, and for a summary historical account of the Christian origins of this concept that can be traced back linguistically to the Latin Bible's articulation of the parable of the Good Samaritan (Lk. 10:35), David Heyd, *Supererogation: Its Status in Ethical Theory* (Cambridge: Cambridge University Press, 1982), 15–34. It is important to recall, with Heyd, that the specifically Catholic doctrine of supererogatory works—indissolubly linked as it was to the cult of the saints—was one of the principal targets for vituperative attack on the part of the reformers of the sixteenth century. Heyd quotes Luther himself

(from his "Explanation of the Ninety-Five Theses"): "No saint has adequately fulfilled God's commandments in this life. Consequently, the saints have done nothing which is superabundant." The Anglican Church would go even further again. According to Thomas Becon, *opera supererogationis* should more appropriately be termed *opera superarrogantiae*. See Heyd, *Supererogation*, 27–28.

55. Ambrose, *De officiis* 3, 2, 10; 358–59 (trans. modified). See, again, the important remarks in Davidson, *Ambrose: De officiis*, II:481–82.

56. In this shift, the respective limits both of Roman imperialism and of Christian universalism are both laid bare: While in the former a part purports to count for the whole (the Roman republic for the whole of humanity), in the latter the whole is effectively absorbed by a particular part that thereby separates itself from it (the salvation of all by the salvation of the clergy).

57. See Marcia L. Colish, *The Stoic Tradition from Antiquity to the Middle Ages, II: Stoicism in Christian Latin Thought through the Sixth Century* (Leiden: Brill, 1985), 69–70.

58. This is where the experience of monasticism appears in sharpest contrast to that of the priesthood. This contrast is treated at length by Agamben in *The Highest Poverty*, xii–xiii, 82–85, and 116–22; but perhaps nowhere is it so powerfully articulated as in the following passage: "If [for the monk] the liturgy is totally transformed into life, then the fundamental principle of the *opus operatum*—which already, beginning with Augustine, sanctioned the indifference of the priest's moral qualities with respect to the efficacy of his office—cannot hold. While the unworthy priest remains in any case a priest, and the sacramental acts he carries out do not lose their validity, an unworthy monk is simply not a monk" (84). In the context of Agamben's own work, it is necessary to add this: if "bare life" is a life that has been separated from its form, the "office" is a form that has been separated from its life. Monasticism, instead, would be that experiment—not always successful, to be sure—that, in attempting to construct a "form-of-life," refuses the separation both of life from form (bare life) and of form from life (office). Cf. Giorgio Agamben, "Form-of-life," in *Means without End: Notes on Politics*, trans. Vincenzo Binetti and Cesare Casarino (Minneapolis: University of Minnesota Press, 2000), 3–12.

59. See Aristotle, *Politics* 1260a35–36, in *CW* 2:2000.

60. Agamben, *Opus Dei*, 87 (trans. modified).

61. In truth, however, if the minister—qua minister—indeed acts, he does so neither in the sense of a *poiēsis* nor of a *praxis* (to employ the classic Aristotelian distinction). He neither *facit* nor *agit*, but rather, as Agamben has suggested, borrowing a third category from Varro, he *gerit*: he "bears" and "sustains" the action of the principal cause, thereby once again affirming that indistinguishability of passivity and activity, of potentiality and actuality, which we have argued is the enduring contribution of the ministerial paradigm to the history of power. See Agamben, *Opus Dei*, 82–83. Cf. Varro, *De lingua latina* 6, 77; *On the Latin Language, I: Books V–VII*, trans. Roland J. Kent (London: William Heinemann, 1938), 244–45.

62. The contrast with Aristotle is again illuminating. Since action, according to Aristotle, is a matter of "deliberation" (*bouleutōn*) and "choice" (*prohairetōn*), the exercise of virtue—and of vice—is something that is very distinctly "in our power" (*eph'hemin dē kai ē aretē*). And since where things are in our power we are free both to act and not to act, where acting is good and not acting is bad that will be in our power, and where acting is bad and not acting is good that too will in our power. Hence both virtue and vice wholly depend upon us. See Aristotle, *Nicomachean Ethics* 1113b3–14; *CW* II:1758.

63. The foundational work, in this regard, is certainly Jacques Derrida's 1997 seminar at Cerisy, *The Animal That Therefore I Am*, ed. by Marie-Louis Mallet, trans. David Wills (New York: Fordham University Press, 2008).

64. See Erik Peterson, "Book on the Angels," in *Theological Tractates*, trans. Michael J. Hollerich (Stanford, Calif.: Stanford University Press, 2011), 138.

CONCLUSION

1. Carl Schmitt, *Political Theology: Four Chapters on the Concept of Sovereignty*, trans. George Schwab (Chicago: University of Chicago Press, 2005), 65 (trans. modified).

2. See Carl Schmitt, *The Concept of the Political*, trans. George Schwab (Chicago: University of Chicago Press, 2007), 69–73.

3. See Carl Schmitt, "The Age of Neutralizations and Depoliticizations," trans. Matthias Konzett and John P. McCormick, in *The Concept of the Political*, 89–94.

4. Schmitt, "The Age of Neutralizations and Depoliticizations," 90.

5. Schmitt, "The Age of Neutralizations and Depoliticizations," 91.

6. Carl Schmitt, *Roman Catholicism and Political Form*, trans. G. L. Ulmen (Westport, Conn.: Greenwood Press, 1995), 14.

7. See Reinhard Mehring, *Carl Schmitt: A Biography*, trans. Daniel Steuer (Cambridge: Polity Press, 2014), 110.

8. Schmitt, *Political Theology*, 46 (trans. modified).

9. Schmitt, *Political Theology*, 36, 37; 51–52.

10. See Michael Allen Gillespie, *The Theological Origins of Modernity* (Chicago: Chicago University Press, 2009).

11. See Roberto Esposito, *Two: The Machine of Political Theology and the Place of Thought*, trans. Zakiya Hanafi (New York: Fordham University Press, 2015). The reference here is to Hegel's theory of sovereignty, Weber's notion of charismatic authority, and Schmitt's artful combination of the two in his decisionism.

12. See Hannah Arendt, *On Violence* (New York: Harcourt, Brace, Jovanovich, 1970), 38–39: "Today," she writes, "we ought to add the latest and perhaps most formidable form of such domination: bureaucracy or the rule of an intricate system of bureaus in which no men, neither one nor the best, neither the few nor the many, can be held responsible, and which could properly be called rule by Nobody."

13. Hannah Arendt, *The Human Condition* (Chicago: University of Chicago Press, 1958), 40.

14. As Arendt is careful to specify, "no-man rule" is not be confused with "no-rule"; importantly, it remains a rule, perhaps even the most tyrannical form of all. See Arendt, *On Violence*, 39: "If, in accord with traditional political thought, we identify tyranny as government that is not held to give account of itself, rule by Nobody is clearly the most tyrannical of all, since there is no one left who could even be asked to answer for what is being done."

15. Hannah Arendt, "Introduction into Politics," in *The Promise of Politics*, ed. Jerome Kohn (New York: Schocken Books, 2005), 138–41.

16. Cf. here the recent book of Dotan Leshem, *The Origins of Neoliberalism: Modeling the Economy from Jesus to Foucault* (New York: Columbia University Press, 2016).

17. Cf. Stathis Gourgouris, "Political Theology as Monarchical Thought," *Constellations* 23, no. 2 (2016): 145–59.

BIBLIOGRAPHY

Agamben, Giorgio. *Altissima povertà: Regole monastiche e forma di vita.* Homo sacer, IV, 1. Vicenza: Neri Pozza, 2011. Translated by Adam Kotsko as *The Highest Poverty: Monastic Rules and Form-of-Life.* Stanford, Calif.: Stanford University Press, 2013.

———. Introduction to *Angeli: Ebraismo Cristianesimo Islam,* edited by Giorgio Agamben and Emanuele Coccia, 11–21. Vicenza: Neri Pozza, 2009.

———. *Homo Sacer: Sovereign Power and Bare Life.* Translated by Daniel Heller-Roazen. Stanford, Calif.: Stanford University Press, 1998.

———. *Means without End: Notes on Politics.* Translated by Vincenzo Binetti and Cesare Casarino. Minneapolis: University of Minnesota Press, 2000.

———. *Il mistero del male: Benedetto XVI a la fine dei tempi.* Bari: Laterza, 2013.

———. *Opus Dei: Archeologia dell'ufficio.* Homo sacer, II, 5. Turin: Bollati Boringhieri, 2012. Translated by Adam Kotsko as *Opus Dei: An Archaeology of Duty.* Stanford, Calif.: Stanford University Press, 2013.

———. *La potenza del pensiero. Saggi e conferenze.* Vicenza: Neri Pozza, 2005.

———. *Il Regno e la Gloria: Per una genealogia teologica dell'economia e del governo.* Homo sacer, II, 2. Vicenza: Neri Pozza, 2007. Translated by Lorenzo Chiesa and Matteo Mandarini as *The Kingdom and the Glory: For a Theological Genealogy of Economy and Government.* Stanford, Calif.: Stanford University Press, 2011.

———. *The Time That Remains: A Commentary on the Letter to the Romans.* Translated by Patricia Dailey. Stanford, Calif.: Stanford University Press, 2005.

Andia, Ysabel de. *Henosis: L'Union à Dieu chez Denys l'Aréopagite.* Leiden: Brill, 1996.

Arendt, Hannah. *Eichmann in Jerusalem: A Report on the Banality of Evil.* London: Penguin Books, 1963.

———. *The Human Condition.* Chicago: University of Chicago Press, 1958.

———. *On Violence.* New York: Harcourt, Brace, Jovanovich, 1970.

———. *The Origins of Totalitarianism.* 2nd ed. London: Allen and Unwin, 1958.

———. "Introduction *into* Politics," in *The Promise of Politics,* edited by Jerome Kohn, 93–200. New York: Schocken Books, 2005.

———. "What Is Authority?" In *Between Past and Future: Eight Exercises in Political Thought*, 91–141. New York: Viking Press, 1968.

Aristotle. *The Complete Works of Aristotle*. Edited by Jonathan Barnes. 2 vols. Princeton: Princeton University Press, 1984.

Assmann, Jan. *Politische Theologie zwischen Ägypten und Israel*. Munich: Carl Friedrich von Siemens Stiftung, 1992.

———. *The Price of Monotheism*. Translated by Robert Savage. Stanford, Calif.: Stanford University Press, 2010.

Aubry, Gwenaëlle. "L'impuissance de Dieu." *Revue philosophique de la France et de l'étranger*, 135, no. 2 (2010): 307–20.

Augustine. *De civitate Dei*. Translated by Henry Bettenson as *Concerning the City of God against the Pagans*. Harmondsworth, U.K.: Penguin Books, 1972.

———. *Confessiones*. Translated by Henry Chadwick as *Confessions*. Oxford: Oxford University Press, 1991.

———. *De Doctrina Christiana*. Edited and translated by R. P. H. Green. Oxford: Clarendon Press, 1995.

———. *Enarrationes in Psalmos*. In *The Works of Saint Augustine*, III:16–19. 4 vols. New York: New City Press, 2000–2003.

———. *Epistula*. In *The Works of Saint Augustine*, II/1–4. Translated by Ronald J. Teske. 4 vols. New York: New City Press, 2001–5.

———. *De Genesis Contra Manichaeos*. In *The Works of Saint Augustine*, I:13. Translated by Edmund Hill. New York: New City Press, 2002.

———. *Sermo*. In *The Works of Saint Augustine*, III:1–11. 11 vols. New York: New City Press, 1990–97.

Austin, J. L. *How to Do Things with Words*. Edited by J. O. Urmson and Marina Sbisà. Oxford: Clarendon Press, 1962.

Austin, M. M., ed. *The Hellenistic World from Alexander to the Roman Conquest*. Cambridge: Cambridge University Press, 2006.

Balibar, Étienne. "*demos/ethnos/laos*." In *Dictionary of Untranslatables: A Philosophical Lexicon*, edited by Barbara Cassin, 201–3. Princeton: Princeton University Press, 2014.

Barrow, R. H., ed. and trans. *Prefect and Emperor: The Relationes of Symmachus, A.D. 384*. Oxford: Clarendon Press, 1973.

Basil of Caesarea. *Sur le Saint-Esprit*. Edited and translated by Benoît Pruche. Paris: Cerf, 1968.

Benveniste, Émile. "Remarks on the Function of Language in the Freudian Discovery." In *Problems in General Linguistics*, trans. Mark Elizabeth Meek, 75–87. Coral Gables: University of Miami Press, 1971.

———. *Vocabulaire des institutions indo-européennes*. 2 vols. Paris: Minuit, 1969. Translated by Elizabeth Palmer as *Indo-European Language and Society*. London: Faber and Faber, 1973.

La Bible d'Alexandrie. Multivolume. Paris: Cerf, 1986–.

Bietenhard, Hans. "People." In *The New International Dictionary of the New Testament Theology,* II, edited by Colin Brown, 788–805. Exeter: Paternoster Press, 1976.

Blankenhorn, Bernard. "The Instrumental Causality of the Sacraments: Thomas Aquinas and Loius-Marie Chauvet." *Nova et Vetera* (English edition) 4, no. 2 (2006), 255–92.

Boethius. *The Theological Tractates and The Consolation of Philosophy.* Translated by E. K. Rand, H. F. Stewart and S. J. Tester. Cambridge, Mass.: Harvard University Press, 1973.

Boureau, Alain. "Droit et théologie au XIIIe siècle." *Annales HSS* 47, no. 6 (1992): 1113–25.

Boyarin, Daniel. *Border Lines: The Partition of Judaeo-Christianity.* Philadelphia: University of Pennsylvania Press, 2004.

Braude, William G., trans. *The Midrash on Psalms.* 2 vols. New Haven: Yale University Press, 1959.

Brown, Peter. *Poverty and Leadership in the Later Roman Empire.* Hanover, N.H.: University Press of New England, 2002.

———. *Through the Eye of a Needle: Wealth, the Fall of Rome, and the Making of Christianity, 350–500 AD.* Princeton: Princeton University Press, 2012.

Büttgen, Philippe. "Théologie politique et pouvoir pastoral." *Annales HSS* 62, no. 5 (2007): 1129–54.

Chenu, M.-D. *La théologie au douzième siècle.* Paris: Vrin, 1976.

Cicero. *De finibus bonorum et malorum.* Translated by H. Rackham. London: William Heinemann, 1931.

———. *De natura deorum; Academica.* Translated by H. Rackham. London: William Heinemann, 1967.

———. *De officiis.* Translated by Walter Miller. London: William Heinemann, 1928.

———. *De re publica; De legibus.* Translated by Clinton Walter Keyes. London: William Heinemann, 1970.

Coccia, Emanuele. Introduction to *Angeli: Ebraismo Cristianesimo Islam,* edited by Giorgio Agamben and Emanuele Coccia, 435–513. Vicenza: Neri Pozza, 2009.

———. "La legge della salvezza: Bernardo di Clairvaux e il diritto monastico." *Viator* (English and Multilingual Edition) 41 (2010): 127–46.

———. "*Potestas dicitur multipliciter.* Le pouvoir et la nature." In *Un histoire du présent: Les historiens et Michel Foucault,* edited by Damien Bouquet, Blaise Dufal and Pauline Labey, 262–81. Paris: CNRS, 2013.

———. *La vita sensibile.* Bologna: Mulino, 2011.

Colish, Marcia L. *The Stoic Tradition from Antiquity to the Middle Ages.* 2 vols. Leiden: Brill, 1985.

Courtine, Jean-François. "A propos du 'problème théologico-politique.'" *Droits* 18 (1993): 109–18.

Daniélou, Jean. *Origen*. Translated by Walter Mitchell. New York: Sheer and Ward, 1955.

———. "Les sources juives de la doctrine des anges des nations chez Origène." *Recherches de science religieuse* 38 (1951): 132–37.

Davidson, Ivor J., ed. and trans. *Ambrose: De officiis*. 2 vols. Oxford: Oxford University Press, 2001.

Davies, J. K. *Athenian Propertied Families, 600–300 B.C.* Oxford: Clarendon Press, 1971.

Dean, Mitchell. "Governmentality Meets Theology: 'The King Reigns, but He Does Not Govern.'" *Theory, Culture and Society*, 29, no. 3 (2012): 145–58.

Debray, Régis. *Transmitting Culture*. Translated by Eric Rauth. New York: Columbia University Press, 2000.

Denys l'Aréopagite. *La hiérarchie céleste*. Translated by Maurice de Gandillac. Paris: Cerf, 1970.

Derrida, Jacques. *The Animal That Therefore I Am*. Edited by Marie-Louis Mallet and translated by David Wills. New York: Fordham University Press, 2008.

de Vries, Hent, and Lawrence E. Sullivan, eds. *Political Theologies: Public Religions in a Post-Secular World*. New York: Fordham University Press, 2006.

The Digest of Justinian. Translated and edited by Alan Watson. 2 vols. Philadelphia: University of Pennsylvania Press, 1985.

Diogenes Laertius. *Lives of Eminent Philosophers*. 2 vols. Translated by R. D. Hicks. London: William Heinemann, 1925.

Dondaine, H.-F. "A propos d'Avicenne et de Saint Thomas: de la causalité dispositive à la causalité instrumentale." *Revue Thomiste* 51 (1951): 441–53.

duBois, Page. *Torture and Truth*. New York: Routledge, 1991.

Ducrot, Oswald. *Dire et ne pas dire: Principes de sémantique linguistique*. 2nd edition. Paris: Hermann, 1991.

Ehrman, Bart D, ed. and trans. *The Apostolic Fathers*. 2 vols. Cambridge, Mass.: Harvard University Press, 2003.

Esposito, Roberto. *Categories of the Impolitical*. Translated by Connal Parsley. New York: Fordham University Press, 2015.

———. *Immunitas: The Protection and Negation of Life*. Translated by Zakiya Hanafi. Cambridge: Polity Press, 2011.

———. *Living Thought: The Origins and Actuality of Italian Philosophy*. Translated by Zakiya Hanafi. Stanford, Calif.: Stanford University Press, 2012.

———. *Two: The Machine of Political Theology and the Place of Thought*. Translated by Zakiya Hanafi. New York: Fordham University Press, 2013.

Finley, M. I. *Ancient Slavery and Modern Ideology*. London: Chatto and Windus, 1980.

————. *The Ancient Economy.* Updated edition. Berkeley: University of California Press, 1999.

Foucault, Michel. *Histoire de la sexualité, I: La volonté de savoir.* Paris: Gallimard, 1976. Translated by Robert Hurley as *The History of Sexuality, Volume 1: The Will to Knowledge.* London: Penguin Books, 1998.

————. *"Omnes et singulatim*: Toward a Critique of Political Reason." In *Essential Works of Michel Foucault, 1954–1984, Volume 3: Power*, edited James D. Faubion, 298–325. London: Penguin, 2000.

————. *Sécurité, territoire, population: Cours au Collège de France (1977–1978).* Edited by Michel Senellart. Paris: Gallimard/Seuil, 2004. Translated by Graham Burchell as *Security, Territory, Population: Lectures at the Collège de France, 1977–78.* Houndmills, U.K.: Palgrave Macmillan, 2007.

Freud, Sigmund. "The Antithetical Meaning of Primal Words." Translated by Alan Tyson in *The Standard Edition of the Complete Psychological Works of Sigmund Freud, Vol. XI (1910): Five Lectures on Psycho-Analysis, Leonardo Da Vinci and Other Works*, edited by James Strachey, 155–61. London: The Hogarth Press, 1957.

Gaius. *The Institutes of Gaius.* Edited and translated by W. M. Gordon and D. F. Robinson. London: Duckworth, 1988.

Galli, Carlo. *Genealogia della politica: Carl Schmitt e la crisi del pensiero politico moderno.* Bologna: Mulino, 1996.

————. "Le teologie politiche di Carl Schmitt," in *Lo sguardo di Giano: Saggi di Carl Schmitt*, 52–84. Bologna: Mulino, 2008.

Gehlen, Arnold. *Der Mensch: Seine Natur und sein Stellung in der Welt.* Wiesbaden: Akademische Verlagsgesellschaft Athenaion, 1978. Translated by Clare McMillan and Karl Pillemer in *Man: His Nature and Place in the World.* New York: Columbia University Press, 1988.

Geréby, György. "Political Theology versus Theological Politics: Erik Peterson and Carl Schmitt." *New German Critique* 35, no. 3; issue 105 (Fall 2008): 7–33.

Gillespie, Michael Allen. *The Theological Origins of Modernity.* Chicago: Chicago University Press, 2009.

Goldschmidt, Victor. "La théorie aristotélicienne de l'esclavage et sa méthode." In *Zetesis: album amicorum door vrienden en collega's aangeboden aan Prof. Dr. E. de Strycker ter gelegenheid van zijn 65e verjaardag*, 147–63. Antwerp: Der Nederlandsche Boekhandel, 1973.

Gourgouris, Stathis. "Political Theology as Monarchical Thought," *Constellations* 23, no. 2 (2016): 145–59.

Gregory the Great. *Homiliae in Evangelium.* Translated by David Hurst as *Forty Gospel Homilies.* Kalamazoo, Mich.: Cistercian Publications, 1990.

Gregory of Nazianzus. *Discours.* 9 vols. Paris: Cerf, 1978–92.

Grundmann, Herbert. *Religious Movements in the Middle Ages: The Historical Links Between Heresy, the Mendicant Orders, and the Women's Religious Movement in* the Twelfth and Thirteenth Centuries, with the Historical Foundations of German Mysticism. Translated by Steven Rowan. Notre Dame, Ind.: University of Notre Dame Press, 1995.

Habermas, Jürgen. *The Structural Transformation of the Public Sphere: An Inquiry into a Category of Bourgeois Society*. Translated by Thomas Burger. Cambridge: Polity Press, 1989.

Hathaway, Ronald H. *Hierarchy and the Definition of Order in the "Letters" of Pseudo-Dionysius: A Study in the Form and Meaning of the Pseudo-Dionysian Writings*. The Hague: Martinus Nijhoff, 1969.

Haubold, Johannes. *Homer's People: Epic Poetry and Social Formation*. Cambridge: Cambridge University Press, 2000.

Heidegger, Martin. *Gesamtausgabe, 33: Aristoteles, Metaphysik Θ 1–3: Von Wesen und Wirklichkeit der Kraft*. Frankfurt am Main: Vittorio Klostermann, 1981. Translated by Walter Brogan and Peter Warnek as *Aristotle's* Metaphysics Θ *1–3: On the Essence and Actuality of Force*. Bloomington: Indiana University Press, 1995.

Heron, Nicholas. "The Ungovernable." *Angelaki* 16, no. 2 (2011): 159–74.

Heyd, David. *Supererogation: Its Status in Ethical Theory*. Cambridge: Cambridge University Press, 1982.

Hippolytus of Rome. *Contra Noetum*. Edited and translated by Robert Butterworth. London: Heythrop Monographs, 1977.

Hobbes, Thomas. *Leviathan*. Edited by Richard Tuck. Cambridge: Cambridge University Press, 1996.

Hohendahl, Peter. "Political Theology Revisited: Carl Schmitt's Postwar Reassessment." *Konturen* 1 (2008): 1–28.

Homer. *The Iliad*. Translated by A. T. Murray, revised by William F. Wyatt. 2 vols. Cambridge, Mass.: Harvard University Press, 1999.

Horkheimer, Max. *Eclipse of Reason*. New York: Oxford University Press, 1947.

Illich, Ivan, and David Cayley. *The Rivers North of the Future: The Testament of Ivan Illich*. Toronto: House of Anansi Press, 2005.

Irenaeus of Lyon. *Contre les hérésies*. Edited by Adeline Rousseau and Louis Doutreleau. 10 vols. Paris: Cerf, 1968–82.

Jakobson, Roman. "Signe zéro." In *Selected Writings*, II:211–19. The Hague: Mouton, 1971.

Jaeger, Werner. *Aristotle: Fundamentals on the History of His Development*. Translated by Richard Robinson. Oxford: Clarendon Press, 1934.

Jeanmaire, Henri. *Couroi et Courètes: Essai sur l'éducation spartiate et sur les rites d'adolescence hellénique*. Lille: Bibliothèque Universitaire, 1939.

Jeremias, Joachim. "*poimen*." In *Theological Dictionary of the New Testament*, vol. 6, edited by Georg Friedrich, translated by Gregory Bromiley, 485–99. Grand Rapids: Eerdmans, 1968.

John of Damascus. *Writings*. Translated by Frederick H. Chase Jr. Washington, D. C.: Catholic University of America Press, 1958.

Jonas, Hans. "The Concept of God after Auschwitz: A Jewish Voice." *Journal of Religion*, 67, no. 1 (1987): 1–13.

Jordan, Mark D. *Rewritten Theology: Aquinas after His Readers*. Oxford: Blackwell Publishing, 2006.

Kant, Immanuel. *Practical Philosophy*. Edited and translated by Mary J. Gregor. Cambridge: Cambridge University Press, 1996.

Kantorowicz, Ernst H. *"Deus per Naturam, Deus per Gratiam*: A Note on Mediaeval Political Theology." *The Harvard Theological Review* 45, no. 4 (1952): 253–77.

———. *The King's Two Bodies: A Study in Mediaeval Political Theology*. Princeton: Princeton University Press, 1957.

———. *Laudes Regiae: A Study in Liturgical Acclamations and Mediaeval Ruler Worship*. Berkeley: University of California Press, 1946.

Karsenti, Bruno. "Agamben et le mystère du gouvernement." *Critique* 744 (2009): 355–75.

King, Karen L. *What Is Gnosticism?* Cambridge, Mass.: The Belknap Press of Harvard University Press, 2003.

Kittler, Friedrich. "Toward an Ontology of Media." *Theory, Culture and Society*, 26, nos. 2–3 (2009): 23–31.

Koselleck, Reinhart. "Volk, Nation, Nationalismus, Masse." In *Geschichtliche Grundbegriffe: Historisches Lexikon zur politisch-sozialen Sprache in Deutschland*, VII, edited by Otto Brunner, Werner Conze and Reinhart Koselleck, 141–431. Stuttgart: Klett-Cotta, 1992.

La Potterie, Ignace de, and Stanislaus Lyonnet. *La vie selon l'esprit: Condition du chrétien*. Paris: Cerf, 1965. Translated by John Morriss as *The Christian Lives by the Spirit*. Staten Island, N.Y.: Alba House, 1971.

Lactantius. *The Minor Works*. Translated by Mary Frances McDonald. Washington, D. C.: Catholic University of America Press, 1968.

Le Boulluec, Alain. *La notion d'hérésie dans le littérature grecque IIe-IIIe siècles*. 2 vols. Paris: Études Augustiniennes, 1985.

Leshem, Dotan. *The Origins of Neoliberalism: Modeling the Economy from Jesus to Foucault*. New York: Columbia University Press, 2016.

Lewis, Naphtali. *The Compulsory Public Services of Roman Egypt*. Florence: Gonnelli, 1982.

———. "*Leitourgia* and Related Terms." *Greek, Roman and Byzantine Studies* 3 (1960): 175–84.

Long, A. A., and D. N. Sedley, eds. *The Hellenistic Philosophers*. 2 vols. Cambridge: Cambridge University Press, 1987.

Lucretius. *De rerum natura*. Translated by W. D. Rouse; revised by Martin Ferguson Smith. London: William Heinemann, 1975.

Maes, Baziel. *La loi naturelle selon Ambroise de Milan*. Rome: Presses de l'Université Grégorienne, 1967.

Markus, R. A. *Saeculum: History and Society in the Theology of St. Augustine.* Cambridge: Cambridge University Press, 1970.

Marx, Karl. "Zur Kritik der Hegelschen Rechtsphilosophie." In Karl Marx and Friedrich Engels, *Werke*, vol. 1. Berlin: Dietz Verlag, 1983. Translated by Annette Jolin and Joseph O'Malley as *Critique of Hegel's "Philosophy of Right."* Cambridge: Cambridge University Press, 1970.

McCormick, John P. *Carl Schmitt's Critique of Liberalism: Against Politics as Technology.* Cambridge: Cambridge University Press, 1997.

Mehring, Reinhard. *Carl Schmitt: A Biography.* Translated by Daniel Steuer. Cambridge: Polity Press, 2014.

Meier, Heinrich, *The Lesson of Carl Schmitt: Four Chapters on the Distinction between Political Theology and Political Philosophy.* Translated by Marcus Brainard. Chicago: University of Chicago Press, 1998.

———. "What is Political Theology?" *Interpretation* 30, no. 1 (2002): 79–92.

Mendieta, Eduardo, and Jonathan VanAntwerpen, eds. *The Power of Religion in the Public Sphere.* New York: Columbia University Press, 2011.

Migne, J.-P., ed. *Patrologiae cursus completus: Series graeca.* 161 vols. Paris: 1857–66.

———. *Patrologiae cursus completus: Series latina.* 221 vols. Paris: 1844–65.

Mohrmann, Christine. *Études sur le latin des chrétiens.* 4 vols. Rome: Edizioni di Storia e Letteratura, 1961–77.

Moingt, Joseph. *Théologie trinitaire de Tertullien.* 4 vols. Paris: Aubier, 1966–69.

Moltmann, Jürgen. *The Trinity and the Kingdom: The Doctrine of God.* Translated by Margaret Kohl. Minneapolis: Fortress Press, 1993.

Momigliano, Arnaldo. "The Disadvantages of Monotheism for a Universal State." *Classical Philology* 81, no. 4 (1986): 285–97.

Mondzain, Marie-José. *Image, Icon, Economy: The Byzantine Origins of the Contemporary Imaginary.* Translated by Rico Franses. Stanford, Calif.: Stanford University Press, 2005.

Montevecchi, Orsolina. "Laos: Linee di una ricerca storico-linguistica." In *Actes du XVe Congrès International de Papyrologie* 4, edited by Jean Bingen and Georges Nachtergael, 51–67. Brussels: Fondation Egyptologique, 1979.

Murray, Oswyn. "The Idea of the Shepherd King from Cyrus to Charlemagne." In *Latin Poetry and the Classical Tradition: Essays in Medieval and Renaissance Literature*, edited by Peter Goodman and Oswyn Murray, 1–14. Oxford: Clarendon Press, 1990.

Musil, Robert. *The Man without Qualities.* Translated by Sophie Wilkins and Burton Pike. 2 vols. New York: Vintage International, 1995.

O'Meara, Dominic J. *Platonopolis: Platonic Political Philosophy in Late Antiquity.* Oxford: Clarendon Press, 2003.

Origen. *Contra Celsum.* Translated by Henry Chadwick. Cambridge: Cambridge University Press, 1965.

———. *Traité des principes*. Edited by Henri Crouzel and Manlio Simonetti. 5 vols. Paris: Cerf, 1978–84.

Paléologue, Théodore. *Sous l'œil du Grand Inquisiteur: Carl Schmitt et l'héritage de la théologie politique*. Paris: Cerf, 2004.

Pembroke, S. G. "Oikeiōsis." In *Problems in Stoicism*, edited by A. A. Long, 114–49. London: Athlone Press, 1971.

Peter Lombard. *The Sentences*. Translated by Giulio Silano. 4 vols. Toronto: Pontifical Institute of Medieval Studies, 2007–10.

Peters, Edward. *Limits of Thought and Power in Medieval Thought*. Aldershot, U.K.: Ashgate, 2001.

Peterson, Erik. *Heis Theos: Epigraphische, formgeschichtliche und religionsgeschichtliche Untersuchungen*. Göttingen: Vandenhoeck and Ruprecht, 1926.

———. "Das Problem des Nationalismus im alten Christentum." *Theologisches Zeitschrift* 7, no. 2 (1951): 81–91.

———. *Theologische Traktate*. Munich: Kösel-Verlag, 1951. Translated by Michael J. Hollerich as *Theological Tractates*. Stanford, Calif.: Stanford University Press, 2011.

Philo. *In Ten Volumes*. Translated by F. H. Colson. 10 vols. London: William Heinemann, 1929–62.

Plato. *Laws*. Translated by R. G. Bury. 2 vols. London: William Heinemann, 1968.

———. *Lysis; Symposium; Gorgias*. Translated by W. R. M. Lamb. London: William Heinemann, 1925.

———. *The Statesman; Philebus*. Translated by W. R. M. Lamb. Cambridge, Mass.: Harvard University Press, 1975.

———. *Theaetetus; Sophist*. Translated by Harold North Fowler. London: William Heinemann, 1967.

Plutarch. *Moralia*. 16 vols. Translated by Frank Cole Babbit. Cambridge, Mass.: Harvard University Press, 1927–76.

Porro, Pasquale. "Angelic Measures: *Aevum* and Discrete Time." In *The Medieval Concept of Time*, edited by Pasquale Porro, 131–59. Leiden: Brill, 2001.

Pritchard, James B., ed. *Ancient Near Eastern Texts Relating to the Old Testament*. Princeton: Princeton University Press, 1969.

Proclus. *Commentaire sur le Timée*. 4 vols. Translated by A. J. Festugière. Paris: Vrin, 1967.

———. *The Elements of Theology*. Edited and translated by E. R. Dodds. Oxford: Clarendon Press, 1971.

Reumann, J. "*Oikonomia*-Terms in Paul in Comparison with Lucan *Heilsgeschichte*." *New Testament Studies* 13 (1966): 147–67.

Roques, René. *L'Univers Dionysien: Structure hiérarchique du monde selon Pseudo-Denys*. Paris: Aubier, 1954.

Rorem, Paul and Lamoreaux, John C. *John of Scythopolis and the Dionysian Corpus: Annotating the Areopagite*. Oxford: Clarendon Press, 1998.

Ross, W. D. *Aristotle's Physics*. Oxford: Clarendon Press, 1936.

Rousseau, Jean-Jacques. *The Social Contract and Other Later Political Writings*. Edited and translated by Victor Gourevitch. Cambridge: Cambridge University Press, 1997.

Schmidt, Christoph. "Apokalyptischer Strukturwandel der Öffentlichkeit: Von der politischen Theologie zur Theopolitik: Anmerkungen zu Erik Petersons 'Buch von den Engeln—Stellung und Bedeutung der heiligen Engel im Kultus' von 1935," in *Die theopolitische Stunde: Zwölf Perspektiven auf das eschatologische Problem der Moderne*, 113–42. Munich: Wilhelm Fink Verlag, 2009.

Schmitt, Carl. *The Concept of the Political*. Translated by George Schwab. Chicago: University of Chicago Press, 2007.

———. *Constitutional Theory*. Edited and translated by Jeffrey Seitzer. Durham, N.C.: Duke University Press, 2008.

———. "Dialogue on Power and Access to the Holder of Power." In *Dialogues on Power and Space*, edited by Andreas Kalyvas and Federico Finchelstein, translated by Samuel Garrett Zeitlin. Cambridge: Polity Press, 2015.

———. *The* Nomos *of the Earth in the International Law of the* Jus Publicum Europaeum. Translated by G. L. Ulmen. New York: Telos Press, 2006.

———. *Politische Theologie: Vier Kapitel zur Lehre von der Souveränität*. Berlin: Duncker & Humblot, 1985. Translated by George Schwab as *Political Theology: Four Chapters on the Concept of Sovereignty*. Chicago: University of Chicago Press, 2005.

———. *Politische Theologie II: Die Legende von der Erledigung jeder politischen Theologie*. Berlin: Duncker & Humblot, 1970. Translated by Michael Hoelzl and Graham Ward as *Political Theology II: The Myth of the Closure of Any Political Theology*. Cambridge: Polity Press, 2008.

———. *Roman Catholicism and Political Form*. Translated by G. L. Ulmen. Westport, Conn.: Greenwood Press, 1996.

Schindler, Alfred, ed. *Monotheismus als politisches Problem? Erik Peterson und der Kritik der politischen Theologie*. Gütersloh: Gütersloher Verlagshaus Gerd Mohn, 1978.

Schürmann, Reiner. *Heidegger on Being and Acting: From Principles to Anarchy*. Translated by Christine-Marie Gros. Bloomington: Indiana University Press, 1990.

Seneca. *Ad Lucilium Epistulae Morales*. 4 vols. Translated by Richard M. Gummere. London: William Heinemann, 1917–25.

Sorabji, Richard. *Time, Creation, and the Continuum: Theories in Antiquity and the Middle Ages*. Ithaca, N.Y.: Cornell University Press, 1983.

Stimilli, Elettra. *Il debito del vivente: Ascesi e capitalismo*. Macerata: Quodlibet, 2011.

Strathmann, Hermann. "*laos*." In *The Theological Dictionary of the New Testament*, vol. 4, edited by Gerhard Kittell, translated by Geoffrey Bromiley, 29–57. Grand Rapids, Mich.: Eerdmans, 1967.

Stroumsa, Guy G. "Moses the Lawgiver and the Idea of Civil Religion in Patristic Thought." In *Teologie politiche: Modelli a confronto*, edited Giovanni Firolamo, 135–48. Brescia: Morcelliana, 2005.

Taubes, Jacob. *The Political Theology of Paul*. Translated by Dana Hollander. Stanford, Calif.: Stanford University Press, 2004.

———. *To Carl Schmitt: Letters and Reflections*. Translated by Keith Tribe. New York: Columbia University Press, 2013.

Tertullian. *Adversus Marcionem*. Edited and translated by Ernest Evans. 2 vols. Oxford: Clarendon Press, 1972.

———. *Adversus Praxean*. Edited and translated by Ernest Evans. London: S. P. C. K., 1948.

———. *Apology; De spectaculis*. Translated by T. R. Glover. London: William Heinemann, 1966.

Thomas Aquinas. *Commentary on Aristotle's "Metaphysics."* Translated by John P. Rowan. Notre Dame, Ind.: Dumb Ox Books, 1995.

———. *Commentary on Aristotle's "Physics."* Translated by Richard J. Blackwell, Richard J. Spath and W. Edmund Thirlkel. London: Routledge and Kegan Paul, 1963.

———. *Commentary on Aristotle's "Politics."* Translated by Richard J. Regan. Indianapolis, Ind.: Hackett Publishing, 2007.

———. *Summa contra gentiles*. 5 vols. Notre Dame, Ind.: University of Notre Dame Press, 1975.

———. *Summa theologiae*. 61 vols. London: Blackfriars, 1964–81.

Thomas, Yan. "Le sujet concret et sa personne: Essai d'histoire juridique rétrospective." In Olivier Cayla and Yan Thomas, *Du droit de ne pas naître: À propos de l'affaire Perruche*, 91–170. Paris: Gallimard, 2002.

Tuck, Richard. *The Sleeping Sovereign: The Invention of Modern Democracy*. Cambridge: Cambridge University Press, 2016.

Varro. *On the Latin Language*. Translated by Roland J. Kent. 2 vols. London: William Heinemann, 1938.

Vatter, Miguel, ed. *Crediting God: Sovereignty and Religion in the Age of Global Capitalism*. New York: Fordham University Press, 2011.

Vernant, Jean-Pierre. "Intimations of the Will in Greek Tragedy." In Jean-Pierre Vernant and Pierre Vidal-Naquet, *Myth and Tragedy in Ancient Greece*, translated by Janet Lloyd, 49–84. New York: Zone Books, 1988.

Veyne, Paul. *Bread and Circuses: Historical Sociology and Political Pluralism*. Abridged translation by Brian Pearce. London: Allen Lane, 1990.

Voegelin, Eric. *The New Science of Politics: An Introduction*. Chicago: University of Chicago Press, 1952.

Vogl, Joseph, *The Specter of Capital*. Translated by Joachim Redner and Robert Savage. Stanford, Calif.: Stanford University Press, 2015.

Weber, Max. *Wirtschaft und Gesellschaft*. 2 vols. Tübingen: J. C. B. Mohr, 1925. Translated Ephraim Fischoff et al as *Economy and Society: An Outline of Interpretive Sociology*. Edited by Guenther Roth and Claus Wittich. 2 vols. Berkeley: University of California Press, 1978.

Weber, Samuel. *Geld ist Zeit: Gedanken zu Kredit und Krise*. Zurich: Diaphanes, 2009.

Whyte, Jessica. "'The Kings Reigns but He Doesn't Govern': Thinking Sovereignty and Government with Agamben, Foucault and Rousseau." In *Giorgio Agamben: Legal, Political and Philosophical Perspectives*, edited by Tom Frost, 143–61. London: Routledge, 2013.

Wolfson, Harry Austryn. *Philo*. 2 vols. Cambridge, Mass.: Harvard University Press, 1947.

Xenophon. *Memorabilia and Oeconomicus*. Translated by E. C. Marchant. Cambridge, Mass.: Harvard University Press, 1997.

———. *Scripta Minora*. Translated by E. C. Marchant. London: William Heinemann, 1984.

INDEX

Abel, Carl, 70

acclamations, 45, 50, 156n26, 157–58n45

action, 28, 39, 118, 185n62; angel and, 81, 115; Christian political, 3–4, 10, 11, 41–42, 48, 136 (*see also* liturgy); communicative, 156n26; divine, 21–23, 25, 39, 115; minister and, 12, 90–92, 106–7, 108, 111–12, 115, 116–18, 130–32, 180n8, 184n61; passion and, 107–9, 110–13, 176–77n76, 177n77; slave and, 100, 104, 110, 113. *See also* office, *officium*

administration, 7–8, 24, 26–27, 37, 138

Agamben, Giorgio, 9, 43–44, 132, 184n61; *dynamis*, 108, 147n32, 76n67; economic theology, 5, 8, 9–10, 38, 145n17, 147n33; glory, 11, 85–87; government, 5, 6–8, 11, 23–25, 85, 179n93; instrumental cause, 92–93, 116–17; office, *officium*, 118, 122–23, 130, 179–80n2, 181n28, 182n38; *oikonomia*, 4–5, 6, 7, 10, 23–27, 29, 36, 38; people, 55, 78, 165–66n157; political theology, 2, 4, 5, 2833, 136, 147n33; *The Highest Poverty*, 184n58; *The Kingdom and the Glory*, 23–25, 116; *Opus Dei*, 116

Ambrose of Milan, St., 118, 126–27, 130; *De officiis*, 123–26, 129, 182n36; *De viduis*, 127–29

anarchy, 34, 39, 154n94

Andia, Ysabel de, 167n19

angelology, 11, 81, 87, 170n40

angels: the fall and, 80–81, 90; liturgy and, 43–46, 66–67, 130, 132, 155n11, 155n23, 169n32; morality and, 168n28; power and, 20, 37–38, 79–81, 86, 88, 89, 115, 179n93; time and, 169n31; of the nations, 33–34, 63–65, 153n91, 163n118

antipolitics: Christian, 2, 139

apostolic succession, 69–70

Arendt, Hannah, 145n16; bureaucracy, 10, 138, 148n39, 185n12, 186n14; political theology, 28

Aristotle, 12, 23, 30, 55, 59, 90, 105, 106, 145n16, 185n62; aetiology, 11, 92–94, 97–98, 176n69; distinction between *oikos* and *polis*, 4, 145n16, 153n76; *dynamis*, 107–9, 113, 147n32, 176n67; household management, 24, 26, 35, 99, 151n38, 153n76; liturgy, 47, 156n30, 157n34; *metaxy*, 176n30; munificence, 47; slave, slavery 99–101, 110–13, 130, 151n39, 174n34, 179n83; theology, 33, 35, 39, 75, 170n44, 174n45; *De caelo*, 21; *Eudemian Ethics*, 100; *Metaphysics*, 35, 147n32; *Nicomachean Ethics*, 117–18; *Physics*, 101–4; *Politics*, 99–101, 151n39, 156n30;

Pseudo-Aristotle: *Economics*, 153n76; *De mundo*, 33, 38, 114
Assmann, Jan, 145n15
Athanasius of Alexandria, 105
Augustine of Hippo, St., 18, 43, 96, 123, 125, 179n94, 184n58; angels, 155n11; distinction between *frui* and *uti*, 178n82; distinction between *tempus* and *aeternitas*, 16–17; peace, 3, 32, 35; people, 49, 62, 157n43; sacraments, 94–95; *Confessions*, 15–16; *De civitate Dei*, 15, 17, 20, 49, 144n33; *De Genesis contra Manichaeos*, 15
Austin, J. L., 94, 172n15
Averroes, 17, 98, 104, 176n69
Avicenna, 97–98

Baldus de Ubaldis, 177n78
Balibar, Étienne, 159n74, 162n109, 165n156
Basil of Caesarea, 150n30
Becon, Thomas, 183–84n54
Benjamin, Walter, 85
Benveniste, Émile: *Vocabulaire des institutions indo-européenne*, 56–57
Bible: Hebrew, 3, 32, 51, 54, 59, 65, 161n94, 161n101; Septuagint, 46, 54–61, 64, 65, 66, 69, 71–72, 124, 162n102; New Testament, 25, 54, 61–62, 65, 69, 71, 124, 158n60, 162n102
Bodin, Jean, 146n25
Boethius, 105, 175n61
Bonald, Louis Gabriel Ambroise de, 135
Brown, Peter, 113–15, 181n26
bureaucracy, 10, 138. *See also* Arendt, Hannah; Marx, Karl

career, 88
cause, effect and, 77, 84, 86, 93–96, 104, 107–8, 112–13, 122, 167n10, 173–74n30

cause, types of: advisory, 97; auxiliary, 97; dispositive, 97–99, 106, 173–74n30; efficient, 92–93, 173n28; final, 93, 173n28; formal, 92, 173n28; instrumental, 11–12, 92–113, 116–18, 130, 170n42, 172n7, 173n28, 173–74n30, 176n69, 177n78, 180n8; intermediary, 84, 86; material, 92, 173n28; moral, 106; paradigmatic, 173n28; perfective, 97, 98; principal, 93, 96, 104, 106, 108, 116–17, 173–74n30, 180n8, 184n61
Chantraine, Pierre, 71
charisma: charismatic authority, 57, 160n83, 170n50; objectification of: 163n112
Chenu, M.-D., 173n20
Christology, 105; political, 113–15
Chrysippus, 180n14
Church, 3, 4, 11, 24, 42–46, 48, 50, 52–53, 62, 90, 92, 115, 117, 126, 136, 139, 162n109, 165n155, 170–71n51, 173n63; early, 15, 29, 58, 69; Fathers, 23, 25, 45, 46; history of, 62, 63–64, 67, 114. *See also ekklēsia*
Cicero, 32, 118, 131–32; as model for Ambrose, 123–26, 129–130; *De finibus*, 119–120; *De natura deorum*, 21–23; *De officiis*, 120–23; *De re publica*, 49, 62, 157n40
city, *polis*: earthly, 43–44, 48, 136, 157n40; heavenly, 1, 40, 42–46, 48, 136, 138–39, 155n11. *See also oikos*
civil war, *stasis*, 35, 37, 65
Clement of Alexandria, 72
Clement of Rome, 65–73, 164n129
Coccia, Emanuele: 176n69; on angels, 79–81; on the distinction between *consilium* and *praeceptum*, 128–29, 183n53
Constantine the Great, 32, 34, 48, 163n117

counsel, *consilium*: command, *praeceptum* and: 127–29, 182n48, 182–83n51, 183n53
creation, 15–20, 78–80, 114, 149n14. *See also* salvation
Cyril of Alexandria, 105, 113–15

Davidson, Ivor, 127
Debray, Régis, 170n40
Demosthenes, 55
depoliticization, 2, 133–35, 139, 144n6
Derrida, Jacques, 185n63
Diogenes Laertius, 180n14
Dionysius the Areopagite, Pseudo-, 11, 75–78, 84, 164n129, 166n6, 167n11, 167n19, 168n27
divinization, 78, 167n11; of authority, 87
Domitian, 65
Dondaine, H.-F., 98–99
Donoso Cortés, Juan, 135
doxology, 45, 86, 136. *See also* glory
duBois, Page, 177–78n80
Dumézil, Georges, 57
duty, 30, 52, 113, 138; virtue and, 116, 130, 178n81. *See also* office, *officium*
dynamis, 107–9; *adynamia* and, 108, 147n32; distinction between *dynamis tou pathein* and *dynamis tou poiein*, 102, 108–9; *energeia* and, 108–9, 147n32, 176n67, 176–77n76; of the slave, 101, 113

economic theology, 5, 8, 9–10, 23–29, 38–40, 50, 78, 104, 138–39, 145n17, 150n37, 167–68n17
economy: monarchy and, 8, 36–39, 138–39; political, 6, 89, 138
ekklēsia, 42, 49, 50, 162n109. *See also* Church
Epictetus, 56

Epicurus and Epicureanism, 10, 21–23, 29–31, 149–50n26
Esposito, Roberto, 7, 157n36, 185n11
eschatology, 44, 64; economy and, 165n156; political, 3, 32, 163n117; suspension of, 3, 4–5, 32, 170–71n51
Eusebius of Caesarea, 32, 163n117

Finley, Moses, 156n27, 177–78n80
Foucault, Michel: clergy/laity dimorphism, 63, 162–63n111; counter-conduct, 162–63n111; distinction between sovereignty and government, 6–7, 146n26; governmentality, 5–7, 9, 23–24, 50–53, 57, 89, 136, 181n28; minister, 11, 63, 89; pastoral power, 10, 50–55, 57, 63, 70, 137, 161–62n101, 163n112; power, 6–7, 9, 12–13; population, 159n72; *History of Sexuality*, 6; *Security, Territory, Population*, 50–53
Freud, Sigmund, 70
flock, 65, 69–70; shepherd and, 51–55, 57
Führung, 181n28

Gaius, 165n153
Gehlen, Arnold, 181n28
glory, 17, 44, 67; government and, 7, 11, 85–87
Gnosticism, 18, 29, 37, 149n14
Goldschmidt, Victor, 100–101
governability, 74, 123, 129, 132
governed, 63, 78, 84; governors and, 12–13, 71, 74, 75, 85, 108, 112, 123, 129–30, 137
government, 8, 9, 11, 13, 33–34, 55, 74, 75, 83, 85, 86, 88–89, 123, 131, 138; divine, 22, 39, 84, 115, 136. *See also* glory; sovereignty
governmentality, 9, 11, 55, 85, 162–63n11. *See also* Foucault, Michel

Gregory of Nazianzus, St., 34, 37, 150n30
Gregory the Great, St., 79, 168n27, 169n31

Habermas, Jürgen, 156n26
Harnack, Adolf von, 73
Hathaway, Ronald F., 76, 166n6
Hegel, G. W. F., 87–88, 138, 185n11
Heidegger, Martin, 107–9, 176n67, 176n68
heresiology, 15, 24, 29
Herodotus, 55
Heyd, David, 183n54
hierarchy, 11–13, 75–80, 85–88, 129–30, 137, 162–63n111, 164n29, 166n6, 168n26, 168n27, 173n28; celestial, 168n27; ecclesiastical, 48; liturgy and, 11–12, 67–69, 86–87, 137
Hippolytus of Rome, 24, 26–27, 36–37, 150n37
Hobbes, Thomas, 146n25; *De cive*, 146n25; *Leviathan*, 182n48
Homer, 54–56, 58, 158n69
household management, 6, 23–24, 27, 35, 99–100, 104, 138, 153n76. *See also oikonomia*
Hugh of Digne, 183
Hugh of St. Victor, 95
human: angel and, 79–83, 132, 169n31; animal and, 121–23, 131–32; divine and, 79, 81–83
humanity, 23, 53, 129, 132, 177–78n80, 184n56; Christ's, 105–7, 109–12, 113–15, 175n60, 175n63, 177n78

Iamblichus, 76
idleness: *see* inactivity
Illich, Ivan, 172n7
imitation: of God, 77, 85, 137
immunity, 48, 157n36
impersonality, 79, 138

improvidence: divine, 10, 29–31
inactivity: divine, 10, 17, 19–23, 29, 149n10
Incarnation, 105, 110, 114
industriousness, 12, 81, 131–32
instrumental reason, 112, 178n82
intention: jocular, 171–72n4; ministerial, 90–91, 96, 112, 117, 172n7; perverse, 91, 171–72n4
Irenaeus of Lyons, 20, 29, 36; *Adversus haereses*, 18
Islam, 179n93

John Chrysostom, St., 111
John of Damascus, St., 105, 109–11, 114, 176–77n76, 177n77
John of Scythopolis, 76
Jonas, Hans, 147n32
Judaism: Hellenistic, 3, 28, 32–33, 54, 150n37; Rabbinic, 15, 64, 158–59n60

Kant, Immanuel: ethics, 116, 130, 179–80n2; self-constraint, 180n8
Kantorowicz, Ernst, 9, 17, 145n15, 147n34, 158n46, 177n78
katechon, 86, 170–71n51
Kelsen, Hans, 135
Kittel, Gerhard, 161n9
Koselleck, Reinhart, 165–66n157

La Potterie, Ignace de, 70–71, 73, 165n155
laïcité, 162n109
laikos, 65, 70–73
laity: clergy and, 63, 68, 69–70, 74, 88, 163–63n111
law, 6, 42, 49, 129, 182n51, 183n52; Athenian, 177–78n80
Lactantius, 30, 170–71n51
leader, 35, 57, 60, 63, 67, 71. *See also Führung*

Lewis, Naphtali, 47
liturgy, *leitourgia*, 8–12, 63, 71, 79–81,
    86–87, 113, 117, 124, 130, 132, 136, 137,
    157n30; *a-leitourgia*, 30, 149–50n26;
    Ancient Greek, 11, 42, 46–48, 156n30;
    Christian, 11, 42–46, 48–50, 65, 68–
    70, 170–71n51, 184n58; Roman Egypt,
    47. *See also* hierarchy; office; power
Lucretius: *De rerum natura*, 30–31
Luther, Martin, 183–84n54

Machiavelli, Niccolò, 5
Maistre, Joseph de, 135
Manicheanism, 15, 149n14
Marcion, 29
Marx, Karl: on bureaucracy: 8788
mediality, 109, 176n69
mediation, 5, 38, 50, 52, 81–85, 86, 89,
    115, 137–38, 179n94
minister, 8, 11–12, 63, 83, 85, 89–92, 94,
    96, 106, 111–13, 115, 116–18, 130–31,
    165–66n157, 171–72n4, 174n34, 175n63,
    177–78n80, 180n8, 183n53, 184n61
modernity, 2, 4, 40, 132, 133–35, 138,
    177–78n80; politics and religion in:
    11, 63, 91
monarchy: constitutional, 5; divine, 3,
    28, 32–37, 41, 82. *See also* economy
monasticism, 184n58
Mondzain, Marie-José, 145n17
monotheism, 4, 33–34, 153n91, 179n93;
    political, 41, 136
Montchrestien, Antoine de, 89
Montevecchi, Orsolina, 58–61
Morin, Germain, 72–73

nation, nations, 45, 54–55, 60, 61, 71–72,
    165n156. *See also* angels
nature: convention and, 100–1, 112;
    grace and, 125–28; hierarchy and, 78,
    79–81, 129, 132, 137

Neoplatonism, 76–77, 82, 83, 167n11,
    173n28
Nestorius, 113–14
neutralization: *see* depoliticization
Nietzsche, Friedrich, 112

O'Meara, Dominic J., 167n11
office, *officium*, 12, 47, 69, 113, 118–27,
    129–32, 181n20, 181n28, 182n38,
    184n58; *medium* (*kathēkon*), 119–24,
    126–27, 129–30, 180n14; *perfectum*
    (*katorthōma*), 119–120, 122, 126–27,
    129–30; translation of *leitourgia*, 87,
    113, 124
oikeiōsis, 121, 180n14
oikonomia, 31, 74, 86, 145n17, 147n33,
    150n30, 167–68n19, 177n77; *theologia*
    and, 104, 151n38; Trinitarian, 4–5,
    7, 10, 23–29, 36, 39, 137. *See also*
    economic theology; household
    management
oikos: *polis* and, 28, 145n16, 177–78n80
order, 11, 22, 66, 67–68, 75, 77, 78, 83–85,
    166n3. *See also* hierarchy
Origen, 71, 72; *Contra Celsum*, 64,
    153n91; *De principiis*, 18–20, 149n16
Overbeck, Franz, 32

Passion: Christ's, 20, 29, 111
pastorate: Christian, 6, 7, 52–53, 54, 63,
    162–63n111; institutionalization of,
    11, 53, 55, 63, 65, 70, 75, 163n112
Paul, St., 15, 18, 25, 66, 76, 128, 150n37
Pelagius, 125
people, 74, 159n74; chosen, 51, 60–61;
    66–67; *dēmos*, 47, 55, 56–57, 59;
    ethnos, 55, 56, 57, 59, 60–61; of God,
    45, 54, 56, 59–60, 62, 63, 65, 70,
    73–74, 162n107, 165n155; *laos*, 11, 46,
    48–50, 54–65, 70–74, 157n38, 160n84,
    160–61n90, 161n94, 162n102, 162n109,

165n156; *ochlos,* 50, 61; *plebs,* 73,
165n153; *populus,* 49, 157n43, 165n153
performative, 94–6
person, 175n61; in Christ, 105, 110, 112,
179n93; in the Trinity, 24, 27, 34
Peter Lombard, 95–96, 97
Peters, Edward, 18, 149n14
Peterson, Erik: acclamations, 42, 44–45,
49–50, 147n34, 156n26, 157–58n45;
angels, 43–44, 45–46, 65, 132, 155n23;
angels of the nations, 64–65, 153n91,
163n117; *katechon,* 170–71n51; liturgy,
11, 42–46, 48–50, 86, 132, 136, 147n34;
political theology, 2–5, 10, 28–29, 31–
34, 39, 41–42, 114, 135–36, 143n4, 145n15,
154n1; "Book on the Angels," 42–46,
144–45n14, 154n7; "The Church," 42–
43, 170–71n51; *Heis Theos,* 42, 49–50,
157n40; "Monotheism as a Political
Problem," 2–3, 4, 6, 31–39, 143n4,
144n13, 145n19, 152n70, 154n7, 155n11,
170n44
philanthropy, *philanthropia,* 137,
167–68n19
Philo of Alexandria, 15, 33, 38, 81–82,
125, 152n68
Plato, 12, 21, 23, 38, 55, 173n28;
Statesman, 54, 99; *Symposium,* 82;
Theaetetus, 167n11
Plutarch, 56, 82–83
political theology, 1–10, 27–29, 39–40,
46, 74, 113–15, 134–35, 138–39, 143–
44n4, 145n15, 146n29, 147n33, 177n78,
185n11; Peterson's critique of: 2–5,
10, 31–34, 38, 41–42, 45, 46
Polybius, 56
power: enactment, execution of, 8,
9, 78, 79–81, 83–85, 109, 113, 131, 138,
168–69n28; manifestation of, 77–78,
85–87; types of power: biopower,
12; disciplinary, 12; liturgical, 8–13,

41–74, 79–81, 83, 86–87, 88, 118, 131,
137–38, 156n26; pastoral, 11, 51–53,
54, 55, 57, 63, 89, 137, 161–62n101;
psychiatric, 12; sacramental, 53;
sacred (*see* hierarchy); vicariousness
of: 9–10, 12, 80, 96, 108, 116–17, 131,
137–38, 177n78
priest, priesthood, 50, 53, 67, 68, 69,
71, 72, 74, 76, 88, 91, 124, 129, 130–31,
162n109, 164n29, 184n58. *See also*
minister
Proclus, 76, 77, 166n6, 173n28
providence: divine, 10, 21–23, 24–25,
83–84
Ptolemy II, 59

Roques, René, 167–68n17
Ross, W. D., 101
Rousseau, Jean-Jacques: "Discourse
on Political Economy," 146n25; *The
Social Contract,* 146n25, 146n26
Rufinus of Aquileia, 149n16

sacraments, 43, 90, 115: administration
of, 11, 90, 117; efficacy of, 11, 90–92,
94–96, 97–99, 106, 171–72n4; pastoral
power and, 53; signs and, 94–96
sage: Stoic, 122, 130
salvation, 23, 52, 74, 137, 184n56; creation
and, 29, 77; hierarchy and, 11, 78, 86
Schmitt, Carl, 155–56n25; decisionism,
185n11; depoliticization and
neutralization, 2, 133–34; *katechon,*
170–71n51; political theology, 1–3,
9, 10, 28, 31–32, 41, 48, 134–37, 138,
139, 143n3, 143n4, 145n15, 154n1;
"The Age of Neutralizations
and Depoliticizations," 133–34;
Constitutional Theory, 156n26, 157–
58n45; *Political Theology,* 2, 31–32,
134, 145–46n19

Schürmann, Reiner, 154n94
secularization, 1–2, 4, 41, 42, 45, 135
Seneca, 123, 131
Senellart, Michel, 150n30
service: *see* liturgy
slave, 99–101, 104, 106–7, 111–13, 130,
    174n34, 177–78n80, 178n81, 179n83;
    master and, 28, 99–100, 104, 110–11,
    112, 151n39, 178n81
slavery, 100–1, 102
society: civil, 40, 55m 138–39; classless,
    88
sovereignty, 2, 6, 8, 28, 135, 185n11;
    distinction between government
    and, 6–10, 51, 136, 146n25, 146n26;
    divine, 19–20, 44, 82; popular,
    146n25
Spinoza, Baruch, 143n4
state, 1, 6, 50–51, 87–88, 134–35; civil
    society and, 5, 139
Stobaeus, 120
Stoicism, 10, 22–23, 119–126, 129, 130,
    143n4, 150n37, 180n14
Strathmann, Hermann, 56, 61, 162n102
supererogation, 129, 183–84n54
Symmachus, 163n115

Taubes, Jacob, 32, 145n15
Tertullian, 24, 27, 29, 38, 150n37, 170–
    71n51; *Adversus Praxean*, 36–37,
    151n45; *Apologeticus*, 38
Thomas Aquinas, St., 11, 102, 103,
    104, 112, 114, 116; hierarchy, 75;
    intermediary cause, 83–84;
    instrumental cause, 93–94, 96,

97–99, 101, 105–7, 111, 116–17, 170n42,
    173–74n30; minister, 11, 85, 89–91,
    92, 116–17, 130, 171–72n4, 174n34;
    religio, 178n81; *Commentary on
    Aristotle's Politics*, 113; *Summa
    contra gentiles*, 83; *Summa
    theologiae*, 75, 84, 175n60
Thucydides, 55
time, 17–20, 81, 169n31; creation of,
    16–17; end of, 3, 43, 64; eternity and,
    16–17; motion and, 102
torture, 177–78n80
Trinity, 3, 19, 24–25, 32, 34, 36, 38, 39,
    136, 151n38. *See also oikonomia*
Tuck, Richard, 146n25

universalism, 88; Christian, 184n56;
    Roman, 184n56

Valla, Lorenzo, 166n6
Varro, 184n61
vicariousness: *see* power
virtue, 120, 122–23, 126, 130, 131, 185n62;
    divine, 129–30, 131
Voegelin, Eric, 145n15

Weber, Max, 57, 133, 138, 145n17, 163n112,
    170n50, 185n11
will: divine, 68, 80, 125; free, 90, 129;
    political, 74

Xenocrates, 82
Xenophon, 23, 24, 55; pseudo-
    Xenophon: *Constitution of the
    Athenians*, 47

Roberto Esposito, *Terms of the Political: Community, Immunity, Biopolitics.*
Translated by Rhiannon Noel Welch. Introduction by Vanessa Lemm.

Maurizio Ferraris, *Documentality: Why It Is Necessary to Leave Traces.*
Translated by Richard Davies.

Dimitris Vardoulakis, *Sovereignty and Its Other: Toward the Dejustification of Violence.*

Anne Emmanuelle Berger, *The Queer Turn in Feminism: Identities, Sexualities, and the Theater of Gender.* Translated by Catherine Porter.

James D. Lilley, *Common Things: Romance and the Aesthetics of Belonging in Atlantic Modernity.*

Jean-Luc Nancy, *Identity: Fragments, Frankness.* Translated by François Raffoul.

Miguel Vatter, *Between Form and Event: Machiavelli's Theory of Political Freedom.*

Miguel Vatter, *The Republic of the Living: Biopolitics and the Critique of Civil Society.*

Maurizio Ferraris, *Where Are You? An Ontology of the Cell Phone.*
Translated by Sarah De Sanctis.

Irving Goh, *The Reject: Community, Politics, and Religion after the Subject.*

Kevin Attell, *Giorgio Agamben: Beyond the Threshold of Deconstruction.*

J. Hillis Miller, *Communities in Fiction.*

Remo Bodei, *The Life of Things, the Love of Things.* Translated by Murtha Baca.

Gabriela Basterra, *The Subject of Freedom: Kant, Levinas.*

Roberto Esposito, *Categories of the Impolitical.* Translated by Connal Parsley.

Roberto Esposito, *Two: The Machine of Political Theology and the Place of Thought.* Translated by Zakiya Hanafi.

Akiba Lerner, *Redemptive Hope: From the Age of Enlightenment to the Age of Obama.*

Adriana Cavarero and Angelo Scola, *Thou Shalt Not Kill: A Political and Theological Dialogue.* Translated by Margaret Adams Groesbeck and Adam Sitze.

Massimo Cacciari, *Europe and Empire: On the Political Forms of Globalization.* Edited by Alessandro Carrera, Translated by Massimo Verdicchio.

Emanuele Coccia, *Sensible Life: A Micro-ontology of the Image.* Translated by Scott Stuart, Introduction by Kevin Attell.

Timothy C. Campbell, *The Techne of Giving: Cinema and the Generous Forms of Life.*

Étienne Balibar, *Citizen Subject: Foundations for Philosophical Anthropology.* Translated by Steven Miller, Foreword by Emily Apter.

Ashon T. Crawley, *Blackpentecostal Breath: The Aesthetics of Possibility.*

Terrion L. Williamson, *Scandalize My Name: Black Feminist Practice and the Making of Black Social Life.*

Jean-Luc Nancy, *The Disavowed Community.* Translated by Philip Armstrong.

Roberto Esposito, *The Origin of the Political: Hannah Arendt or Simone Weil?* Translated by Vincenzo Binetti and Gareth Williams.

Dimitris Vardoulakis, *Stasis before the State: Nine Theses on Agnostic Democracy.*

Nicholas Heron, *Liturgical Power: Between Economic and Political Theology.*